CHARTA

THE SQUARE ROOT OF MINUS ONE IS PLUS OR MINUS i

Jaki Irvine: Assembled Works 1993-2008

CONTENTS

Sarah Glennie, Foreword 5

Jaki Irvine, In a World Like This 11

Selected Writings 1993-2008 29

Michael Newman, What makes it hold together:
Jaki Irvine's acknowledgements 69

Biographical Index 151

Jaki Irvine: Assembled Works 1993-2008 . . . .

FOREWORD

Central to this monograph on Jaki Irvine's work is an ambitious multi-screen video installation

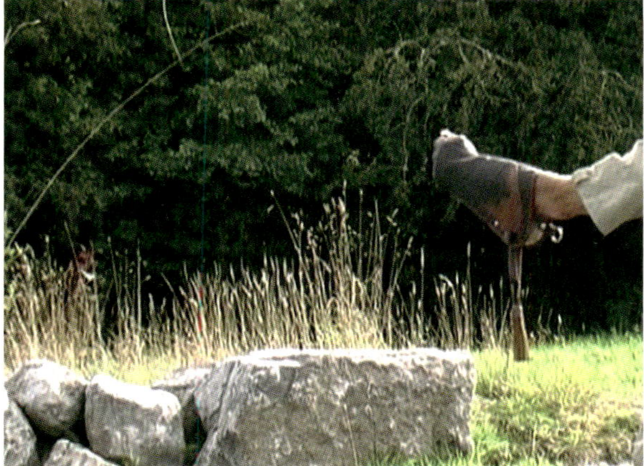

This work developed out of the Model's invitation to Jaki for her to be the inaugural Model Fellow.

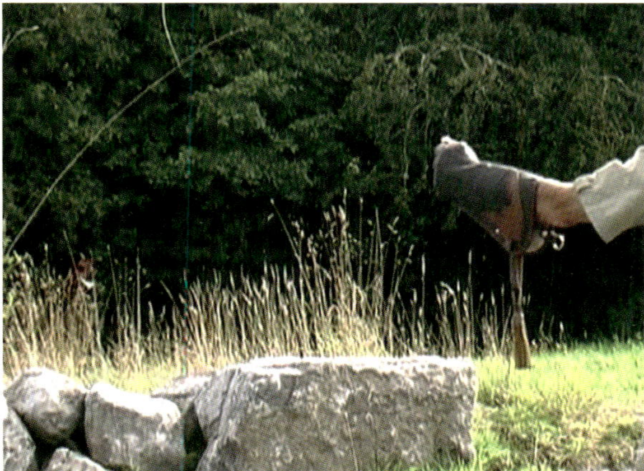

The key resource offered is year-long access to the *Model*'s residency studio and a small stipend,

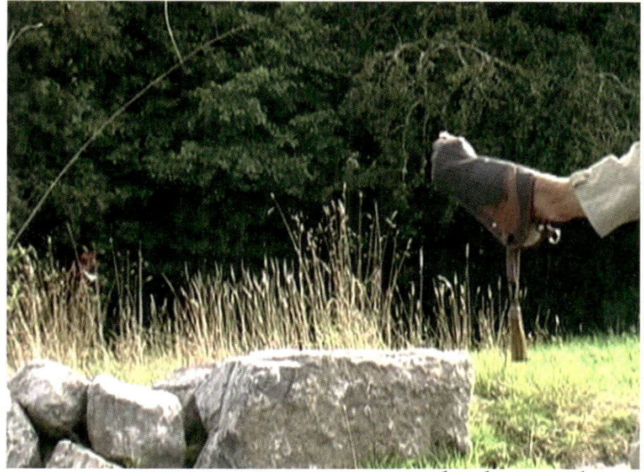

IN A WORLD LIKE THIS, which was shown at *The Model Arts* and *Niland Gallery* in 2006 and the *Chisenhale Gallery*, London in 2007.

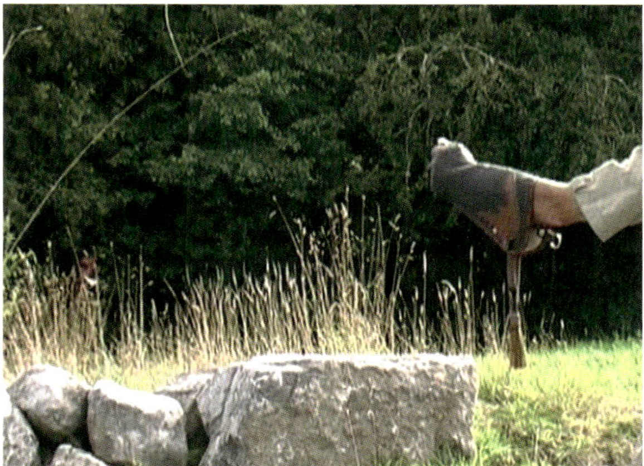

The Fellowship operates on the simple premise of offering artists time and space with few conditions attached.

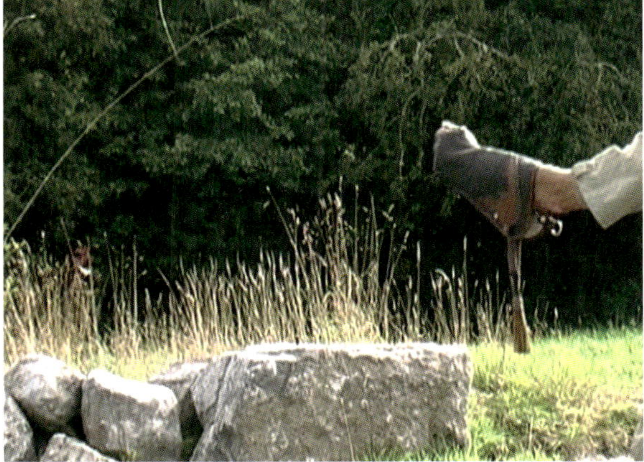

both offered with the main objective of providing artists with research and thinking time away from their day-to-day.

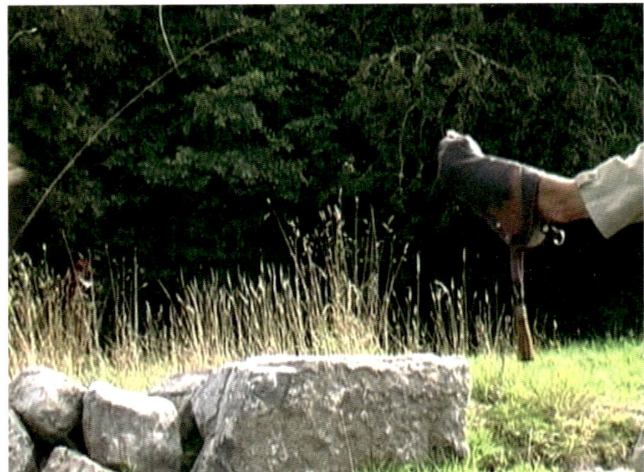

Fortunately for the *Model*, Jaki responded enthusiastically to this invitation

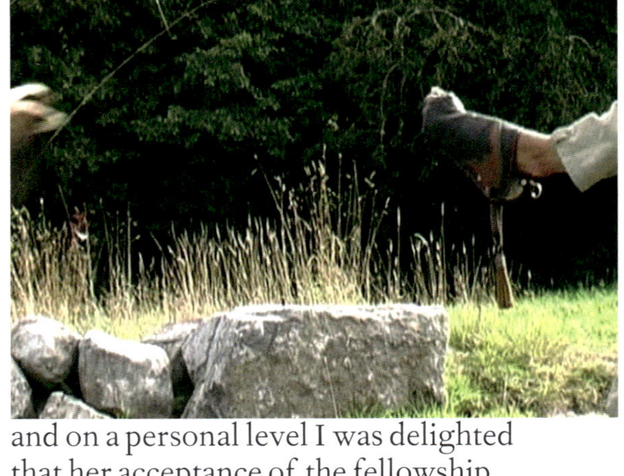

and on a personal level I was delighted that her acceptance of the fellowship

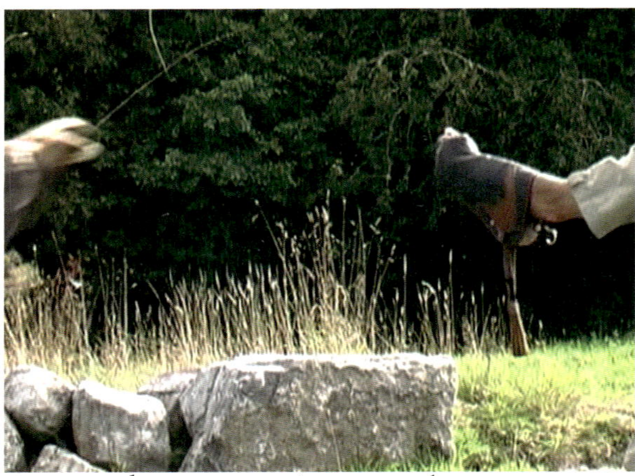

gave me the opportunity to work with an artist whose work I had admired and respected for many years.

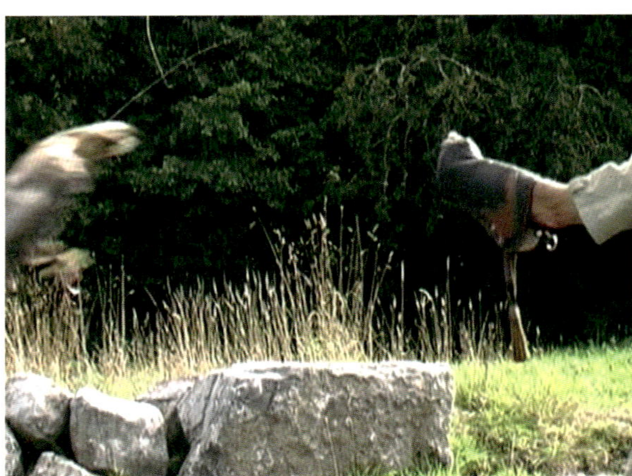

Whilst exploring Sligo, Jaki discovered *Eagles Flying*, *The Irish Raptor Research Centre*,

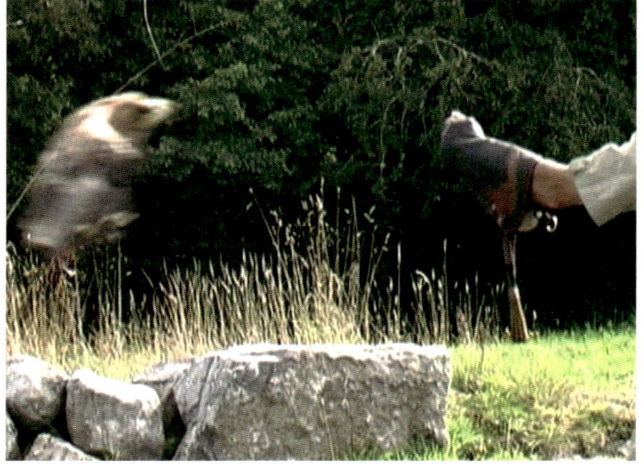

one of the county's lesser known but most intriguing attractions. Whilst open to the public for flying demonstrations,

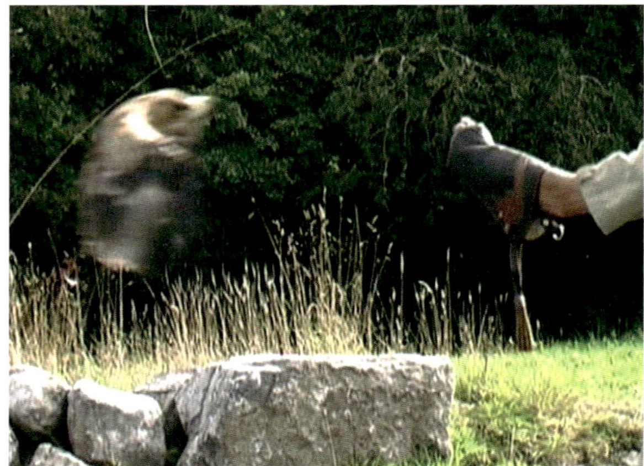

Eagles Flying is primarily a research-led sanctuary for birds of prey.

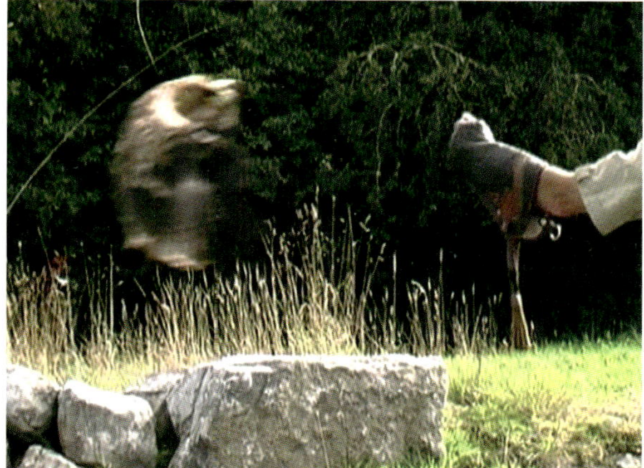

Some of the birds have been damaged through
misuse at other holdings, and have grown
overly aggressive or are physically damaged

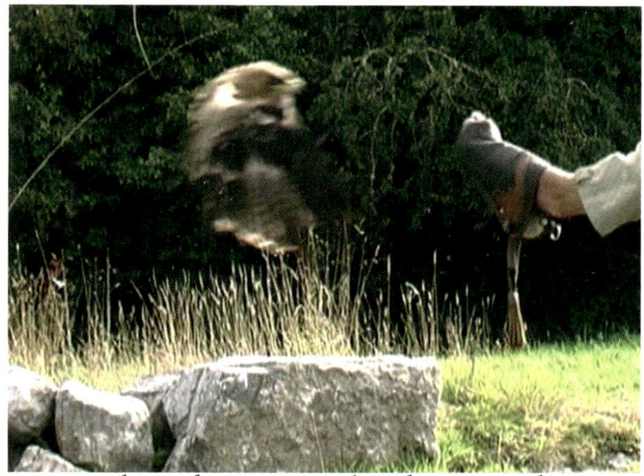

as a result. Others arrived at the centre having
been found with broken wings or other injuries.

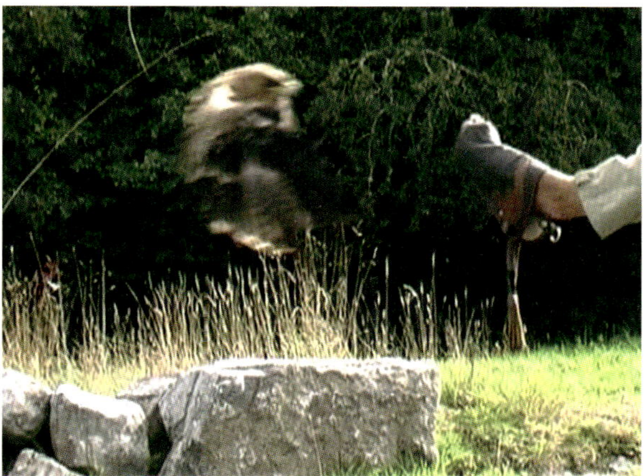

The birds are brought back to health through
the great care and patience of the family who
run the sanctuary

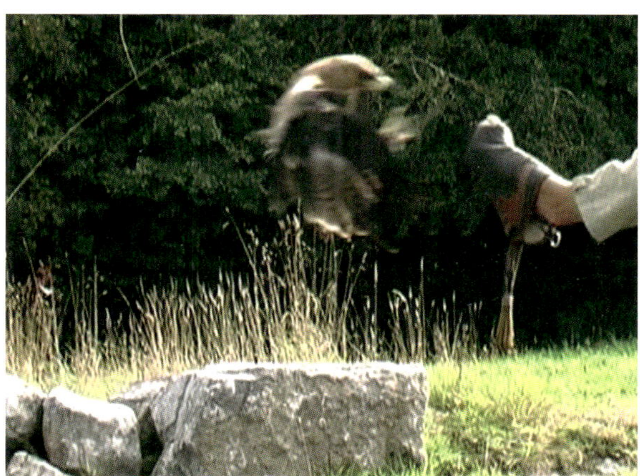

– the three humans portrayed in the work.

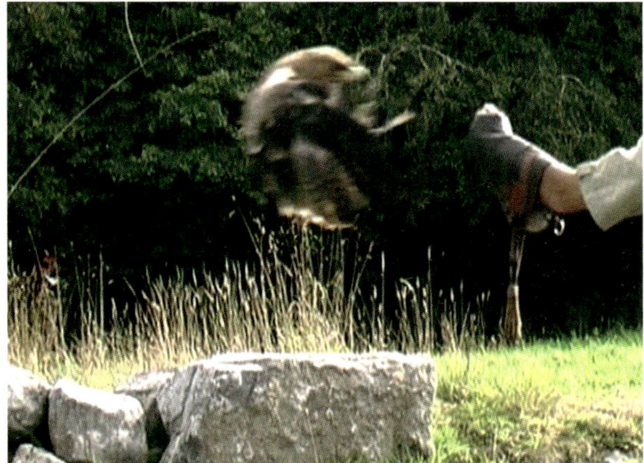

From an initial curiosity sparked
by the sight of the birds of prey
perched calmly in a domestic garden setting,

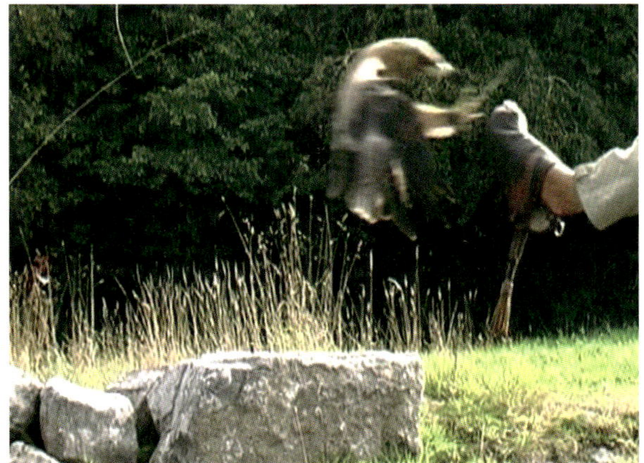

a major new work developed
that is at once located in County Sligo
and in its own distinct reality.

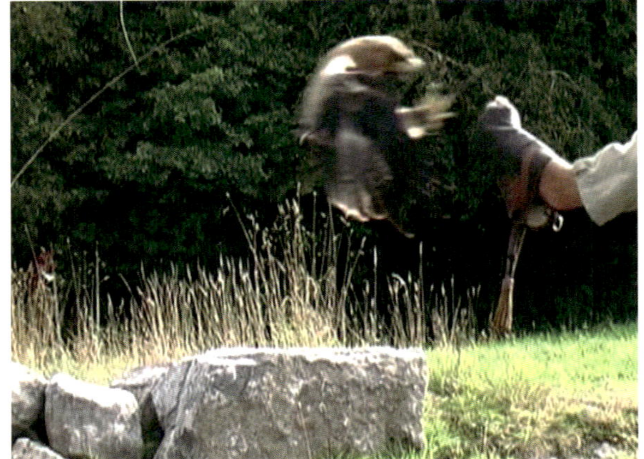
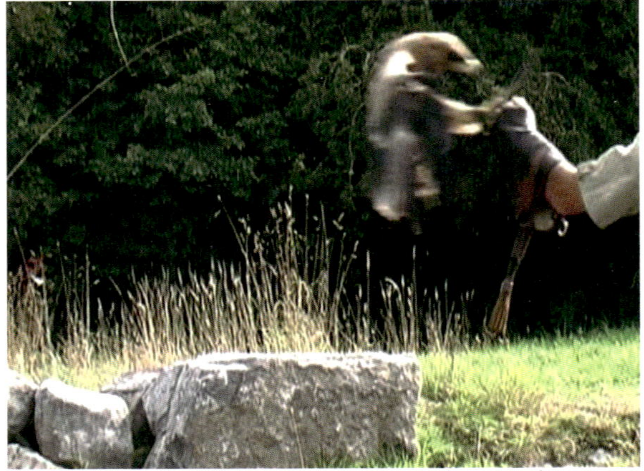

During the summer of 2006 Jaki carefully observed the day-to-day running of *Eagles Flying* and the resulting nine screen video installation traces the delicate relationship between the birds and their handlers. A series of intimate portraits of birds and handlers quietly

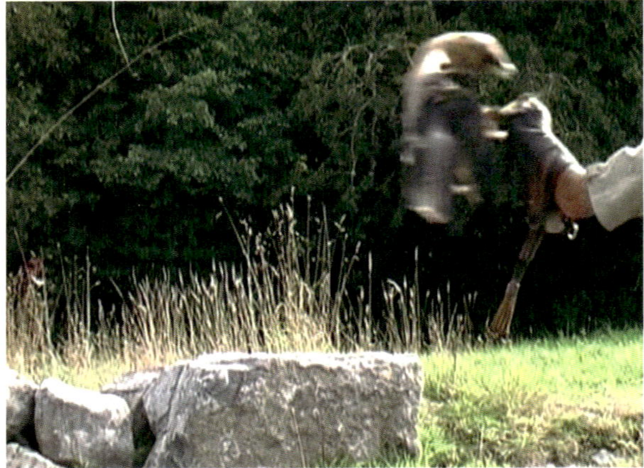
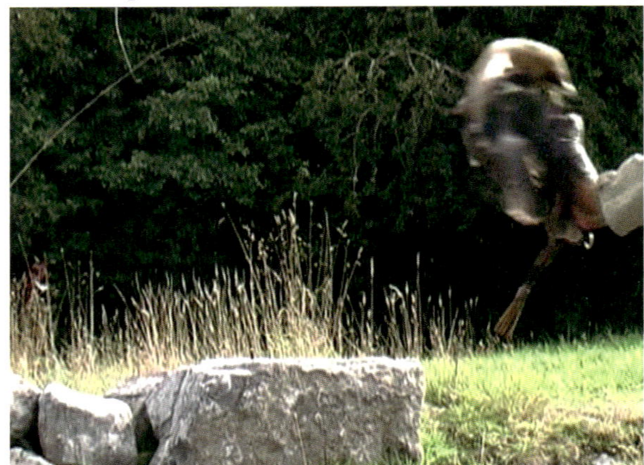

portrays the intense physicality, synergy and fragility of the ties between these wild yet contained birds and the scientists. These are not birds constrained as the zoo-based animals seen in some of her other works are – their wildness and freedom underlies all the films, particularly

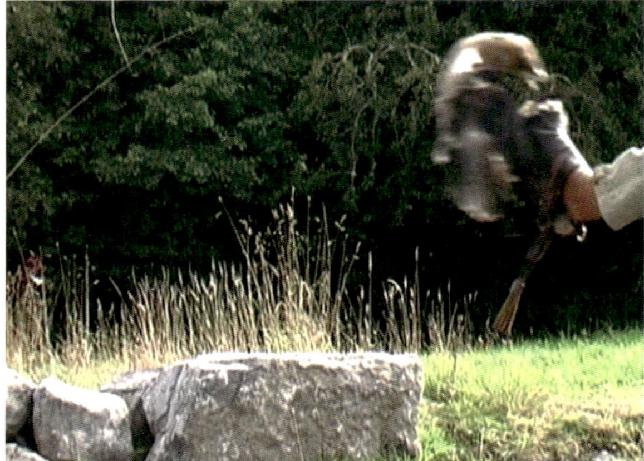
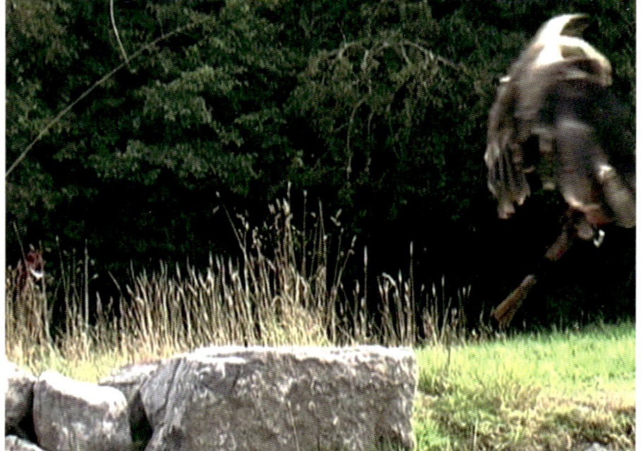

the flying sequences, synched across four screens to demonstrate the physical scope of their flight path, but yet they are operating to the rules of their handlers. Ultimately <u>In a World Like This</u> is concerned with the question of how we might best proceed in circumstances

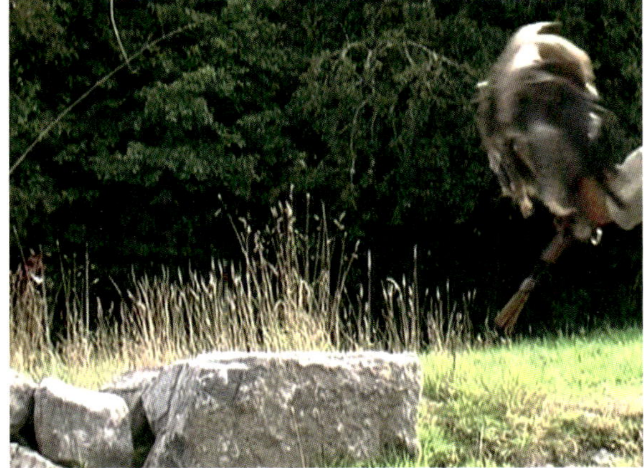

which are not perfect but are possibly the best they're ever likely to be. Tracing the some-times-hesitant flights and landings of

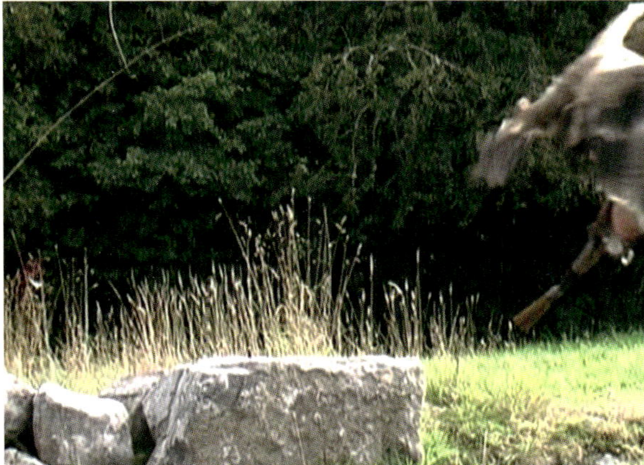

As Michael Newman observes in his thorough and illuminating essay for this book, this por-trayal of 'strangeness', the balance between

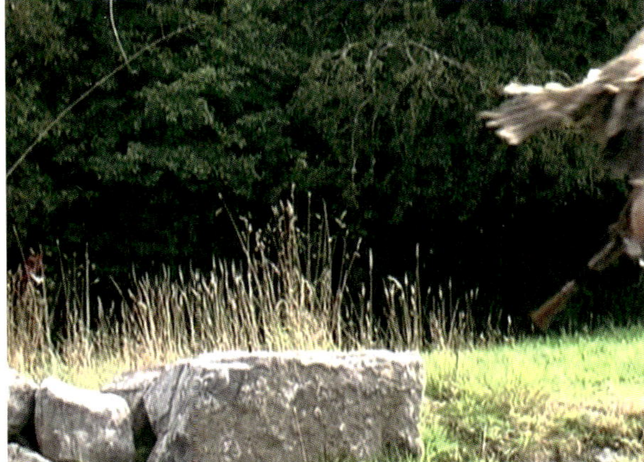

Her films and videos create elusive yet absorbing narratives that explore human interaction with the natural world, with the built environment

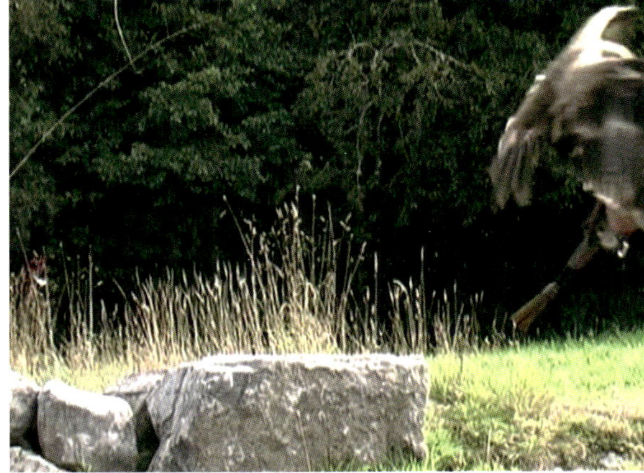

the different birds to and from their handlers, the fragile lines between damage, beauty and trust slowly reveal themselves.

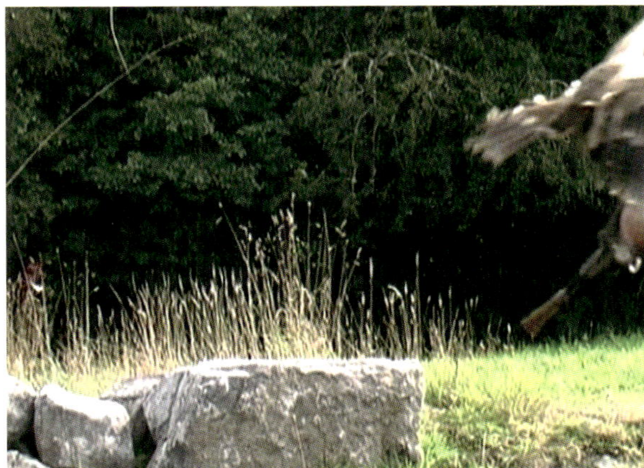

sameness and difference and the blurring of boundaries between different realities are con-cerns that run throughout Jaki's career.

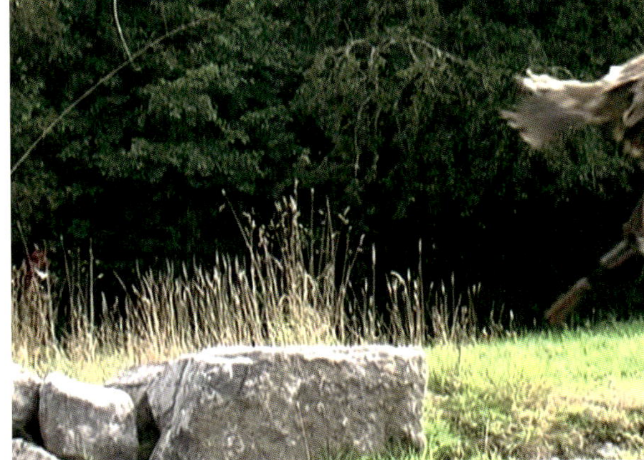

and with other humans. Using a combination of image, sound and voice-over her films sug-gest fragments of larger untold narratives and

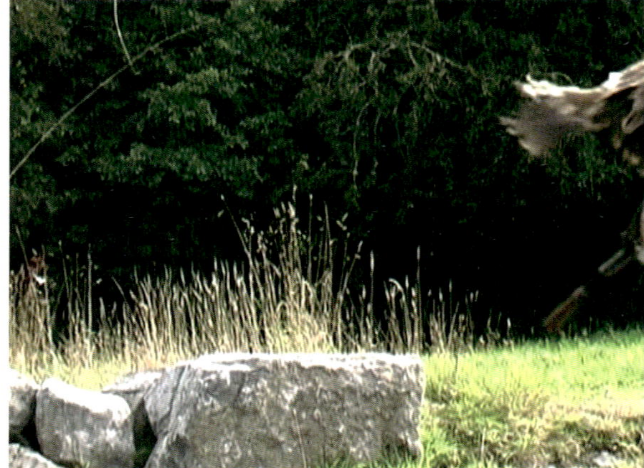

evoke a place where the boundaries between realities and dreams, past and present and animal and human become fluid and permeable.

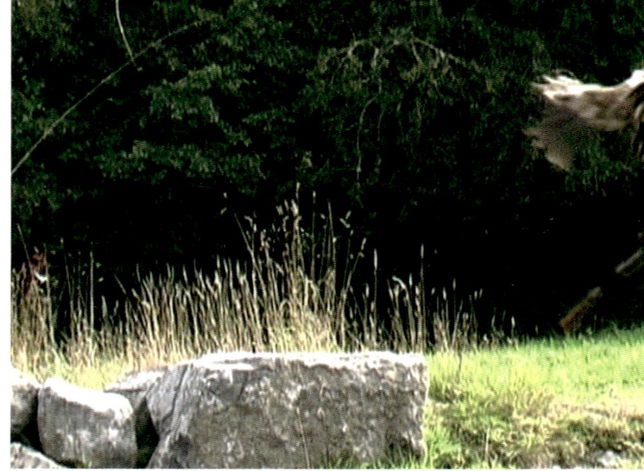

Bringing this work together for the first time, this book provides a unique experience of the depth and strength of her work to date.

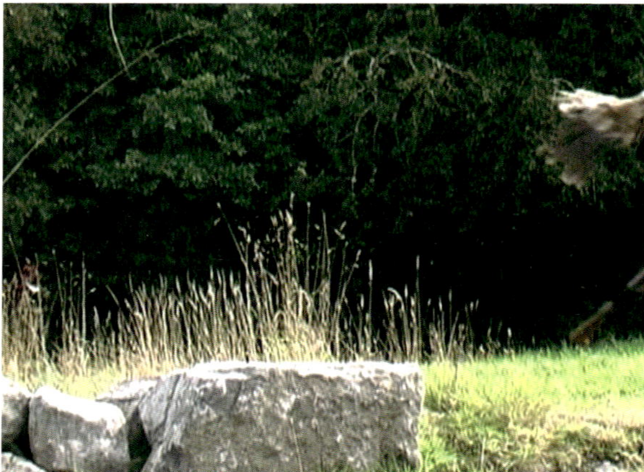

Throughout her practice the use of text has been a driving feature of Jaki's work.
With this in mind a selection of scripts and

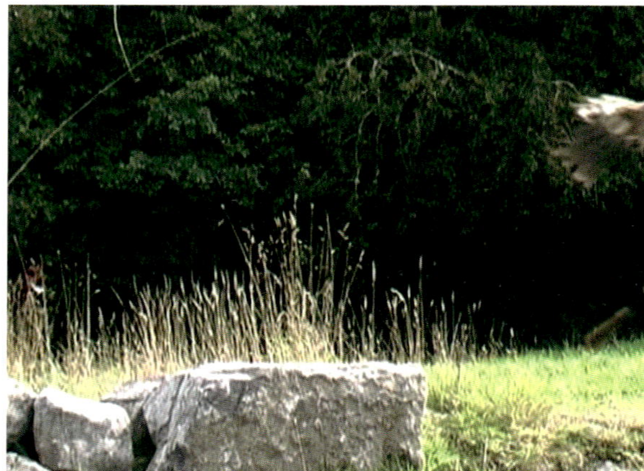

other writings are included in order to complement the images and to give those new to Jaki's work a fuller understanding of her practice.

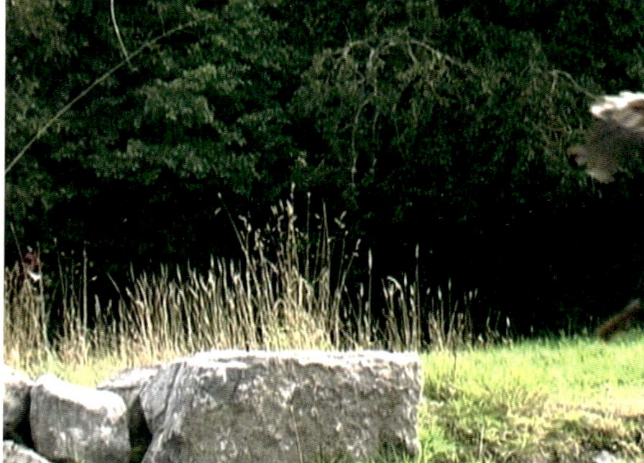

A collaborative project between Jaki and the designer Will Holder, the book has been conceived as a printed equivalent of Jaki's work.

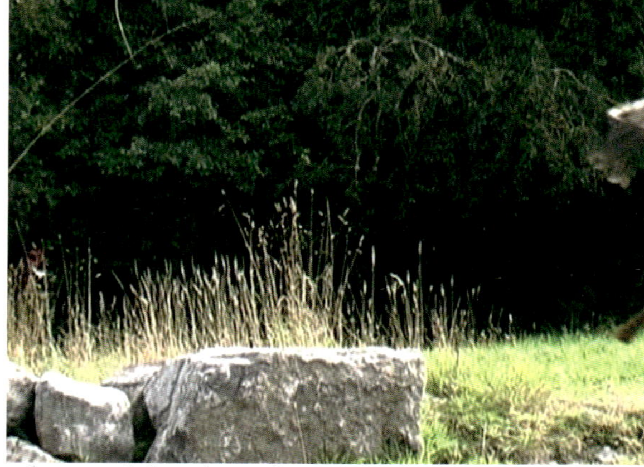

The Model is therefore delighted to continue our relationship with Jaki by publishing this important and timely monograph on her work.
(continued on page 156)

JAKI IRVINE

IN A WORLD LIKE THIS

2006–2007

…I am regarding my inability to enter
my neighbour's mind as something like
an inability to enter his garden;
only as it were, it is a permanent inability,
the garden is sealed or charmed out of reach.

```
.… it was paved over…. flagstones…. something heavy anyway that
took over so much space and now.. they're up …and what's
there?…well you can imagine…but,  well no.. I don't want to put
anything there… no, I don't know what might grow there now…

It will need so much time, effort, energy… what? Yes- of
course…and hope…and of course… it hurts… I want to leave it like
that for now…I'll come back every now and then…see if …ahh…
```

.…For that analogy captures the impression
that I am sealed out; but it fails to capture the
impression (or fact) of the way in which he is
sealed in. He is not in a position to walk in that
garden as he pleases, notice the blooms when he
chooses: he is impaled upon his knowledge.

(Stanley Cavell, *Knowing and Acknowledging*)

I'm invited to do a fellowship at the Model Arts
and Niland Gallery in Sligo.

The process is simple:
in the beginning everything is relevant.

Yve Lomax referred to the "listening eye".

I think it means listening in two directions at once—inside and outside…

a kind of relaxed alertness,

so that a connection can be made—

a leap that will look inevitable in hindsight,

but is as yet unforeseeable from this position.

It's dark.

We go visiting some people and I hear
about a boy who could see no reason
to get up in the morning

but now he's on the road at six every day
because he has started working with falcons.

I think I'll go and visit the falconry,

but I'm told there's a different one…
closer…

and so I set off to take a look.

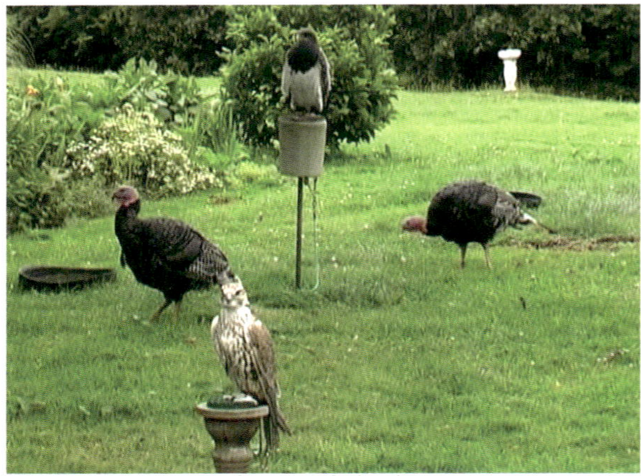

The garden is in front of the house,
laid out for display,
expansive and yet somehow shielded,

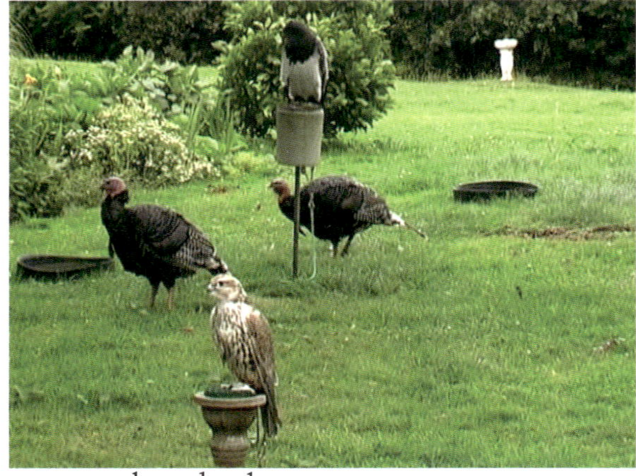

protected, set back,
from the house, from the strangers
who will pass in front of both.

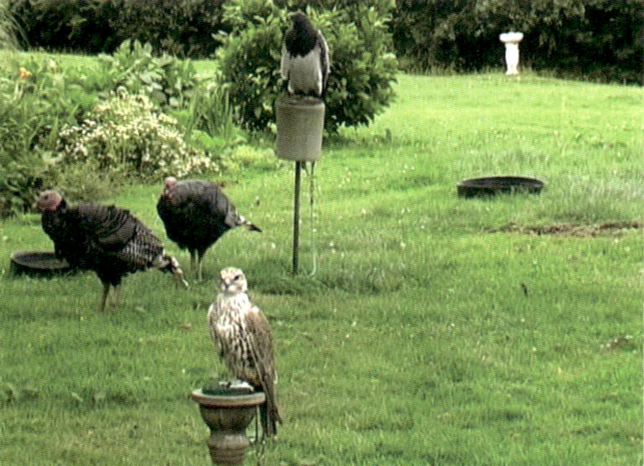

The guests are expected,
factored in to the equation as it were,

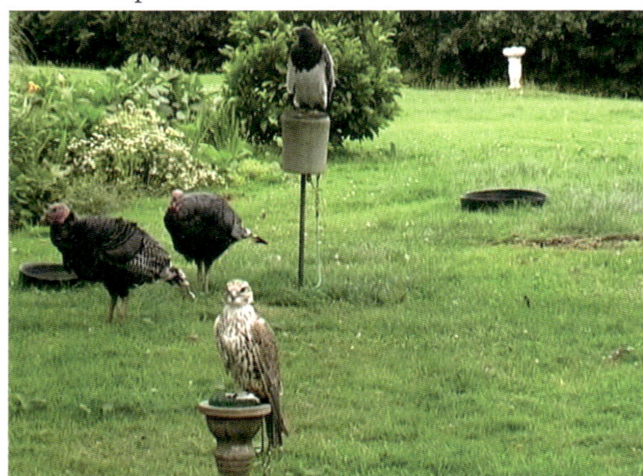

but always they will be slightly removed
from the scene that has been set out
and will unfold for their benefit.

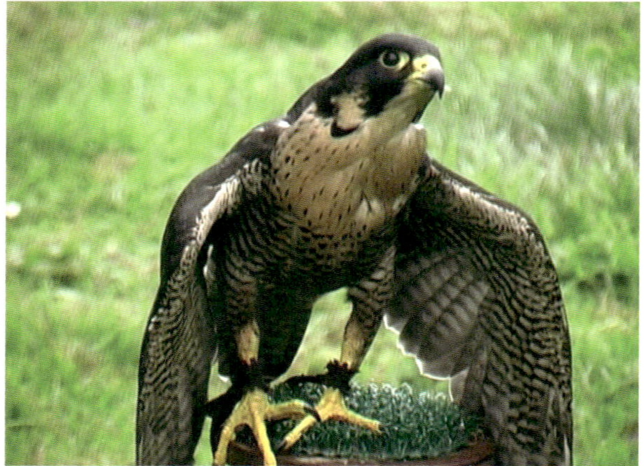

And the birds are there…
Some of them are small, fast,
originally bred by Arabian horsemen for speed.

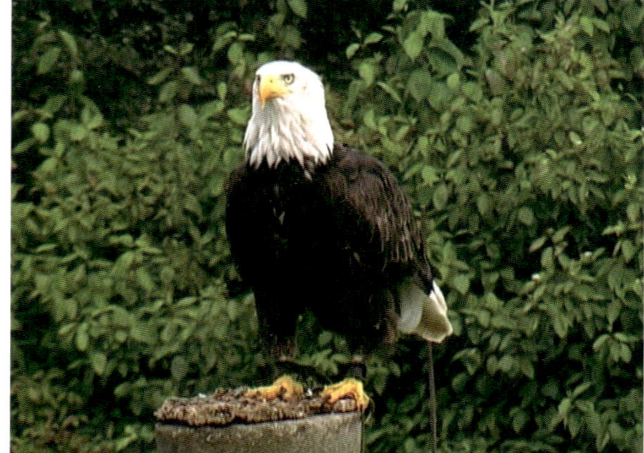

Others are large, majestic and powerful.
Talons and beaks combine razor sharpness
with vice-grip strength.

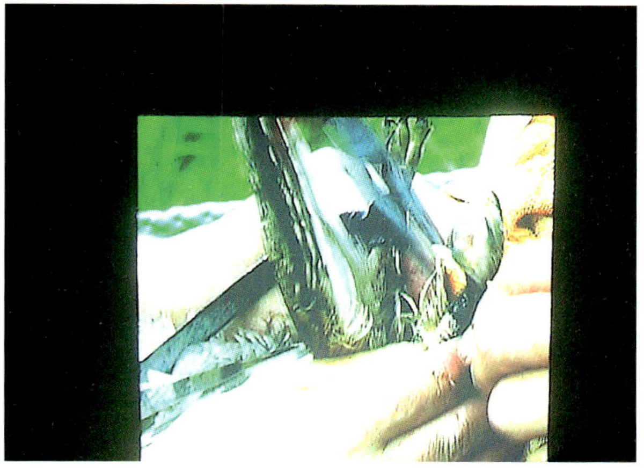

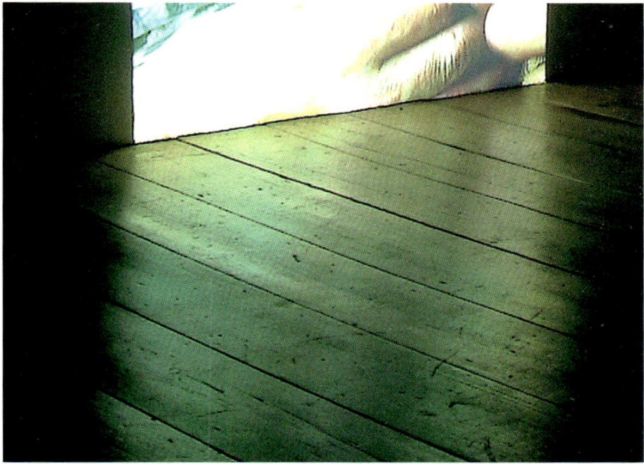

Some months later a small image is projected
low down, in a corner of The Model Arts and
Niland Gallery,

back behind the scenes as it were.

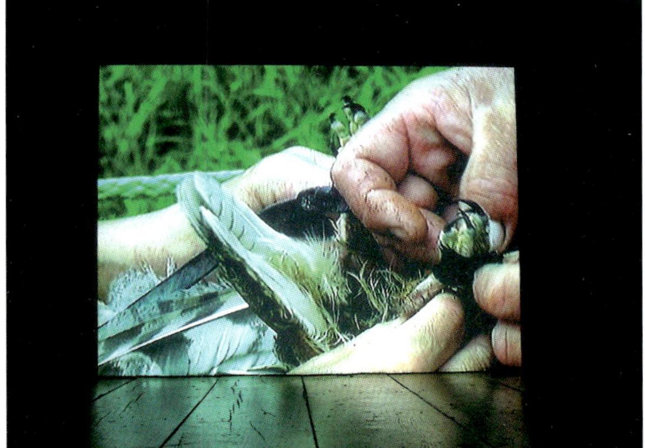

The footage reveals
the slow painstaking process
of attaching new leather jesses to a small bird.

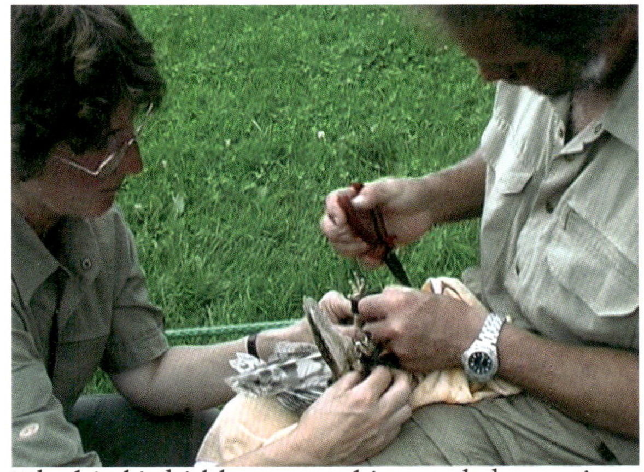

The bird is hidden, squeaking and chuntering
under a towel, while a pliers is being used to
perform the operation.

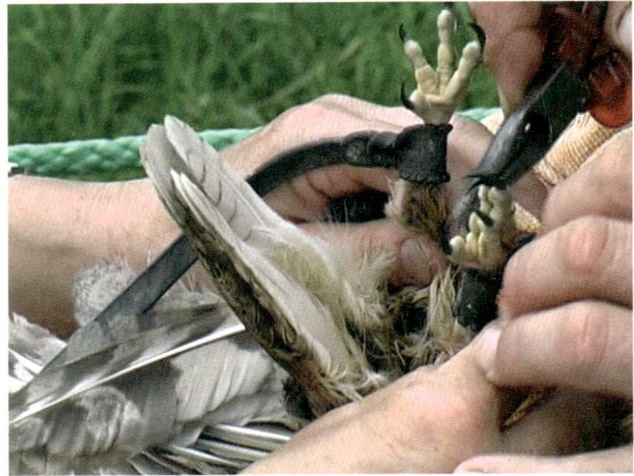

The bird's foot is somehow raw and fragile.
The man and woman working on it
are both firm and careful until,

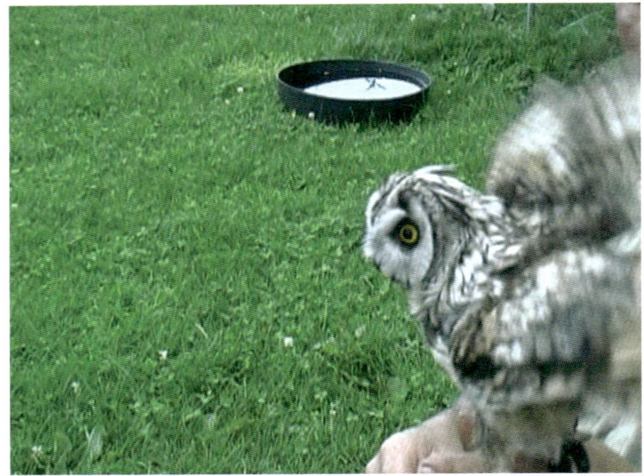

with a flurry, a little owl emerges slightly dazed
from its confines, flapping and fluttering
as it gets soothed back down .

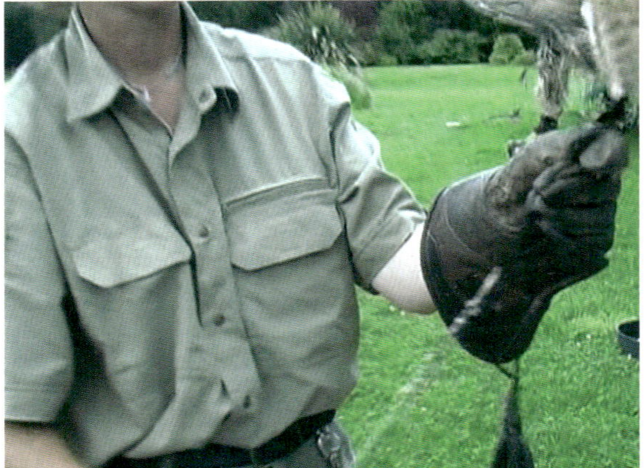

New shoes

says the woman, to no-one in particular,
as she walks away smiling
at the bird on her arm.

On two nearby screens the same man
and woman occupy a separate
but similar space in the garden,

set against thick foliage
that rustles occasionally in the wind.

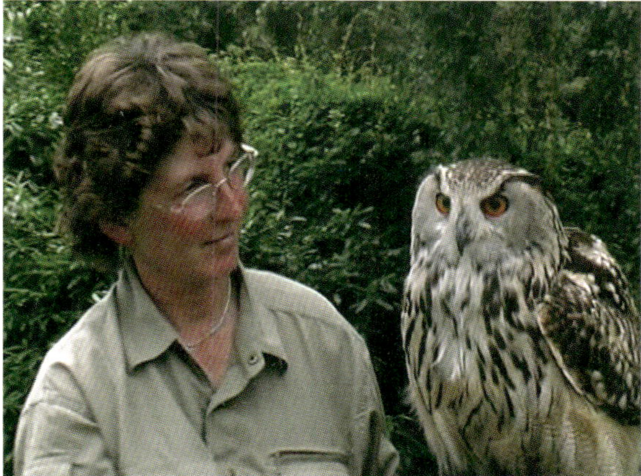

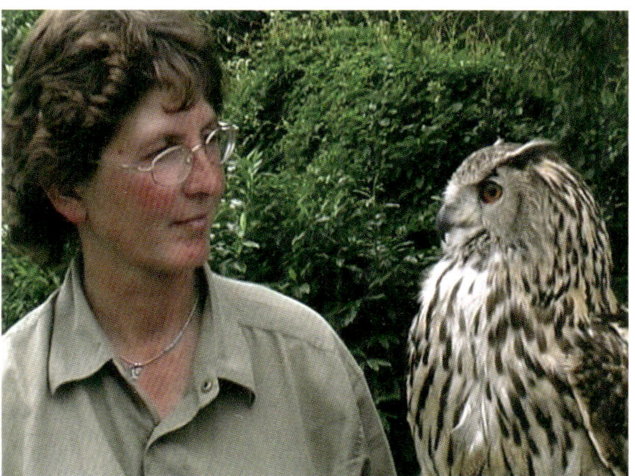

They each hold a different bird.
The woman, Regina, holds a large eagle owl—

one of the birds she calls to her
and feeds and runs from
and calls again in a public display.

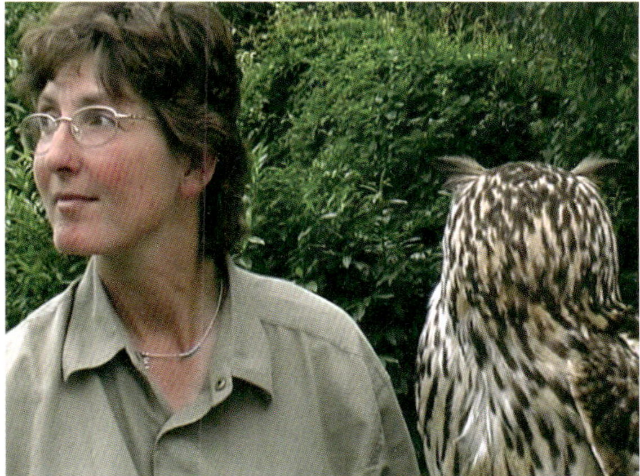

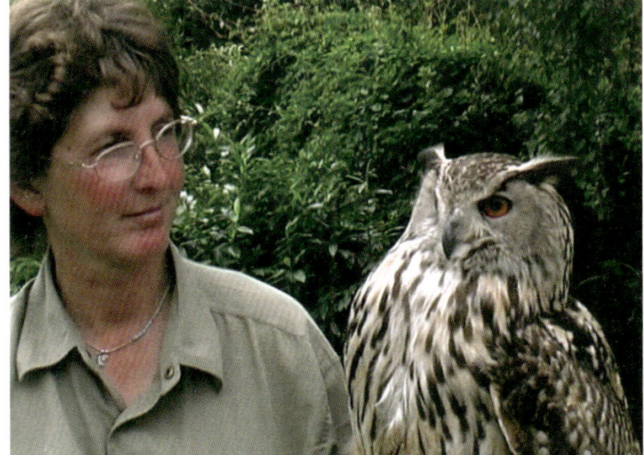

But for now they sit—a double portrait—
both similarly at ease and distracted by what
is unseen, beyond the frame of the camera.

The owl seems settled and almost tame,
knowable, until it flaps its wings and
its sheer scale alone points to something else,

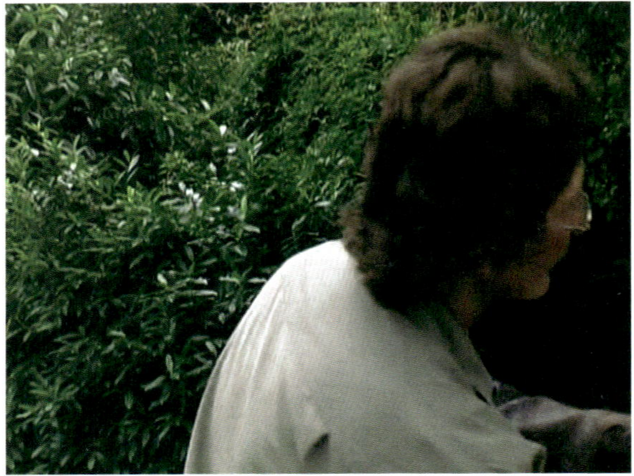

while Regina's watchfulness
and pervasive calm also subtly hint
at an awareness of its nature....

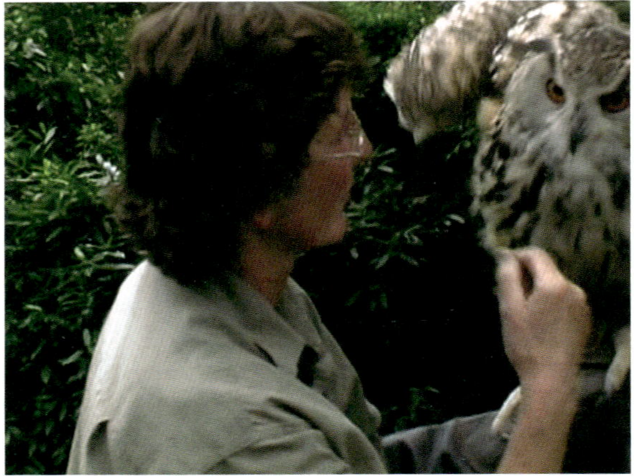

as something knowable but ultimately unknown,
the very silence of which is masked
by bells attached to its legs.

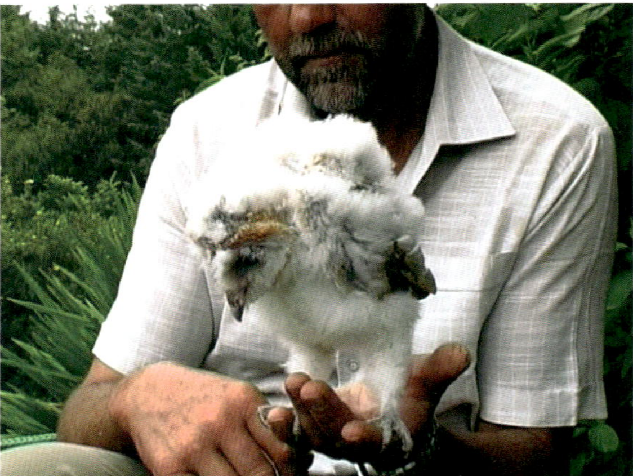

Footage of the man, Lothar,
is projected nearby.

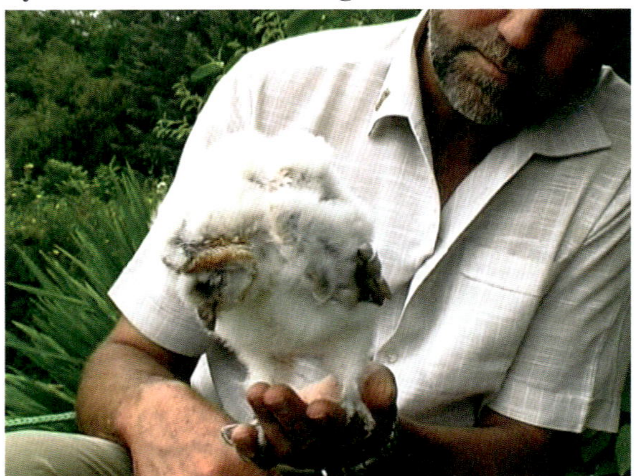

He holds a baby barn owl in his hands, relaxed
but attentive—as lovingly as others might hold
a can of beer, where every drop counts.

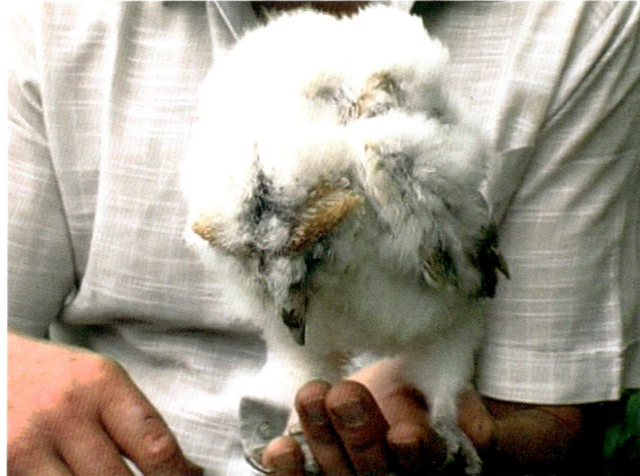

Despite the number of such birds he has held,
Lothar's hand is still and steady
as the tiny creature exerts

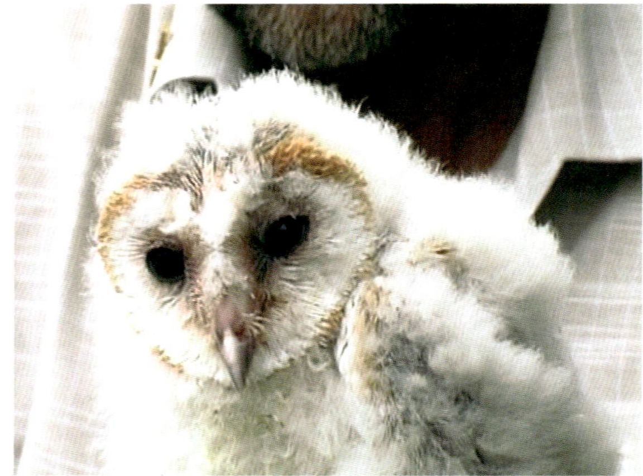

its own peculiar fascination,
weaving and bobbing as it hisses
and glares threats at things it cannot see.

They're standing
in front of the final double portrait,

set slightly apart.

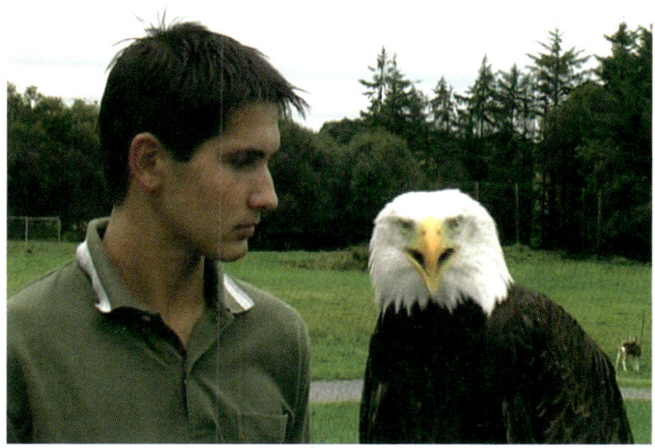

Here a young man, Alex,
stands holding an American bald eagle.

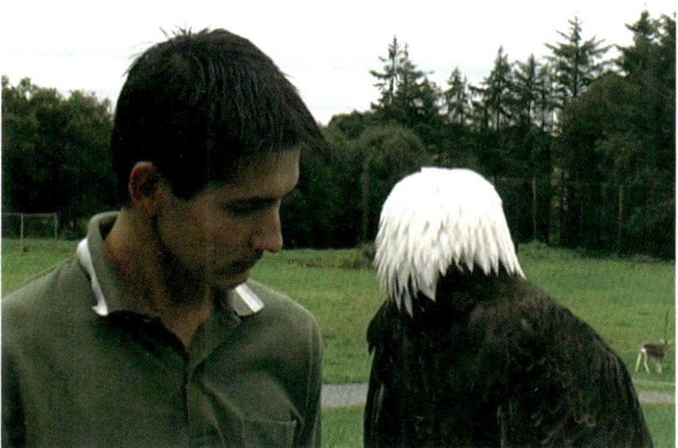

They're standing
in what seems to be an open space.

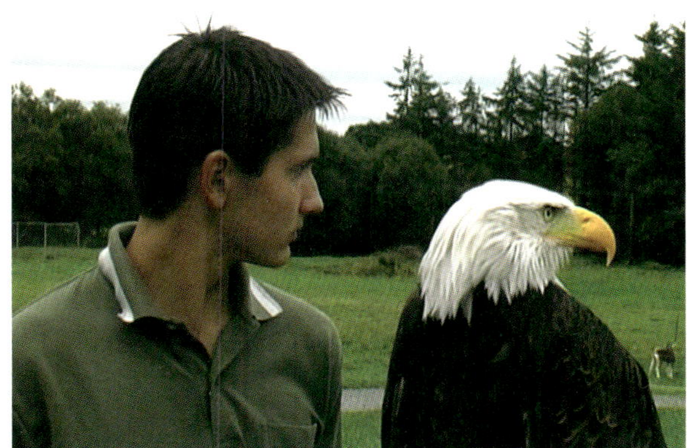

In the distance, treetops wave in the wind
and a goat worries at its tether.

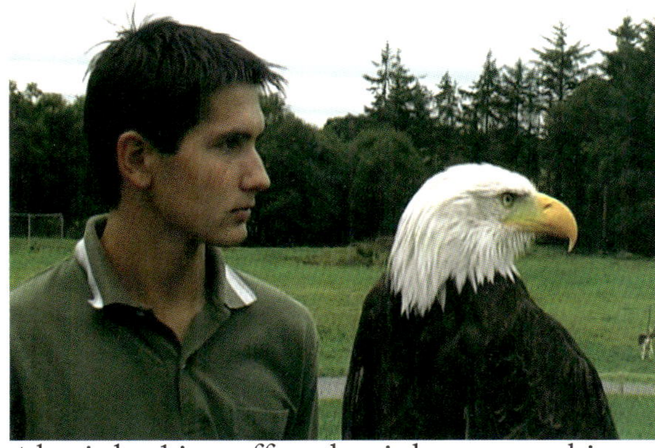

Alex is looking off to the right at something,
so that he is, for a while,

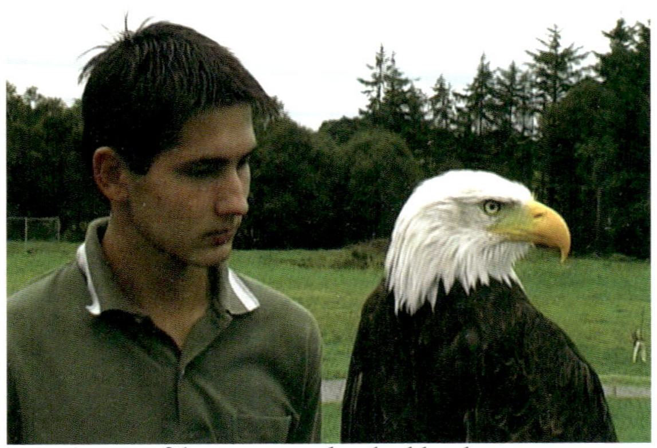

seen in profile—eyes shaded by brows,
clean features and a couple of tufts of hair
spiking up above his head.

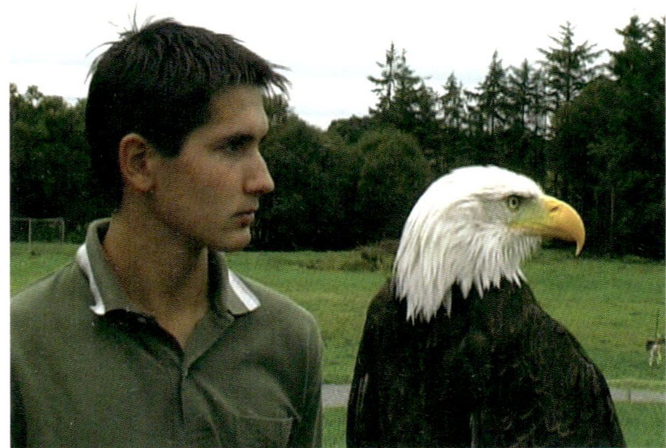

Something about this is echoed
by the eagle's similar attention
to whatever has caught its eye.

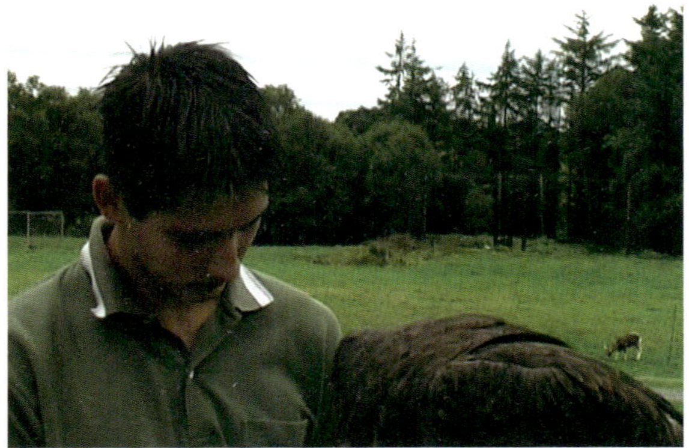

It too presents its profile:

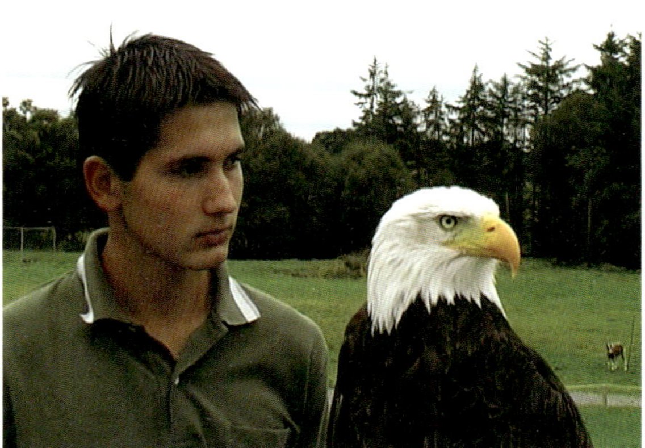

clean strong features, bright yellow beak,
and a forehead that overshadows
piercing eyes.

<pre>
                    GALLERY VISITOR 1
     Hmm, I don't know what it is… maybe it's me projecting,
     but there's some sort of odd connection going on here…
     a kind of doubling up or overlapping of something….

                    GALLERY VISITOR 2
     Yeah… there's some sort of mirroring or…
</pre>

Alex shifts his gaze down, and the eagle follows…
then it turns its head to one side, trying to figure
out the unseen mechanism that is recording it

and he, smiling, does the same, on and on
in a subtle interplay of glances and shifts
of focus and attention between them,

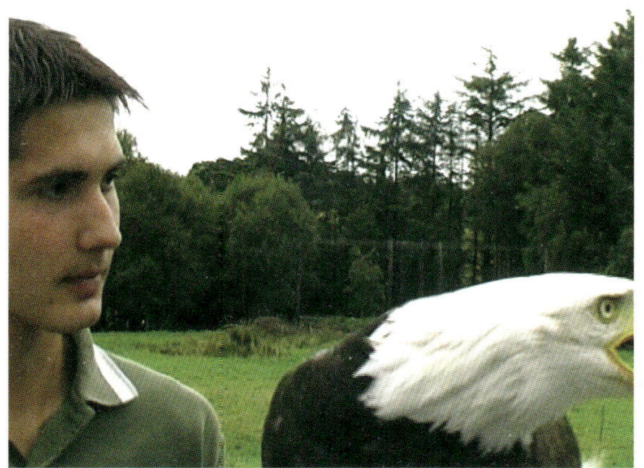

until abruptly, the eagle throws its head up and
sends out a long piercing series of calls that
mark and distance any cosy anthropomorphism,

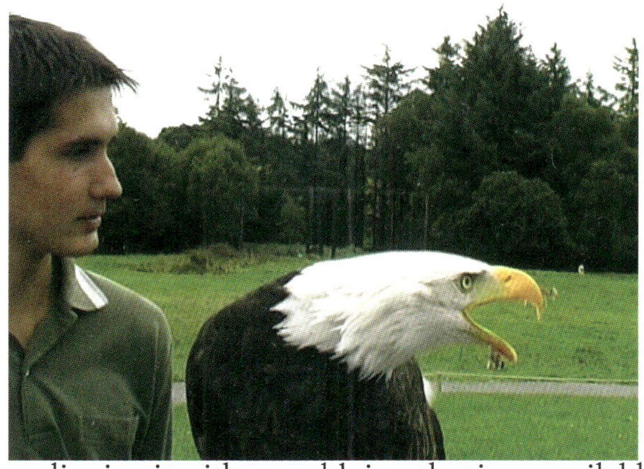

realigning it with a worldview that is unavailable,
for all her apparent acquiescence, held in front
of a still camera and yet, somehow not seen.

§   Tell me about the central space…. the
flights… they're ordinarily done at the Raptor Research Centre
for a paying public aren't they?

-                        Yeah, as a way of funding their
activities.

§   But here… it seems as if even though
an audience is anticipated, something is blocked or withheld?

-                        Well, there are five birds flying here…
but the flights are split across four screens, so I suppose that's
what you're picking up on…

§   Yes-they move across a screen,
from a tree to a perch, but this interruption by black is slightly
disorienting or disruptive, so that I find myself having to relo-
cate myself in the space between the screens, on the one hand,
while facing towards a blank space for a split second that may
or may not be where the bird will land….

-                        Ah yeah…I wanted to leave space
for maybe something between anxiety and desire…

§   And then there's that hesitation…
a hanging on too long, when the bird is called but it doesn't move.
It happens with nearly all of them-a slight but definite resist-
ance.

-                        Yeah, I wanted to let the editing
be paced by the birds themselves, that even when they are staged
for an audience, performing, they are also to some extent, not
entirely tame as it were. Lothar, who runs the centre, tells how
some of them were damaged before they got to the centre and even
though they're healed they won't attain their full speed again
to the point where the can successfully survive for long away from
the centre, although every now and again they do take off, because
they can… and sometimes, they're simply in the wrong place-the
wrong species, and won't be able to survive beyond the centre
for long. But something about that registers for me as kind of
blind spots in what we see of them-gaps where they might disappear
for a fraction of time, before coming back into view

§   On the tree or perch or on the arm
of one of the trainers?

-                         Yeah… but that slight uncertainty
maybe allows a chink of space to become aware of ourselves… our
own shadows caught that can be shifted, our own way of negotiating
and anticipating the world, even by way of projection…. or that we
might block something out by approaching it in the wrong way.

§   Something like how we only see what we
imagine to be there and the world confirms our own version of it,
catching ourselves in the act of imagining?

-                         Mmm…maybe…. or maybe that's too strong
a way of putting it.

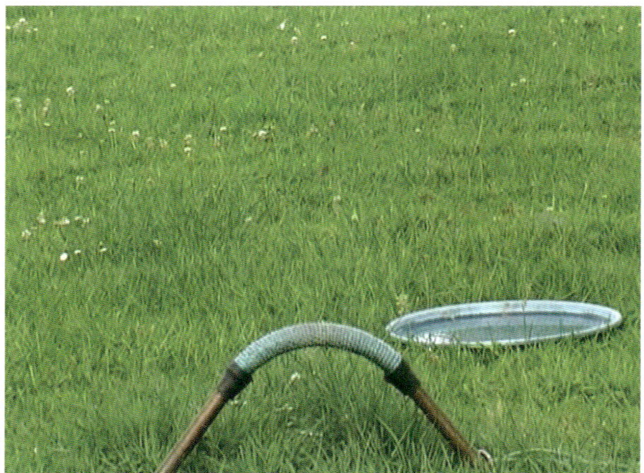

In the large projection of the final darkened space, the birds sit out on the lawn on perches.

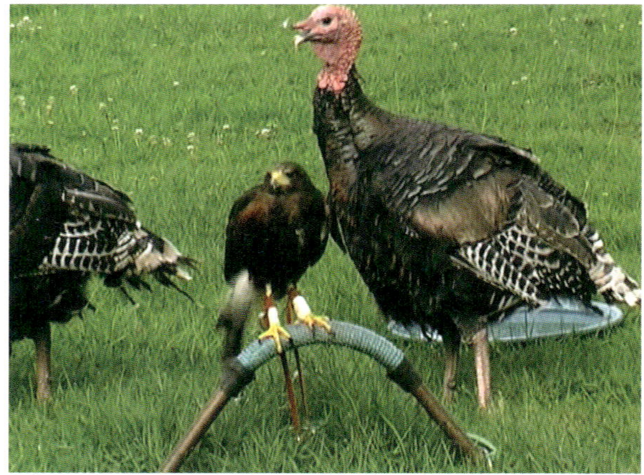

The camera slowly drifts, following a pair of turkeys that wander incongruously through the scene,

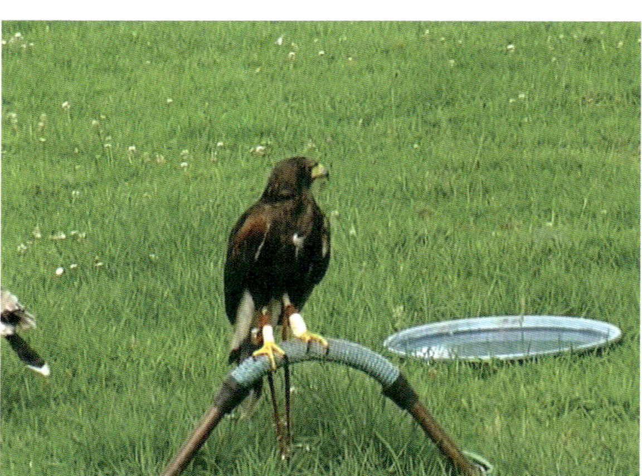

past the raptors that look like creatures of an entirely different order, before switching from one bird and then another…

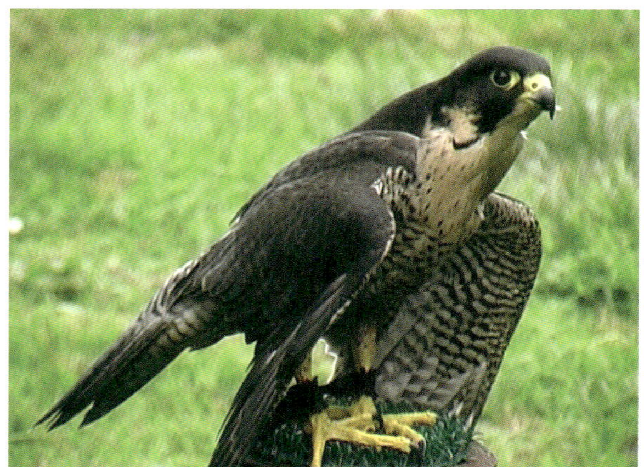

a peregrine falcon,

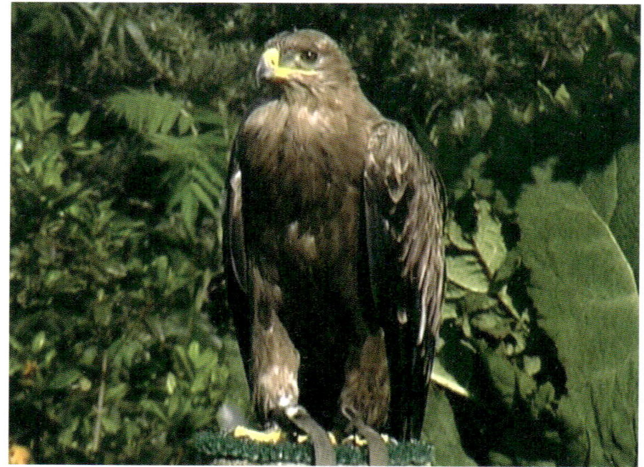

a tawny eagle,

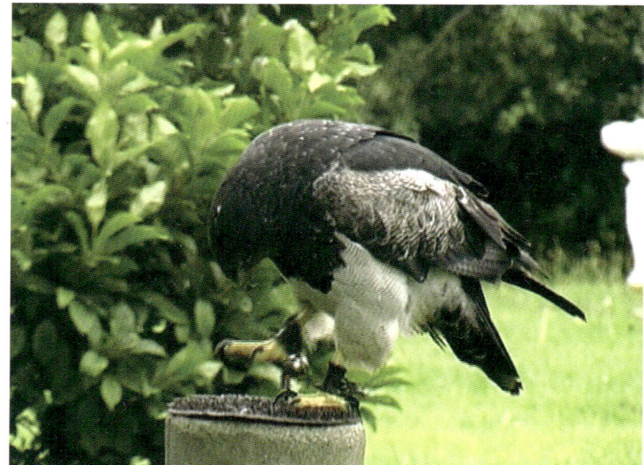

a black chested eagle,

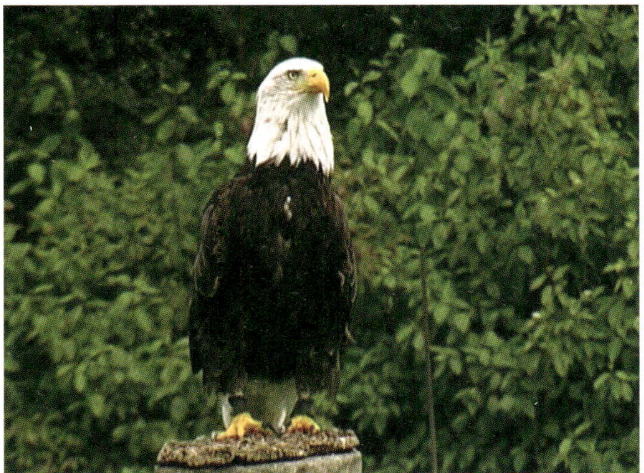

a bald headed eagle…

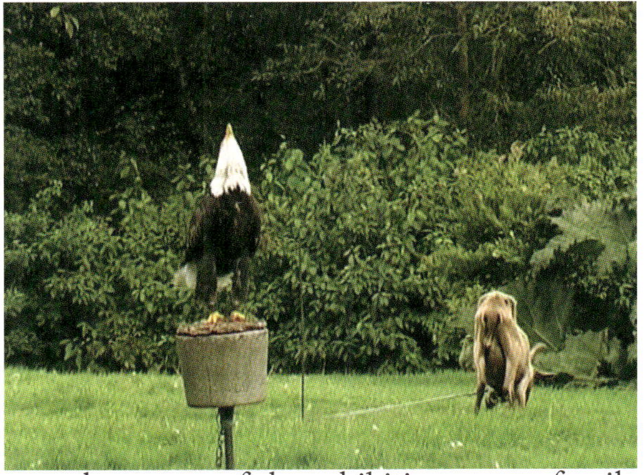

over the course of the exhibition grown familiar, but still somehow alien.

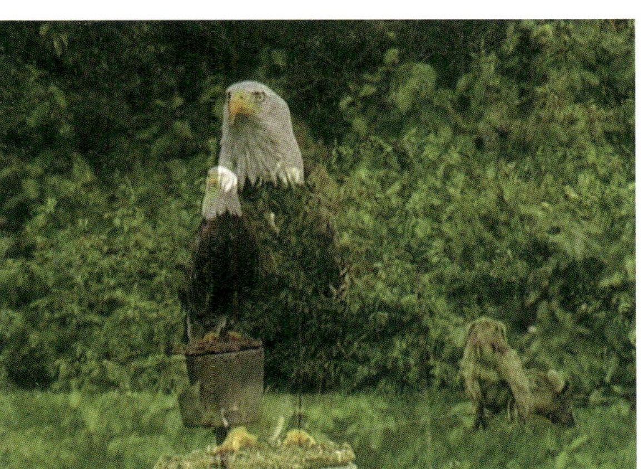

Here the edits coincide with the end of a movement or the turn of a head, picking up on the various attentions of the birds themselves.

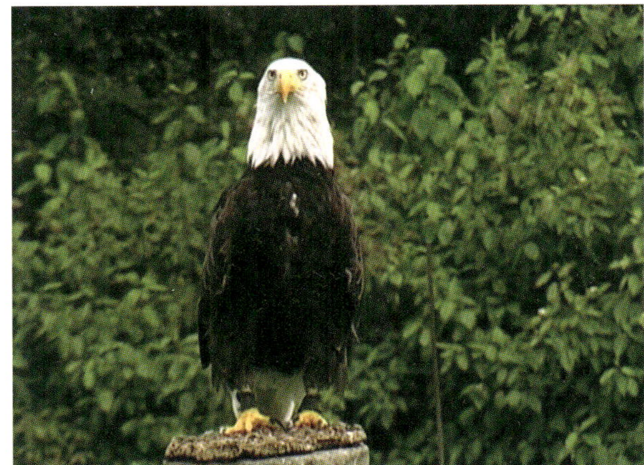

Continuously alert and watchful, time breaks down into an infinite flow of minutiae: blinks, flutters, picking at feathers, jangles of jesses,

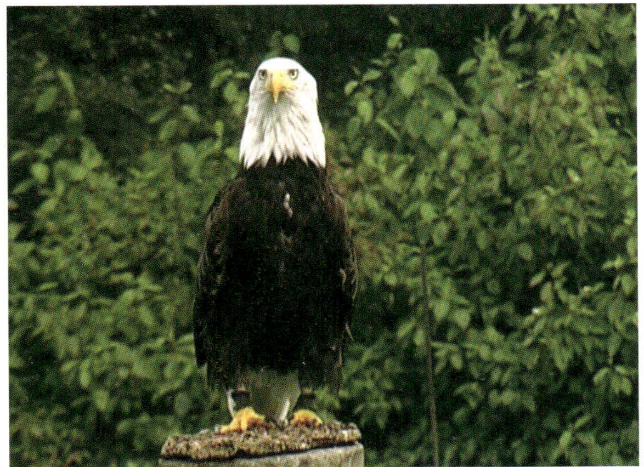

tugging at bells that have been attached to their legs, crows flying overhead, sheep bleating, fragile compromises between damage and free-

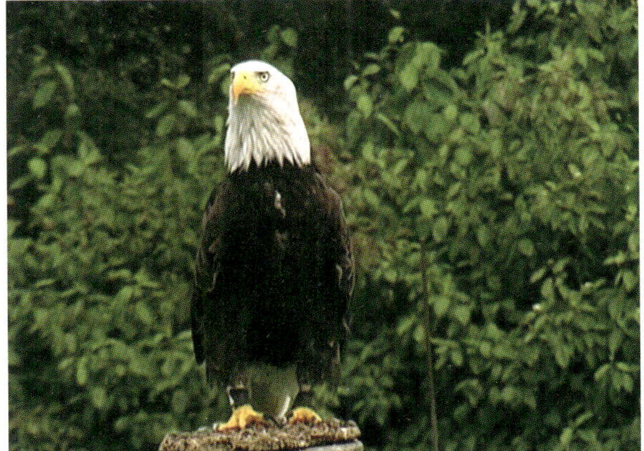

dom, struck and held for a moment or two longer than one might have imagined possible.

SELECTED WRITINGS 1993–2008

0.34   jingle
0.40   wind
0.53   old sheep
       (deep/loud)
1.00   lamb
1.43   jingle
1.50   Alex whistle
2.07   donkey bray-
       ing (long)
3.00   lamb
3.30   tweet
3.53   blackchested
       eagle cry
4.20   jingle
4.34   flap
4.50   jingle
5.01   bells (at
       foot)
5.44   flapping
5.53   crows &
       geese
6.17   geese
6.55   jingle
7.14   lamb
7.44   flutter
8.04   silence
8.44   call
8.50   jingle
8.55   flutter /
       perch?
9.00   bald headed
       eagle
9.20   muttering
9.30   dog growling
9.40   Alex whistle
9.50   dog bark
       (alsatian)
10.20 tawny eagle
       call distant
10.34 jangle
11.10 wing flutter
11.20 tawny eagle
11.24 jangle

11.37 fast flutter
11.50 flutter
12.08 clanking off
       perch
12.36 bell
12.45 big wing
       beat
12.50 lamb
12.55 flutter
13.14 tweet
13.33 tawny eagle
       call
14.05 bell
14.18 peregrine
       falcon call
14.20 clank
       bell
14.49 flap...
       perch
14.57 flap
15.07 flap-
       perch
15.30 tawny eagle
       calling
15.52 lamb
16.10 lamb
16.18 lamb
16.44 geese
17.46 wind
18.09 tawny eagle
       call
18.13 footsteps
18.27 lamb
18.47 lamb
18.55 flutter
19.00 sheep
19.12 owl chunter-
       ing
19.19 long slow
       flapping
19.20 bell
       flutter
19.31 jingle

19.42 flight to
       perch
19.57 jangle
20.06 perch/flap
20.33 sheep
21.08 cheeping
21.23 flutter
       cheep
21.37 flutter
21.50 overhead
       traffic

∫∫

22.30 twittering
       jingle
       (faint)
22.56 footsteps
       on gravel
23.08 flutter
       jangle

.... wind

∫∫

27.51 bucket
       banging
28.00 flapping
29.30 fast light
       flap
29.56 dog panting
30.06 panting
       pawsteps
30.56 tawny eagle
       grumbling
31.24 jingling
31.50 twittering
33.16 flapping
       (persistent)
33.42 bees humming

34.00 bees
35.26 crows (long)
35.30 crows
35.47 cock crowing
36.26 cock crowing
      closer
      crows cawing
36.49 crows in
      flight
      soft flutter
37.21 sheep
37.31 bell
37.39 cock crow
37.44 bell
38.01 wind & cock-
      crow
38.24 crows
38.31 flutter
38.38 crows/ flap-
      ping/flutter
39.00 twitter
      cheap
39.40 eagle call

40.16 car engine
      overhead
      plane

      ∫∫

40.27 flap
40.30 flap / perch
40.43 cockcrow
40.53 flapping-
      long
      slow
41.08 flapping
      cockcrow
41.27 slow flap
41.41 flapping
      cockcrow
41.56 geese
      donkey
42.18 whistle

42.31 hup
42.50 cockcrow
43.00 cockcrow
43.43 footsteps
      jingle
44.05 mutter
44.11 flutter
44.24 twitter
44.43 traffic
      tawny eagle
      calls
      —far away
45.29 bees
45.50 flutter
45.56 flutter at
      bark
46.33 bees
48.08 wind
      small falcon
      chuntering
49.00 flutter
49.20 flutter
50.00 rustle
56.22 jangle of
      ties
56.55 crow
58.29 crows
58'35"
      chuntering
58'53"
      bees
59'00"
      bark
      cockcrow
59'33"
      jangle on
      perch
59'46" cockcrow
59'54"
      dog bark
1:00.36
      jingle
1:00.37
      dog barking
1:00.55
      tweet

1:01:10
      wind
1:1:20
      tweet
1:01:39
      jangle
1:01:49
      geese
1:01:56
      dog
1:01:59
      geese
1:02.10
      wind
01:31:02
      Alex call,
      whistle
01:31:14
      soft flap-
      ping, wind-
      no bell
01:31:26
      tree atmos &
      crows
01:31:54
      hawk eating
01:32.03
      flight jin-
      gle
01:32.47
      small flap-
      ping, flurry
01:33.02
      slow flap
01:33.07
      rustle...
      preen

(previously
published
in "Leaves
and Papers",
a Douglas Hyde
Gallery publi-
cation)

SILENT JAPANESE HORROR

Outside there was a sound that nearly wasn't one at all loud and completely muffled at the same time.
The sound was being made by a Japanese woman who was staring into her bag with her hand over her mouth. The bag was staring right back at her like a street comedian with a wide open mouth and no sound at all coming out.

The woman wasn't laughing. She was looking shocked.

Three other Japanese women were standing around looking worried, their eyes shifting backwards and forwards from their friend's misery to a man in a dirty tracksuit and back again.
He was trying to convince them of something.
One woman stuck her hand into his trouser pocket but it came out again empty.

Their friend kept on trying to shout or cry but no tears would come out. Her voice was still only some heavy breaths left over from a bad movie with the sound turned right down.
  He very deliberately took off his shoes, turning them upside-down like a magician. He shook one first and then the other, saying loudly "Look, I don't have anything of yours...
Look- here's my bag...take it, here's my wallet. "

The woman's mouth was still opening and closing and she had started trying to faint and not faint at the same time, holding onto a nearby pillar in a way that made her look like a forgotten Japanese actress who just couldn't make the move into sound. Once, they said, she had the makings of a star, but that was before...

The man was still talking loudly trying to not enjoy himself:

"I'll go with you", he was saying to one of the women
"I'll go with you...now, I'll go with you"

The women stared from him to their friend and back again like they couldn't believe what was happening. By this time a crowd had gathered attracted by the silent moans.
  Nobody knew what to do. They just stood frozen to the spot and watched how the women didn't want to let this man go even though they couldn't bear to spend another second with him.
And the sound of their friend's muffled moans went on and on, washing over them all so that they felt cold and sick and a long way from home.

A SHORT RED SCARF (!)

Three large freckles sit on the face of an old Chinese man
like a joke.

The waitresses smile as if they've heard it before
and sit him down behind a plate of beans.

The punchline is a short red scarf

THE SMELL OF CHICKEN SANDWICHES

Every time I go into the travel agents
I am reminded that the smell of chicken sandwiches
has gotten there before me.

I've been going in there regularly
and I know it's not connected to any one person,
like someone's favourite lunch that they just can't do without,
not even for one day,
Absolutely not!

It's been hanging around there so long
that I think someone must have hired it
tho' I can't figure out what the boss had in mind.

"So what can you do?"
". . . . .!"
"Ah, very good, you're hired."

Maybe there's been new market research
that shows how people find themselves
more in the mood for long distance holidays
if accompanied by the smell of chicken sandwiches.

All the other staff have changed
but the smell of chicken sandwiches
is working towards its pension.

1. <u>ANOTHER DIFFICULT SUNSET</u>

a.

                         SHE (o.s.)
Tigers-ah tigers! I MUCH prefer them to lions.
(laughing) My living room is full of them.

                         SHE (o.s.)
If a lion could talk we wouldn't understand.
                         HE (o.s.)
Not only that, but if we could understand it we'd be so distracted
by the fact of it talking at all that we wouldn't care what it was
saying. So it's better off roaring.
Especially if it's in discomfort.

b.   MALE (V.O. Irish Accent)
Pauline had gotten me thinking about the tigers. I sat there
and thought about them…how they killed and ate my parents.
I was going to school, I was nine years old and having trouble
with arithmetic.
One morning the tigers came in while we were eating breakfast.
And before my father could grab a weapon, they killed him and
they killed my mother. My parents didn't even have time to say
anything before they were dead.
I was still holding the spoon from the mush I was eating.
"Don't be afraid." One of the tigers said. "We're not going
to hurt you. We don't hurt children. Just sit there where you
are (er) and we'll tell you a story."
One of the tigers started eating my mother. He bit her arm off
and started chewing on it. "What kind of story would you like
to hear?"
"I know a good story about a rabbit…"
"Don't want to hear a story." I said.
"Okay." the tiger said and he took a bite out of my father.
I sat there for a long time with the spoon in my hand, and then
I put it down.

"Those were my folks," I said finally.
"We're sorry." one of the tigers said. "We really are."
"Yeah." The other tiger said. "We wouldn't do this if we didn't
have to. If we weren't absolutely forced to. But this is the only
way we can keep alive."
"We're just like you," the other tiger said. "We speak the same
language you do. We think the same thoughts, but we're tigers."

"You could help me with my arithmetic."
"What's that?" One of the tigers said.
"My arithmetic."
"Oh, your arithmetic."
"Yeah."

"What do you want to know?" One of the tigers said.
"What's nine times nine?"
"Eighty-one." The tiger said.

"What's eight times eight?"
"Fifty-six." The tiger said.
I asked him half a dozen other questions…six times six,
seven times four eccetera
I was having a lot of trouble with arithmetic.

Finally the tigers got bored with my questions and told me to go away.
"Okay, " I said, "I'll go outside. "
"Don't go too far. " One of the tigers said. "We don't want anyone to come up here and kill us. "

"Okay. "
They both went back to eating my parents. I went outside and sat down by the river.
"I'm an orphan. " I said.

[mind the doors please. mind the doors]

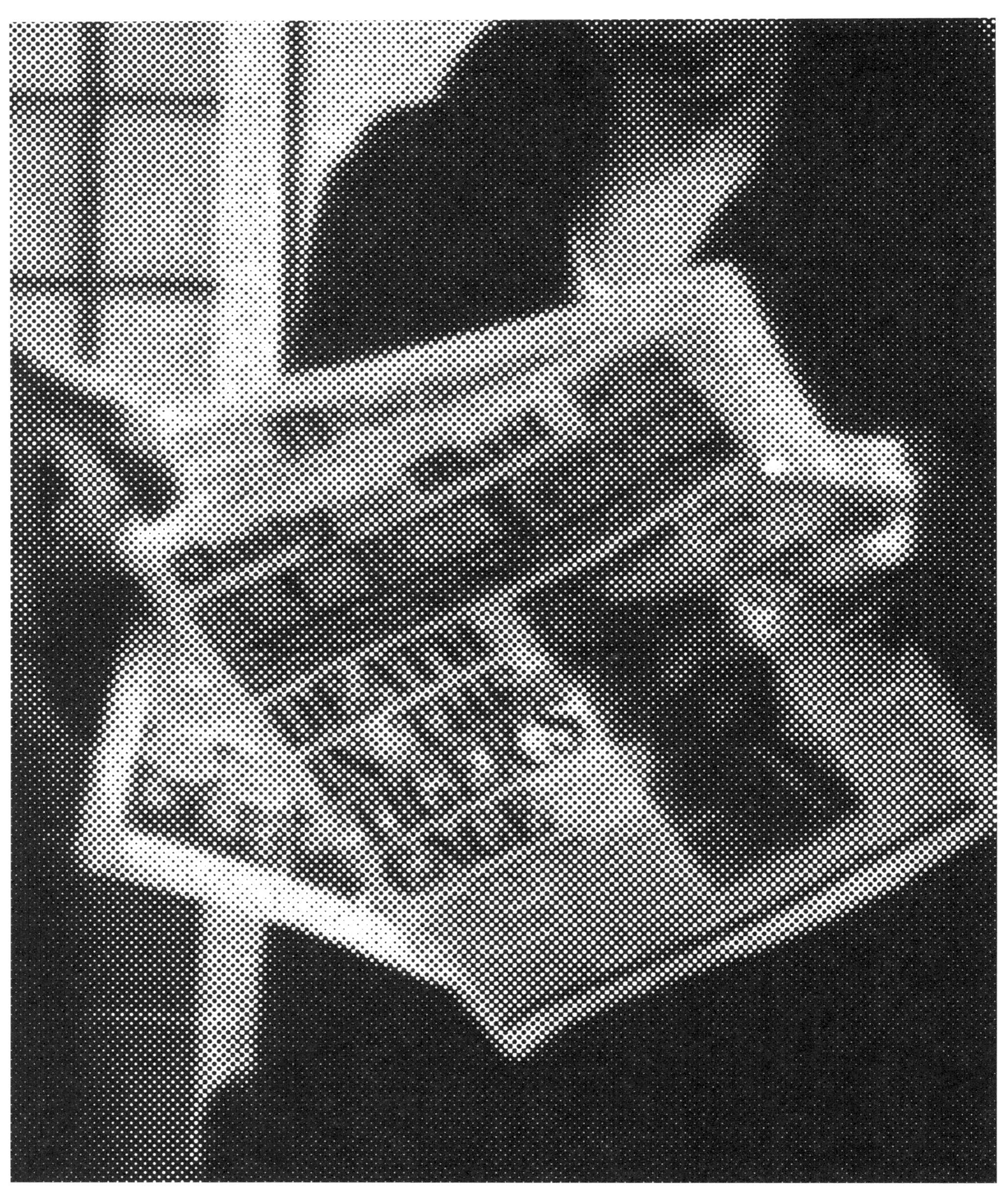

[mind the gap.
mind the gap]

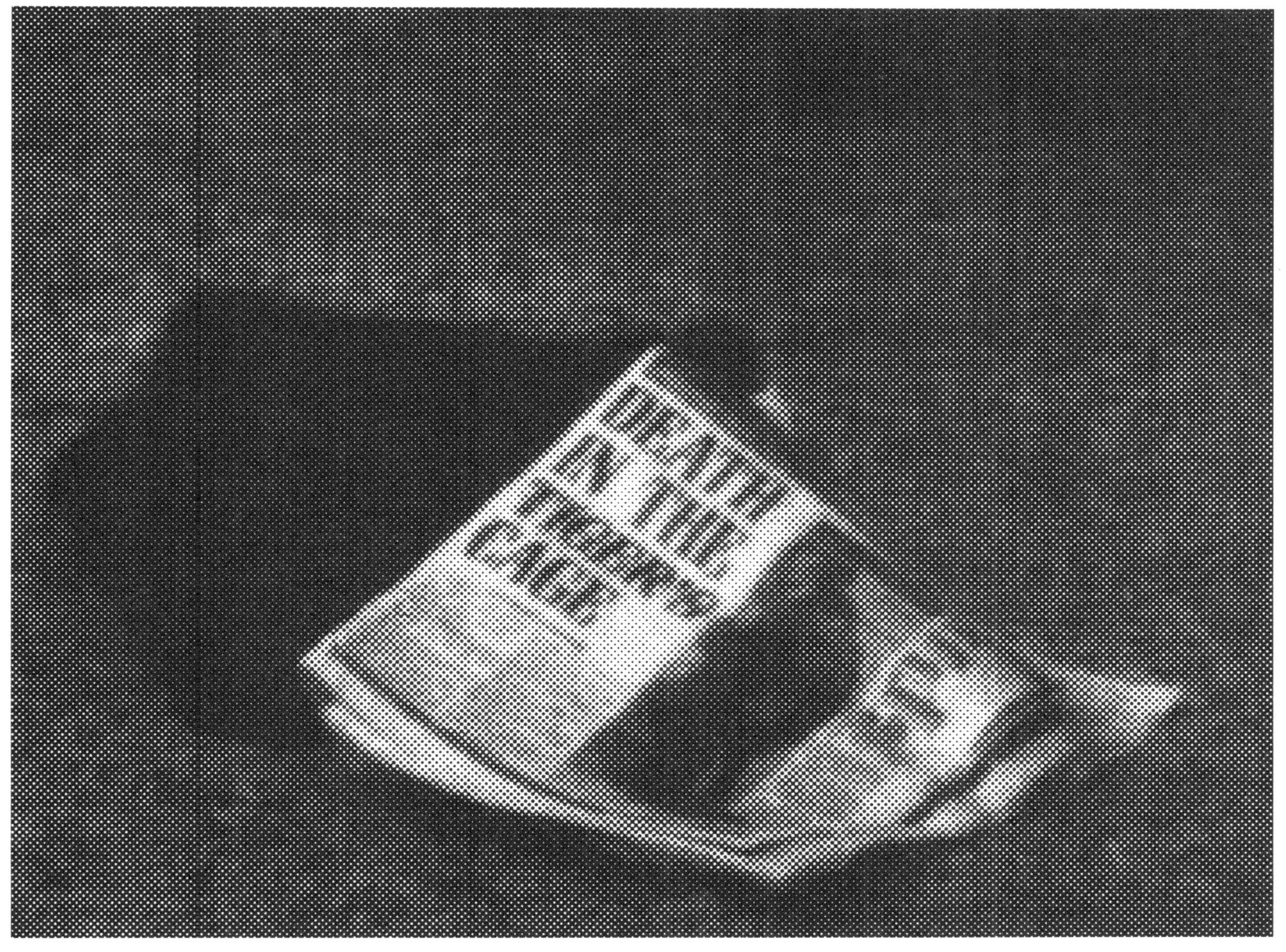

                    SHE (O.S. German accent)
You can't tell everyone everything. But sometimes, if you are
going to speak at all, there are some things that you just have to
say.
                    HER (O.S. German accent)
Yes. And we have to talk to dogs about biting if we are going to
talk to them at all.

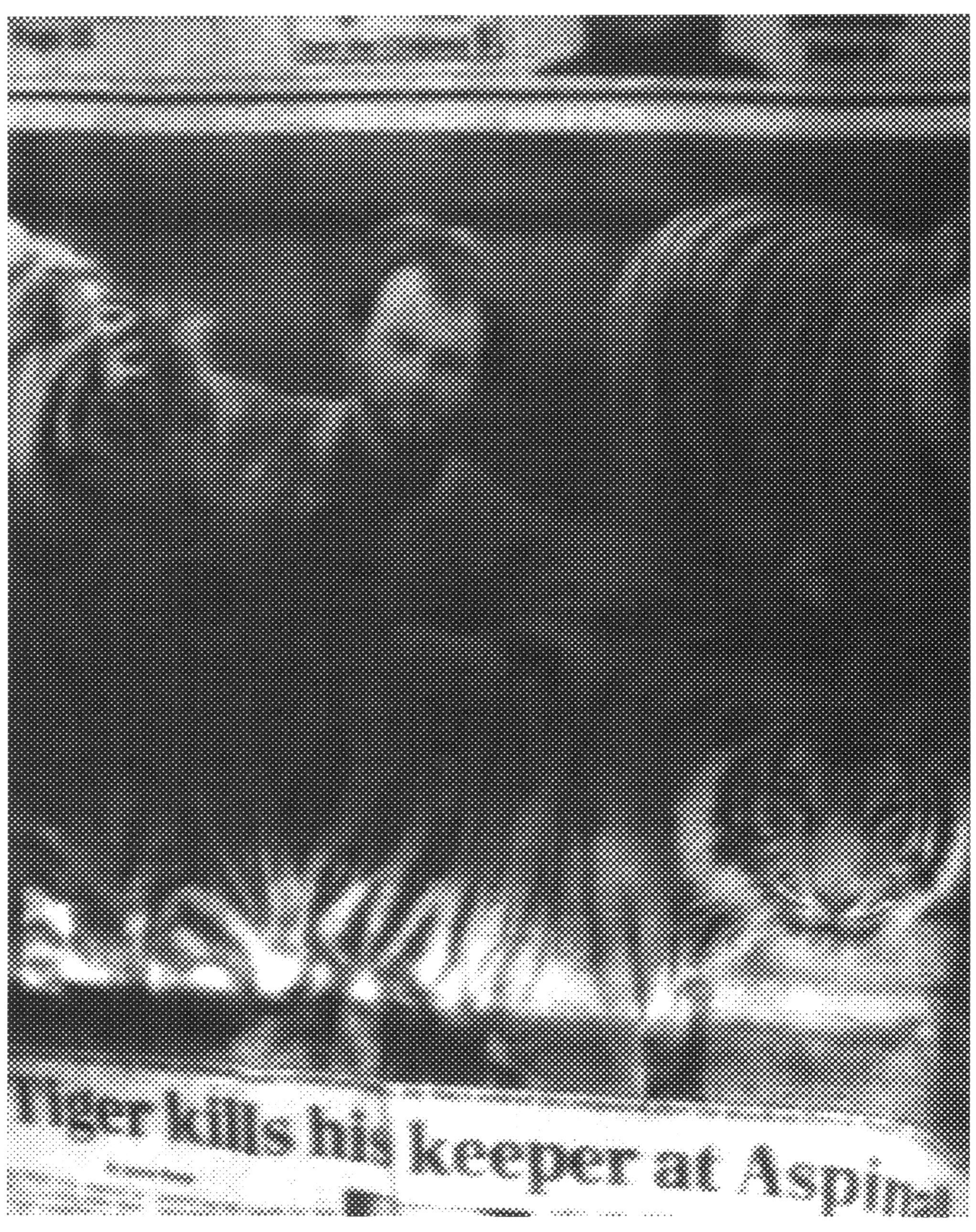
er kills his keeper at Aspin

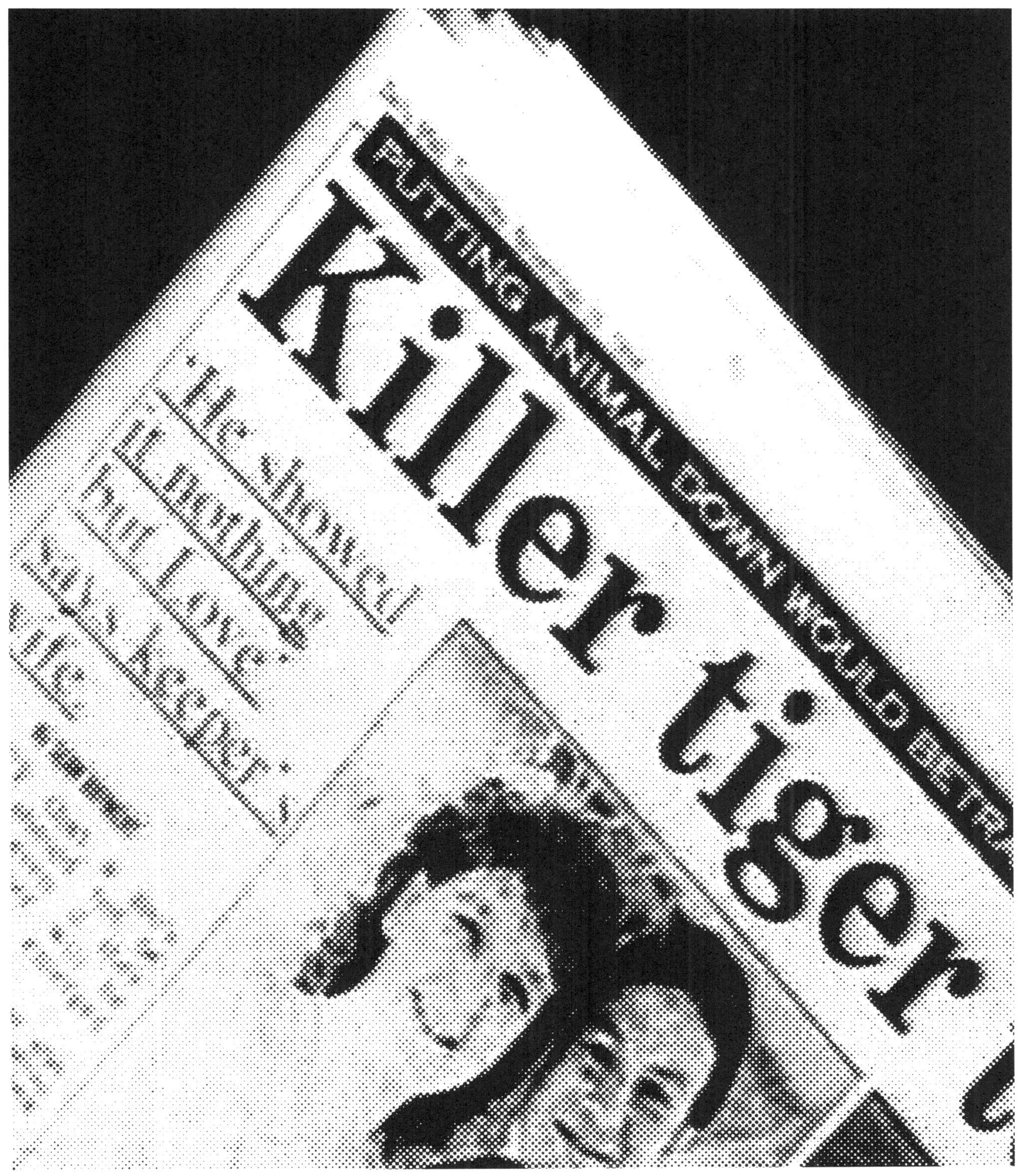

Oh please try and stay upright.
Tiger cub! Tiger cub!

Sometime in the early 70's as far as we can tell, Dr. K. Heinrich's
research began to gain critical attention. It was, to be specific,
his findings that acoustics might be amenable to certain isolating
treatments that heralded a new era.

It would appear that the enthusiasm with which his proposals were
greeted was a product of an increasing concern with what was considered "noise pollution".

Meanwhile in the popularization of some of his methods,
Dr. Heinrich's warning that, "sensational failure may occur in the
field from time to time", was forgotten in the excitement provoked
by his experiments in time space and sound waves. Or perhaps simply misunderstood.

As mentioned, Dr. Heinrich developed a technique to remove what he
termed acoustical defects from a given sound field. The doctor
himself argued with a growing sense of alarm that the methods
employed to determine what might usefully be classified as noise,
should be as sensitive as possible. However, it has been argued
that the chink in his methods which allowed an opening of the
floodgates, was his assertion that in the final analysis, the lis-
tener is always right.

In the subsequent period of often heated debate and general misun-
derstandings and confusion as to where the line lay between sound
and noise, it was agreed at governmental level that all sound
above a certain decibel level, which was not clearly and purpose-
fully organised, fell within what was becoming an ever- expanding
field of noise and should be removed from the audible register.

Despite Dr. Heinrich's insistence that the sound field in a real
physical space is so complicated that it is not open to exact
mathematical treatment, the inherent dangers and possible risks
were considered worth taking.

There then followed a period of what was termed vibrational sweeping - a wide spread radical condensing and simplification of sound
fields with the purpose of controlling or eliminating random elements.

Where these random sound elements do still crop up, the impression
is of sonic weeds or erratic ornaments in a vast perfectly mani-
cured (and muted) aural terrace. Noting his own melancholic fascination in later years with these acoustic outcroppings, Dr.
Heinrich suggested that while this 'lack of uniformity' (which
is its main characteristic), is responsible for many of its diffi-
culties, it also accounts for the continuous power of attraction
these random sound elements exert on a growing number of acousti-
cians.

At the time of writing, one must now contend with the widespread
blanket of oppressive silence which followed in the wake of an
almost total elimination of random sounds.

While the young researcher may lament the sparse information
remaining from the printed sound files of the time, it should be
borne in mind that what survives is due to a process performed in
extremis, when a small number of independent practitioners were
beginning to sense the potentially disastrous impact of vib-
sweeping on the sonic landscape. The difficulty of reconstruction
is compounded by what has been perceived as an apparent reluctance
in literature and scores of the time to adequately account for
these sounds. This must be understood in the context of a world
view that experienced most unstructured sound as noise.

Given the above, while the work of retrieval and reconstitution is
certainly one of the most time-consuming fields, it is also one of
the most creatively challenging research areas of our generation.

SOUND OF JUNGLE BIRD, THEN SHOT OF NOTES BEING MOVED ON A DESKTOP
SCORING PROGRAMME
MORE BIRD SONGS AND SOUND EFFECTS…LONG SOUND OF WATER
SHOT FROM BEHIND OF C AT COMPUTER

                              A (in Chinese with subtitles)
You've got the sound of water…

I haven't been here before. (no subtitles here)

                              C
No, well…it's a bit of an oasis here in the Centre.

                              A
So…what have you found?

                              C
hang on a minute, I'll adjust the levels…

PULLS DOWN LEVEL ON SCREEN
SILENCE…
                              C (GESTICULATING)
…so if the volume on this goes down

                              A
And I tend to mumble…So my voice often drops off the register.
…what have you found?

                              C
Well ,I think they're flights of birds…but it's so crude…it's
written in wav. But I found some other
scribbles attached to it.

C LOOKS TOWARDS THE SCREEN AS A COMBINATION OF MUSIC AND CROW
CALLS ARE HEARD OVER SOME FOOTAGE AS YET NOT PROPERLY SEEN

                              C
It's not really how it sounds. The scribbles say/show something
but this isn't really how it sounds.

                              A
of course…

CLOSE UP OF FOOTAGE OF CROW BEING PREPARED BY TAXIDERMIST
SOUNDS OF PIANO MUSIC, VIOLIN, CROW CALLING, SOME OTHER BIRD CALLS
CAMERA WANDERS AROUND STUDIO ONCE MORE

                              C
ok so…
I think well…you were talking about this idea of sitting
down to write piece of music

                              A
Yes…for the violin

                              C
…and there was a certain kind of sound world attached to
the violin…?

                              A
Yes…that was part of Dr. Heinrich's original theory…that a
room could be constructed like an instrument, like a violin for
example.

CAMERA WANDERS TOWARDS AN OPEN BOOK SHOWING IMAGE OF A REVERBERA-
TION CHAMBER…THE TEXT BENEATH REFERRING TO ERRORS OF SOME SORT

                              C
Well that's not really what I meant.
What I meant was, there are certain ways you can describe how
they might make sounds using an instrument.
                              A
Yes…you mean the score?
                              C
Yes…yes.

CAMERA WANDERS, CUT TO C IN B&W, FLICKER & GRAIN.

                              C
(VOICEOVER ON HER OWN IMAGE AS SHE LOOKS DOWN AT SCORE, DESCRIBES
IT, PLAYS NOTES ON PIANO…)
Well, I never encountered scores before I came to the institute.
I was really intrigued by the notion of learning musical notation
and scoring stuff. But I became disenchanted really quickly
because I realized that practically none of the sound that
I had imagined had survived in written form.

                                    A
No, all of the old texts presume that you have no need of that,
that you know what everything sounds like.
That's taken for granted.

                                    C
If the score is the same set of instructions then…why?
We don't know why one musician plays it better than another.

                                    A
Yes…certain musicians did do it better, but it's hard to say what
that was…when it was essentially the same piece of music.
We think that there must have been a tiny amount of space and some
people moved in that space a bit better than others.

                                    C
So there's a little bit of space in between. Em, it's a kind of
space where people can move a little bit more freely, where they
have a little bit more space to play around with it…in the
gaps…and that's where they make it their own.

THE PIANO MUSIC GRADUALLY INCLUDES A BLOWING ELEMENT.
A LOOKS AT THE WAV FILE AND HIS ATTENTION SLOWLY SHIFTS TO AN OLD
PRINT SHOWING A LARGE WIND INSTRUMENT.

                                    C
Now all I see are gaps and silences.

A LOOKS UP AT C, THEN BACK DOWN AT SOMETHING IN HIS HAND.
C TURNS HER ATTENTION BACK TO THE SCREEN. THE CROW IS NOW BEING
STITCHED UP
                                    A
Well, there were other attempts…there was an electronic
group…and they spoke between
themselves……making shapes in the air…talking about the
sounds being like a cube or a square or something…developing their
own language to describe the sound world they
were thinking about.

SHOT OF CROWS IN A FIELD.

                                    C
Yeah…an air language-so, like an invisible world alongside the
visible, and we're in the middle of it somehow.

                         C (STANDING AT DOOR LOOKING OUT
THROUGH A STRAW)
So when we try to look at something so vast,
When we try to reconstruct it, with such primitive means…
well, it's like looking at the world through a straw.

SHOT OF FIELD OF CROWS, LAYERED AND SHIFTING. C FRAMED BY A CLOS-
ING IN CIRCLE, HERSELF LOOKED AT THROUGH A STRAW AS SHE LOOKS
UNTIL SCREEN CLOSES IN TO THE SOUND OF CROWS CALLING.

56" FANTASY   (FEMALE V/O WITH GERMAN ACCENT)

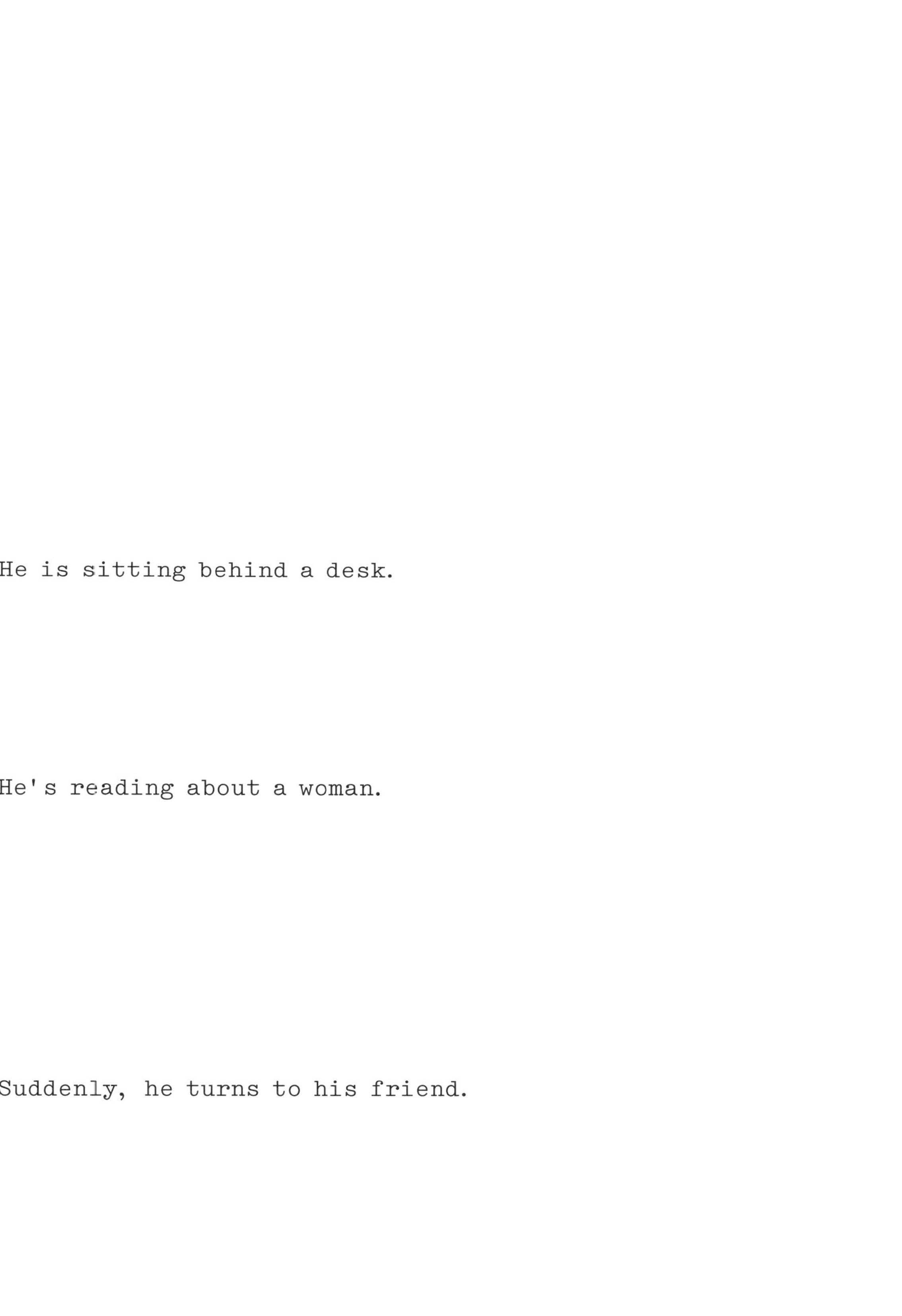

He is sitting behind a desk.

He's reading about a woman.

Suddenly, he turns to his friend.

"Listen," he says. "This woman's fifty-six inch bust is a tax
asset."

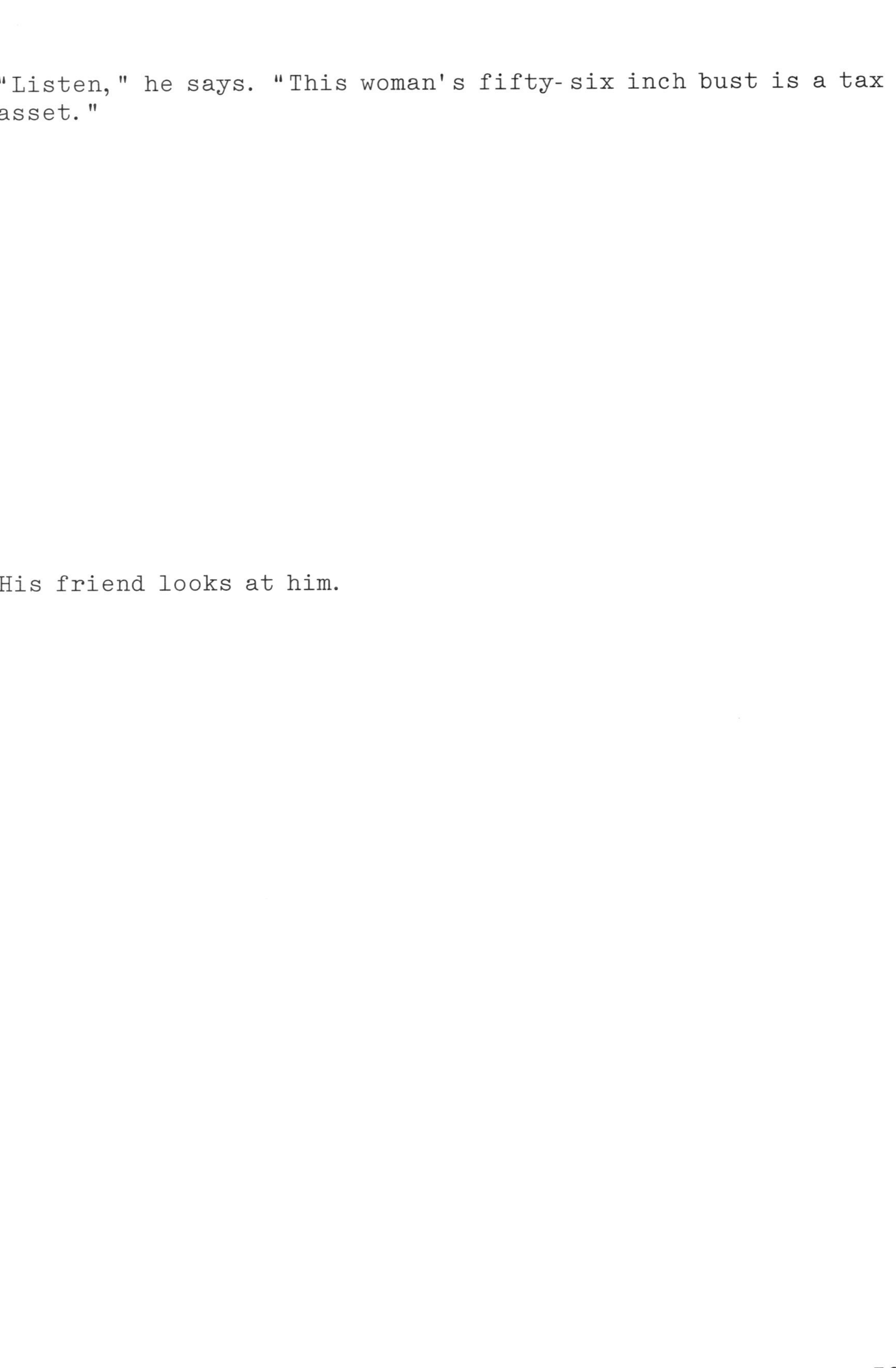

His friend looks at him.

Then, his amazement turns to excitement.
"Imagine," he said. "Imagine if she fell."

POMPEII DINNER

She stopped eating her dinner so suddenly that it looked as if it
belonged in Pompeii next to some chess players who haven't got
very long left.
"Hey, did you hear that?"
"No, what?"
"Oh, never mind…
it's probably nothing. "
"Your move"
She looked down at what had been her dinner just a split second
ago. There was a kind of bewildered expression on her face.
"I don't know", she said, "I don't know what it is…
I just can't eat another mouthful. "

FISH

He tells her how he's been to a place where the fish swim right up
to you "all sizes and colours-red…orange…striped
Then he lifts his hand and a fish swims over and brushes off her
face.

BAT SMILE

Darwin was rushing through some trees
with his coat-tails flapping and his mouth full of insects.
He passed by a young girl with a look on her face
that could have been a pet bat.
It was moving about awkwardly,
trying to get some sleep.
Darwin mumbled something
and a blue-bottle flew out of his mouth.
The bat yawned and stretched its wings like a smile.

SPACE 2

Finally I clear two free hours in the day and I sit looking at
them. They look back at me like aliens, small and unblinking.
What do you do with two free hours?

NOODLES

He's like a letter from a thousand years ago,
sitting on a bench in a bright wooden restaurant.

It was written in some kind of old fashioned style that must have
taken a lot of time and a quiet mastery of the ways of small flour-
ishes and spikes. Whoever wrote it really knew a few things about
ink.

The letter is full of earthquakes and dinosaurs and women with
faded faces.

"Noodles," he says

ERIC'S SUIT

He's so comfortable in his suit that it makes people nervous.
"This suit" he says, "some people just can't get over it they just
can't - for them there's no way around it." Then he laughs good and
loud, "But I say to myself, Why should I change?"

ELVISES

She's thinking about Elvises, Sixteen Elvises walking down the
street in suits made especially to fit Elvises of any shape or
size. The Elvises are waiting for something. They've stopped and
are just chatting to one another when an old man passes by. He'd
love to see someone kill all of those Elvises. "Stupid bastards,"
he says. One of the Elvises laughs. "Ha ha ha." Stupid bastards.

HEADING NORTH

All the girls take off their shoes and sit on the bus as if they're
sitting on sofas—a great herd of sofas galloping north.

all texts on pps. 52-53 originally published as the collection
"Past and Future Films" in Feint Magazine, (ed. Vaari Claffey &
Isabel Nolan) 2007

<u>A LONG WAY FROM FLORIDA</u>

The bee's legs are cold
It walks slowly down the street
like an old man
every now and then it stops and coughs
it sure is a long way from Florida.

<u>PROD PROD PROD</u>

An old man passes by
with a stick in each hand
he pokes the cement path
as if he doesn't quite believe it
prod prod prod

<u>ELISE ALONE AGAIN</u>

Elise is crying fast blonde tears
down her face.
"It's not as if I'm a stranger here", she says.
She wipes her eyes
and looks around
as if she's just woken up.
Everyone tries to look somewhere else.

Dear Chris,

       It's a long time since I've visited this place, but when you asked about sculpture parks this is the one I return to in my mind's eye. The road to it is long and dusty, like a film running backwards, splitting off the main road and then again, getting smaller and more fragile and worn with time as it makes its way further and further into the faded sun-baked mountains. A sharp turn splits off, leading down to two rubbish bins.

Trees and bushes sit behind the bins. A river runs nearby out of sight. Despite the dead heat, the ground deep down is still not so hard on account of being near the river. There are no houses or people, but a dirt trail shows where someone was used to going past the bins, disappearing in through the foliage.

In there, surrounded by trees, dark red leatherette chairs and sofas, formica tables, dark brown ashtrays and stiff newspapers sit around ready for business, like a pub catering for some invisible long lost clientele. The light filtering through the leaves lends the place a kind of muted underwater feeling. Every now and then something rustles quickly through dead leaves.

A small trail leads off through the trees.

We're at the end of that trail, by the water. It's cold even in this dead heat—wide and shallow with deep brown pools scattered with boulders and rocks and stones. I'm distracted by something that looks like black puddles of heavy oil near the water's edge. Hunkering down, the spillage turns into squirming masses of tadpoles, filling all the shallower parts of the bank.

Nearby somebody has hung a metal mobile with many parts out over the river. Altogether it gives the impression of a bit of three-dimensional bar-room banter…The river's winning hands down making the sculpture look a bit foolish and inarticulate. The water is saying many profound things about life and change and transience, stopping for a sip every now and then, before continuing on in a simple and elegant manner while the sculpture hangs about awkwardly trying to say something smart and sculptural about reflections. Beads of rust are already beginning to break out along its surfaces.

Together tho' the relationship between the complicated sculpture
and the water seems to perfectly reflect something else. I look
down to where my girlfriend sits on a rock. She's silent and
appears to grow further away at every passing second, flickering
in and out of focus. She turns her face towards me, then gazes off,
back up at the mountains that climb steeply from the floor of the
valley.

Something's gone and it won't be coming back. Not now, not ever.

We both know it although it is going to take a while for things to
crystallize. Right now, all we know is that we have found the
right place.

We have buried Diego further back up the trail. He is wrapped in
a blanket. We had to go pretty deep to keep animals from digging
him up in the night. Then we scattered leaves and dry earth.
We did such a good job that the leaves and twigs have become
statues of themselves and it will be hard to find the next time
we visit, even tho' we know exactly where he is.

When we walk back to the car the sound of dogs howling follows us.

I think we buried something else there as well although we only
came to know that later and by then it was too late to do anything
about it. It has grown as dark as the ground around it now and all
but disappeared.

(originally published in "Magnetic Promenade and Other Sculpture
Parks", ed. Chris Evans, Studio Voltaire 2006)

THE FEELING THAT SOMETHING'S WRONG

        THE FEELING THAT SOMETHING'S WRONG FOLLOWS HER AROUND.
          SOMETIMES SHE THINKS SHE'S GOT IT FIGURED OUT.
               OTHER TIMES SHE'S NOT SO SURE.

She was wearing a white coat when he arrived, as if she was star-
ring as a famous cheese surgeon in a play whose only other charac-
ters were lesser known but well thought of international cheeses.
The cheeses had come from all corners of the globe after many long
hours of experimentation in countless small laboratories. Each
one was the very special brain-child of long hours and sleepless
nights. The cheeses were sitting around in small groups when he
came in. One or two of them were humming something that had nothing to do with dancing.

"This cheese, " he said, taking a small cheese out of his bag,
"There's something not right about it. "

She turned around as if she had been concentrating very hard on
something that was nearly not there and now it was gone. Damn!

"What?" she said. And it was not a happy question.
In fact it had a lot in common with a large block of cheese that
stuck off a shelf close to his head.
"What?" she said again, using a voice that had been coated in a
thin layer of green wax.
"It's like, emm, ahem…it's just not right. "
She pushed her glasses up her nose and took a well refrigerated
look at him.
"You don't understand, " she said, "this mould is its skin…look…
here…and here…" and she took up one of her prodigies and then
another, tracing her finger along the various black and blue veins
running through them…
Finally, gently, with two hands completely at odds with the look
on her face, she removed the cheese from his hands and placed it on
a nearby shelf, in a way which caused him to question the value of
spending long hours with international cheeses as your only com-
panions.

"You simply don't understand", she slowly repeated.
And it was true. He didn't.
But he was beginning to get the picture.

Something flickered

It may have been a secret, not
a foreign body,
active still
long after its forcible entrance

She smiled dryly

A foreign body does not enter into any relation
with the layers of tissue that surround it
But it may modify them and provoke

An inflamed reaction ?

In fact it does not behave like a foreign body,
but far more like
an infiltrate

Ripples of tension crawled through the muscles across his shoulders
and longer and more lovingly as they reached his throat

He swallowed hard
like someone suffering
from hydrophobia

But there the caress fixed itself

It was a long time ago, he began uneasily

She watched the vein pulsating in his neck

It was in the summer during a period of intense heat
I was suffering very badly from
thirst

She licked her curiously dry lips,
aware of the slight tremor in his voice

For without being able to account for it in any way,
I suddenly found it impossible to drink

(The removal of a foreign body
from living tissue...   It will not be cleanly extirpated

His throat tightened

Sometimes there came a sensation as if a hand was drawn softly
Along my cheek and neck

*She was aware of being slightly distracted by the thin slit of chest
with its splay of hair revealed in the opened shirt*

For a fleeting moment he had the distinct feeling that she was

absent

He laughed nervously
(a shallow sound that was only a quick rush of air)

*I would take up the glass of water I longed for
and as soon as it touched my lips
I would push it away*

A faint smile played about her lips

(The boundary between the two is fixed purely conventionally ...Now at one point ...now at another ...It passes over in every direction
Again I lifted the glass to my lips

...And in some places
It cannot be laid down at all

They were cold and stiff now and seemed no more a part of me than the glass

And things
fragmented and orderless
floated to the surface

It can become increasingly alien
she remarked, continuing in a similar vein

Panic lurched convulsively in his throat
leaving gaps unfilled and riddles unanswered

. . . .

Seconds became minutes became hours
and poured off his face in a
cold dripping sweat

Later...

She put the glass to my lips and drank a great quantity

The Portrait

(V.O.) JANE HAMLYN
(approx. mid-forties,
English Kentish/
Sussex accent. Speaks
slowly, and consider-
ately)

It was in, erm,
nineteen ninety
five, er, I invit-
ed Craigie
Horsfield to do an
exhibition here at
the gallery.
One of the works
which we showed in
the front room of
the gallery was a
portrait of the
woman called Mary
Machinska.
[nb "Mary" is pro-
nounced with the
same intonation as
"Mary" but with the
"a" of Marry.]
The portrait was a
very beautiful
black and white
image of a woman…
I'm not sure
whether she
was sitting
or standing.

You are not here

(V.O.) KARON HEPBURN
(approx. mid-twenties,
soft New Zealand
accent. Speaks
deliberately)

Every morning I
awake to find your
ghost self has
wrapped its arms
around me in the
night.

Slowly I undo its
cold fingers and
put them down.

Sometimes your
ghost self wakes
up and watches as
I leave.

All I know is that
one day I will wake
up and forget that
you are not here.

If the Earth

SOUND OF TYPING ON COM-
PUTER KEYBOARDS.
(V.O.) CHARLOTTE SCHEPKE
(approx. mid-thirties,
German accent. Speaks
deliberately)
Such extensive
water. So barren a
country. Dreadful.

(V.O.) DALE McFARLAND
(approx. mid-twenties,
soft Northern Ireland
accent. Speaks fast)
If the earth opens
and swallows me up,

this doesn't prove
that my trust in it
was misplaced.

What better place
for my trust could
there be?

<u>Blind Building</u>

(V.O.) JANE HAMLYN
Two crows were
killed. A gloom
spread.

One man cannot bear
to be left alone.

He looks wild,
ghastly.
Surprised us by
getting up and
walking.

Samandre lay down,

died before day-
light

<u>The Sound of your
Wings</u>

(V.O.) CHARLOTTE SCHEPKE

You have taken
me to a place
I'd only ever heard
of.

<u>Whenever the Ices
Shift</u>

(V.O.) CHARLOTTE SCHEPKE

October 19th
Patched snowshoes
for the journey.
Packed journals.
Charts.
Documents.
Letters.

(V.O.) JANE HAMLYN
<u>A</u> sent out to examine
the water.

Lost his way.

Erm rather sad,
her head was
sort of bent down
slightly… erm
very fragile
frail- like-like
a little sparrow.
And it was a very
very beautiful
portrait.

And, erm, I think
it was on a
Saturday I was
working in the
gallery on my own,
and I became aware
that there were
various people
standing outside
the gallery in the
street, looking
in, looking at this
portrait. After
a few minutes the
doorbell rang and
three men came in,
and just stood
looking at the por-
trait for a long
time, sort of whis-
pering to them-
selves.

- - - - - - - - - - - - - -

- - - - - - - - - - - - -

I am lying on the
floor, inside this
building.
Listening to it
creak and shuffle
about in the dark.

A light will change
nothing.

- - - - - - - - - - - - -

And now that
you're gone,

I walk through
this dead land

watching the
skies

for the sound
of your wings.

- - - - - - - - - - - - -

(V.O.) DALE McFARLAND
There was not one sin-
gle passage. Rather the
intricate maze of
islands and shoals pro-
vided a number of
potential passages,
whenever the ice shift-
ed to open the door.

(V.O.) CHARLOTTE SCHEPKE
Ice- perfectly smooth-
Slipped at every step-
Blown down by the wind.

One man lost all hope.
All arguments failed.

(V.O.) DALE McFARLAND
The party is reduced to
four persons.

(V.O.) KARON HEPBURN
F could go no further,
overwhelmed with grief.

Antonio Fontano was an
Italian.

Then they walked
around the
gallery… didn't
really… they
weren't really
interested in the
other work, and
then came back to
the portrait and
kept looking.

And they told me
the story that,
erm, the three men
who'd come into the
gallery had known
Mary. And one of
the… men… who'd
seen the portrait
had actually lived
here in the house.
And Mary had come
to the house on
several occasions
to meet him, so it
was rather extra-
ordinairy that
Mary from this por-
trait had been to
this house. And
many many many
years later there
she was again in
the house, but as a
portrait.

- - - - - - - - - - - - - -

(V.O.) DALE McFARLAND
The whole party shed
tears.

(V.O.) JANE HAMLYN
Dear me, If we are
spared to return, I
wonder if we shall ever
recover our understand-
ing.

                - - - - - - - - - - - - - -

<u>LOST QUOTATIONS</u>

Outside the National Poetry Library
there's a notice-board labelled "Lost Quotations".
People go there to ask if anyone can help them to find a poem.
The board is full of lost pieces of poetry.
Some of them have a neglected air,
like the leg of a stuffed dog
left in an old cardboard box in the attic.

Humpty Dumpty went out for a walk
Armed with only a knife and fork.
"Learnt around 1910" was written under this.
That's 88 years or more.
"Author?Source?Title??"
88 years.
You could get well and truly lost in that kind of time.

Others linger on like the desolate ghost of a little known actor,
returning every now and then to find itself recognised by nothing
and nobody.

"I have lost my way,
This is the wrong city
and the wrong midnight."

The man who works at the poetry library
wears the kind of smile
you'd give to a stray dog along with a piece of bread.
He believes that these lines, having somehow gotten themselves
disconnected from the original poems,
have been misremembered…
slowly deforming in the minds of the people who lost them
until they bear little or no resemblance
to the poems they once came from.

All the same, he carefully types them up
and sticks them on the board.

Someone's torn the curtain,
I think it must be me.

I wish I were a bigly hole
And bigly hole were me.

<u>3:17 FOREVER</u>

I have avoided this moment for as long as I could,
but it's arrived.
She hands everyone in the room a government form.

When she asks what time it is,
we all look at our watches with dull bewildered expressions
as if it's centuries since we've last seen them
and we're kind of surprised to find them still there after all
this time,
attached to long ago wrists
like faithful ticking dogs lying at their masters' graves.

Someone has been using the passing years
to perfect a look of mild surprise
that was found on the face of someone buried and uncovered who
once
stood in a long ago queue looking at grey flakes floating down
into the streets.
"Hey… look at that… I wonder…"

At that the professor of time telling jerks his head up off the
table
where he had been using it as a paperweight for government forms.

"SEVENTEEN MINUTES PAST…it's 3:17"
Two thousand slow years later there's no quarrel with that…
It's 3:17 3:17 3:17 3:17 3:17 3:17 3:17 3:17 3:17 3:17 3:17
3:17 3:17 3:17 3:17
3:17 3:17 3:17 3:17 3:17 3:17 3:17 3:17 3:17 3:17 3:17
3:17 3:17 3:17 3:17 3:17
 3:17 3:17 3:17 3:17 3:17 3:17 3:17 3:17 3:17 3:17 3:17
3:17 3:17 3:17 3:17 3:17
3:17 3:17 3:17 3:17 3:17 3:17 3:17 3:17 3:17 3:17 3:17
3:17 3:17 3:17 3:17 3:17
3:17 3:17 3:17 3:17 3:17 3:17 3:17 3:17 3:17 3:17 3:17
3:17 3:17 3:17 3:17 3:17
3:17 3:17 3:17 3:17 3:17 3:17 3:17 3:17 3:17 3:17 3:17
3:17 3:17 3:17 3:17 3:17 3:17 3:17 3:17 3:17 3:17 3:17 3:17
3:17 3:17 3:17 3:17 3:17 3:17 3:17 3:17 3:17
3:17 forever.

MICHAEL NEWMAN

WHAT MAKES IT HOLD TOGETHER:

JAKI IRVINE'S ACKNOWLEDGE-MENTS

PART I

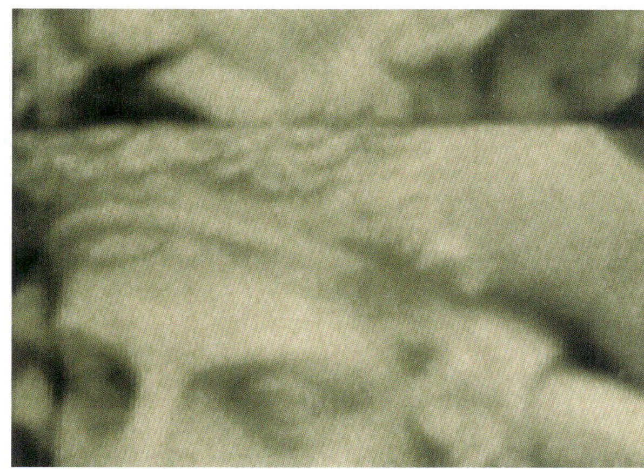

From the toothless girl in <u>SWEETTOOTH</u> (1993-94),

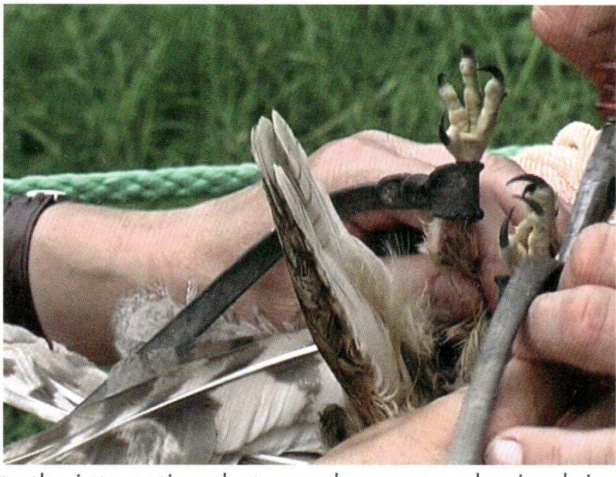

to the interactions between humans and animals in <u>IN A WORLD LIKE THIS</u> (2006)

Jaki Irvine's art has to do with the acknowledgment of strangeness.

How odd other people are.

How the world seems full of coincidences and signs meant just for me one moment, and utterly meaningless the next.

How everything seems coherent, and then suddenly falls apart.

How animals can seem like us, and we like them, yet at the same time we know that they have a perception of a world that we can never inhabit.

Irvine's work explores not only the extremes of passion, of love and hate, of possession and loss—

to the point at which these emotions touch on the limits of representation—

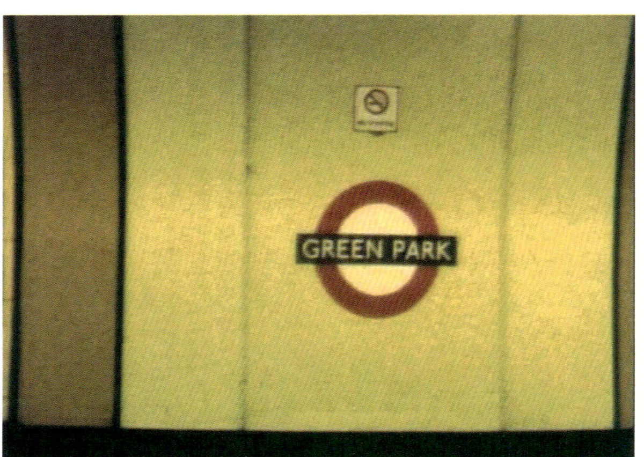

but also the mundane and the everyday, the things that occur on a walk to the park,

or a trip on the underground, where people pass each other by, and encounters are missed yet something happens.

In Irvine's work our link with the world, with others, and with animals is always in question.

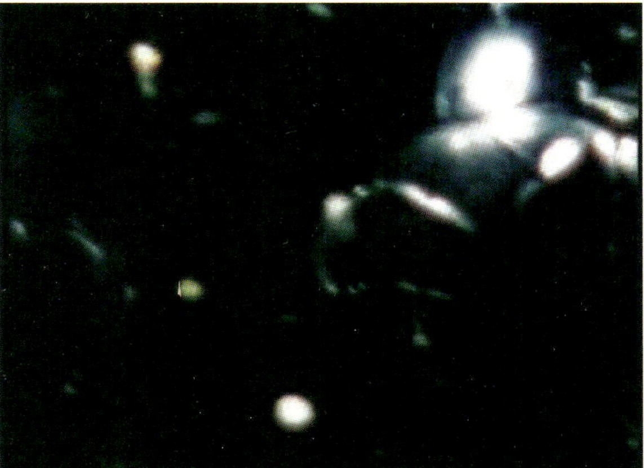

This happens as early as the Super 8 colour film <u>STAR</u>(1973), where a man and woman meet in a pub, but don't connect:

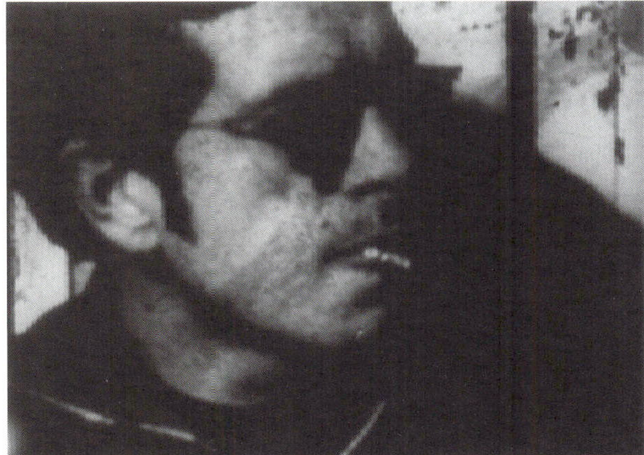

In <u>MARCO, ONE AFTERNOON</u>,
 the first film of the installation of five short 16mm films shot during 1998-99

Paths may cross without meeting, connections misfire, yet this very clinamen, this swerve, is what creates the work.

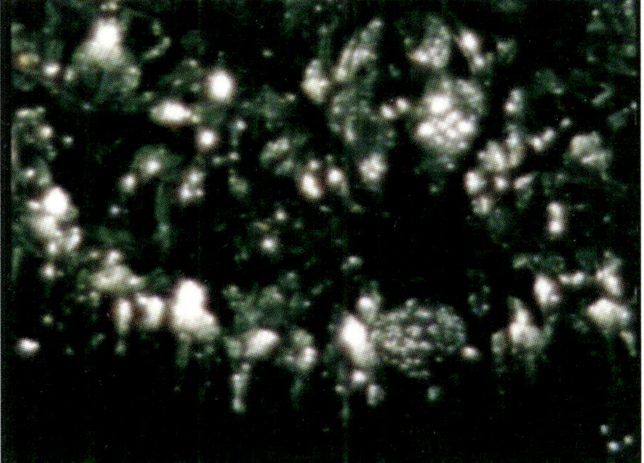

`Hey, handicap, would you like another vodka?` she repeats three times, and falls down to the ground.

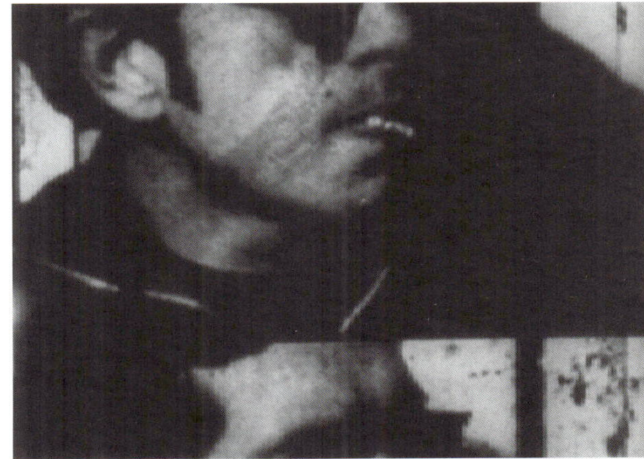

collectively titled <u>THE HOTTEST SUN, THE DARKEST HOUR</u>, a man recounts meeting another 15 years older who looks like he himself will look in fifteen years time;

but if they are, in this narcissistic sense, the "same", did they ever really encounter each other?

Or, on the other hand, is this very sameness the condition for their encounter?

Even face to face in a room together, two people can pass each other by, as we see in <u>EYELASHES</u> (1996),

where a man, obsessed with another woman's eyelashes, seems to be failing to relate to the woman that he is talking to.

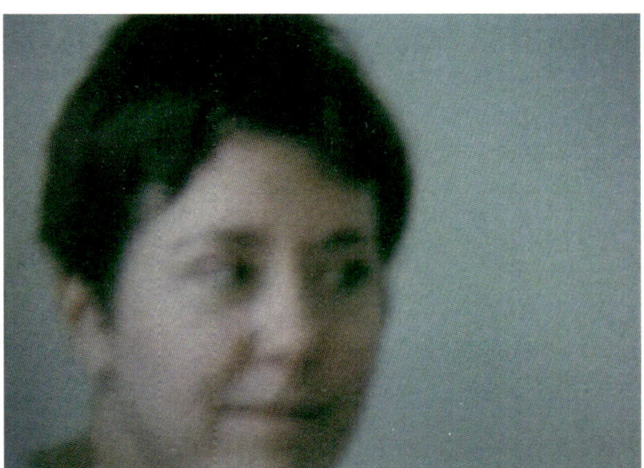

Affect is discharged in compulsive, involuntary micro-gestures, like the twitching of his feet and the tapping of her hand.

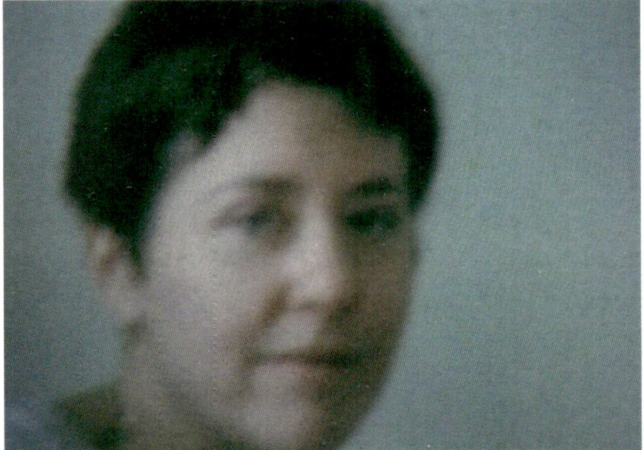

It involves putting oneself at risk.

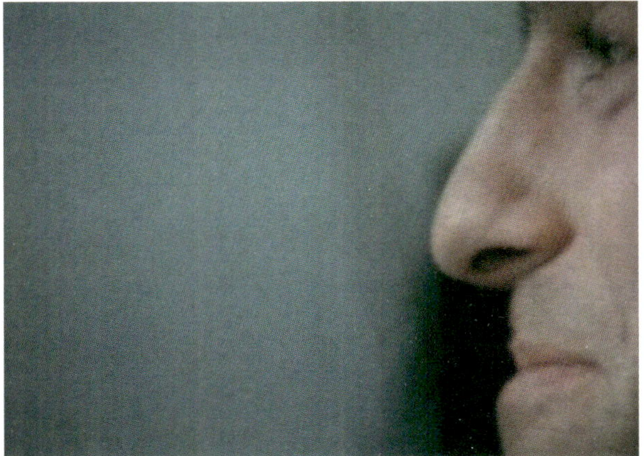

The relation to the other is not something that is benign or easy.

To acknowledge the other person also means exposing oneself.

PART II

Shame is the negative side of the presence to others that is the condition for acknowledgment.

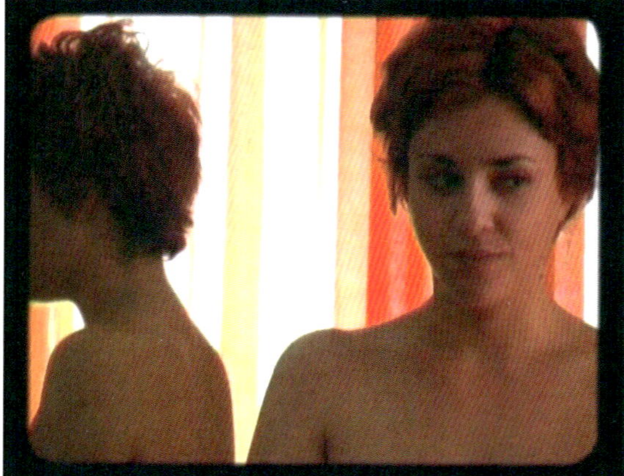

<u>THE ACTRESS</u> (2003) begins with a head-and-shoulders shot of a woman with dyed red hair, dark at the roots, shown in front of an orange curtain.

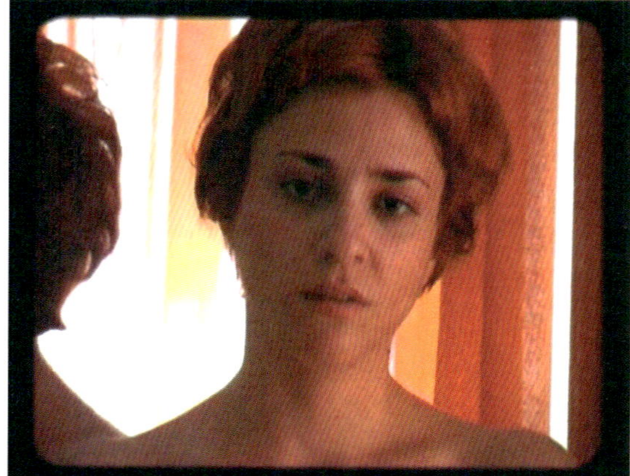

She nods to the camera and says `ok`.

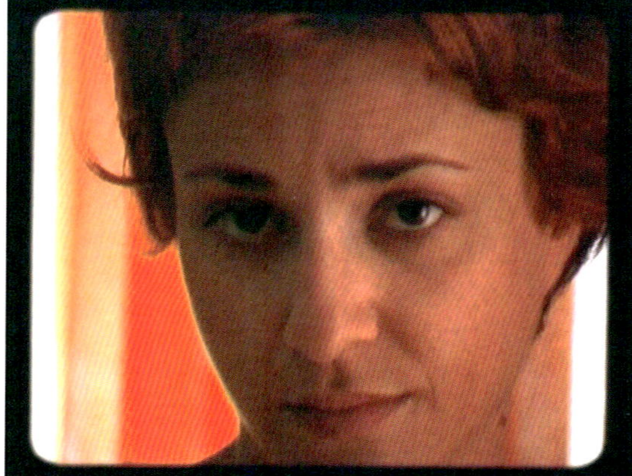

The screen goes blank, and a heavily accented Italian woman's voice–narrating in the third person,

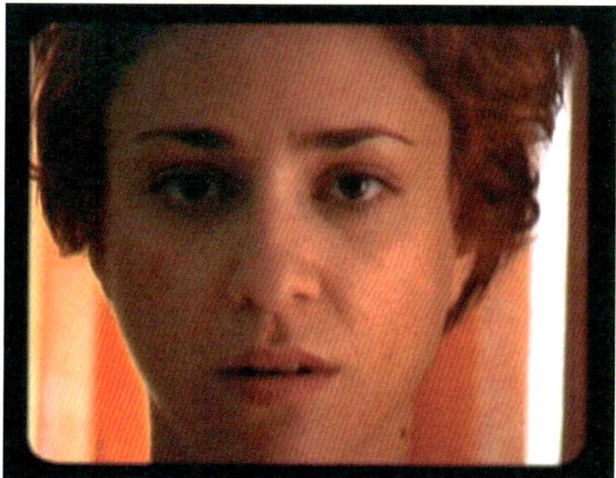

yet it could be the voice of the woman we see— says that she always wanted to be an actress.

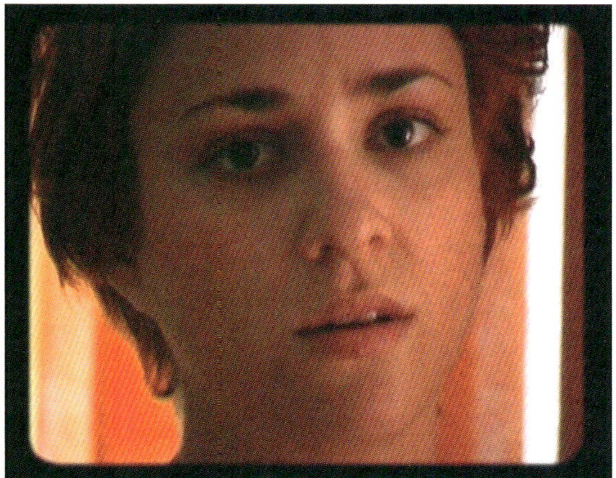

Then there are a series of shorter shots—each of which fades to black, as if a different take—with the woman seeming not quite settled into a role.

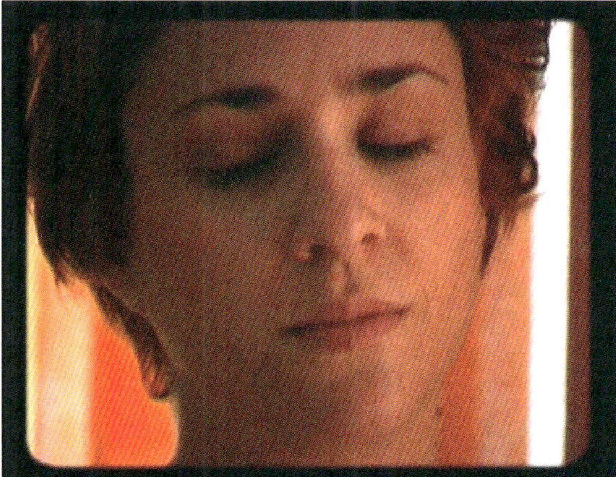

Is she performing for the camera, or for herself in front of a mirror?

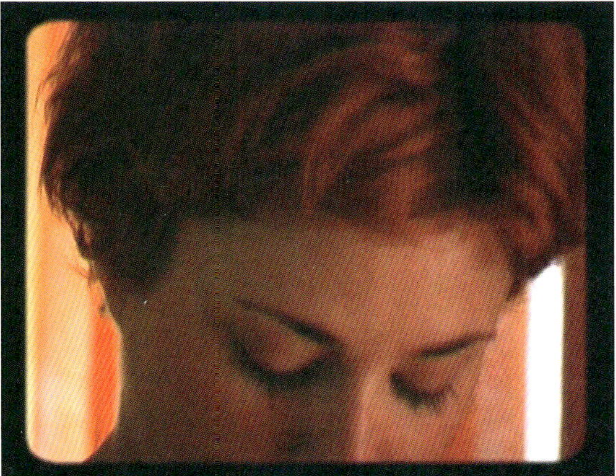

After years of hard work, she finally larded a small part in a film....

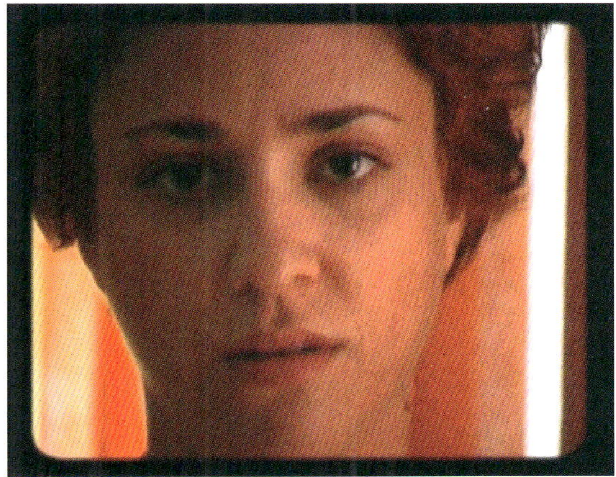

At this point a mirror is behind her,
so we see both her face and shoulders from the front,
and her head from behind.

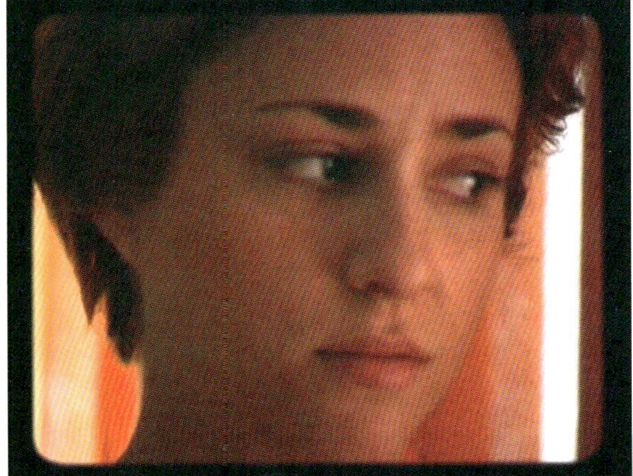

She sighs, grimaces, looks towards the camera and then away.

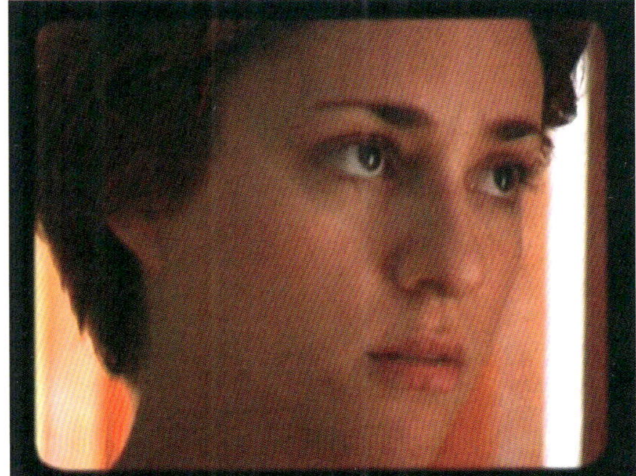

We are told that her father, the mayor of a small town, booked a hall and arranged for a copy of the film to be sent from Rome.

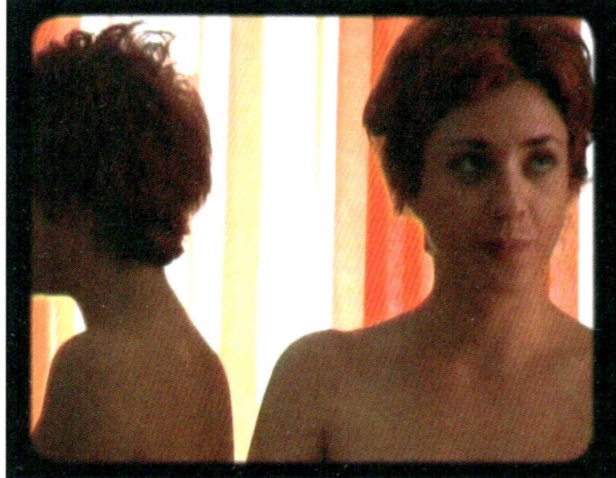

Now, in relation to this paternal authority figure.

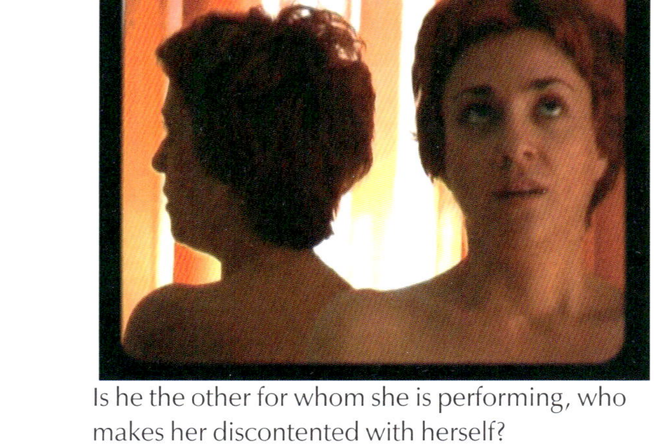

Is he the other for whom she is performing, who makes her discontented with herself?

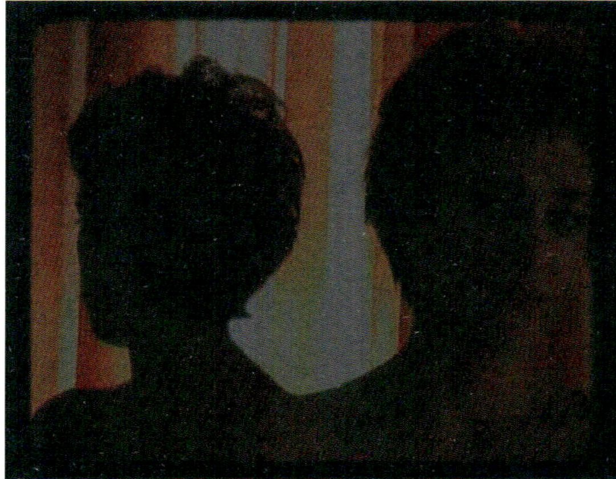

Finally, the whole town was gathered, waiting. .

Her extended posing has put the viewer, too, into the position of the townspeople who are waiting.

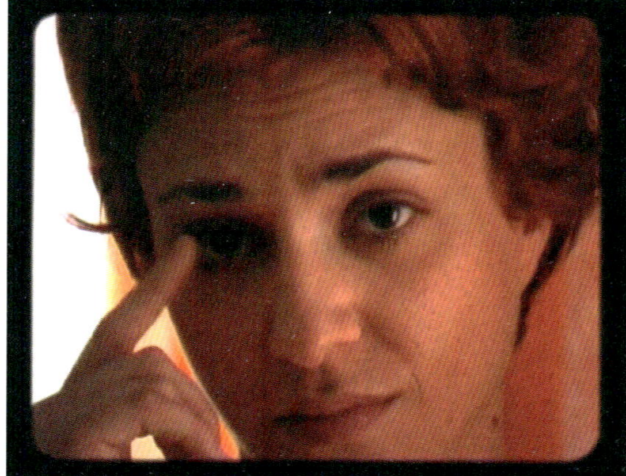

At last she looks directly at the camera, and makes what appears to be a resigned confession:.

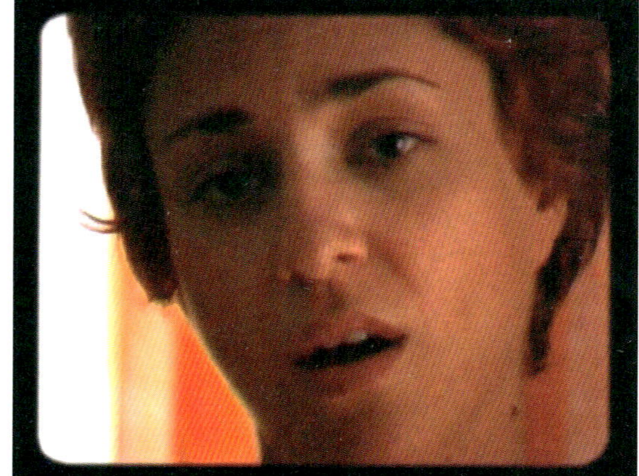

I have ugly breasts.

Who is experiencing shame here, and why?
Stanley Cavell—who writes that .

> it is one of the inconveniences of shame,
> that it is generally inaccurate, attaches to
> the wrong thing[1]

—discusses Gloucester's shame about his son in
<u>KING LEAR</u>:

...if the failure to recognize others is a failure to let others recognize you, a fear of what is revealed to them, an avoidance of their eyes, then it is exactly shame which is the cause of his withholding of recognition.[...]

For shame is the specific discomfort produced by the sense of being looked at, the avoidance of the sight of others is the reflex it produces.[...] Under shame, what must be covered up is not your deed, but yourself. It is a more primitive emotion than guilt, as inescapable as the possession of a body, the first object of shame.[2]

He continues:

"Shame [...] is the emotion whose effect is most precipitate and out of proportion to its cause [...] what mortifies one person seems wholly unimportant to another [...].
Shame [...] is also the most primitive of social responses.

With the discovery of the individual, whether in Paradise or in the Renaissance, there is the simultaneous discovery of the isolation of the individual; his presence to himself, but simultaneously to others.[3]

To anticipate that the proud moment of the woman in
<u>THE ACTRESS</u>
will be precisely a *performance* of shame

is to undercut the authority of the paternal projection.

Is she performing or rehearsing?

Is she practicing her part, this side of a performance, or is she already performing for an other?

Is she looking at herself, or directing her gaze towards the father who will see the film, causing him to be ashamed?

The position of the viewer as addressee oscillates between being that of the actress performing to herself in the mirror,

the father in the narrative who will have been watching the film,

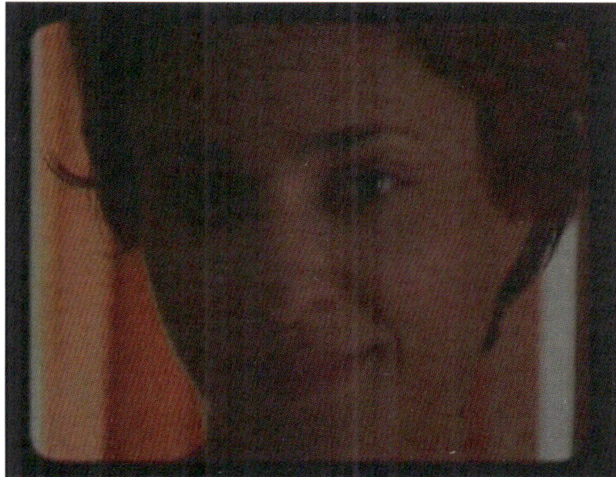

and the artist or filmmaker behind the camera: each of the positions gives rise to a different interpretation of the act.[4]

The woman ends the film with a snort and a little smile, suggesting the hint of a distance from her self-relation before the other, and a mocking defiance

which is also collusion.

It is left open whether her statement "I have ugly breasts" is a comment on herself, or her line for the small part in the film, and that the whole thing we have seen is her rehearsal for it, where she tries to put herself in the position of a woman saying that line, while telling the story in her own voice.

Or she could be an actress acting the actress acting—or rehearsing, or acting rehearsing.

This work could be taken as an extended portrait of the actress,

and indeed many of Irvine's works could be understood as portraits,

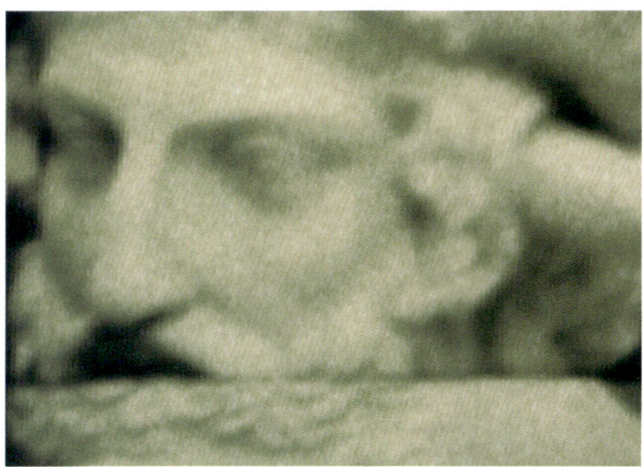

from the black-and-white 8mm film SWEETTOOTH—the indirect portrait of a woman who had all her teeth removed—

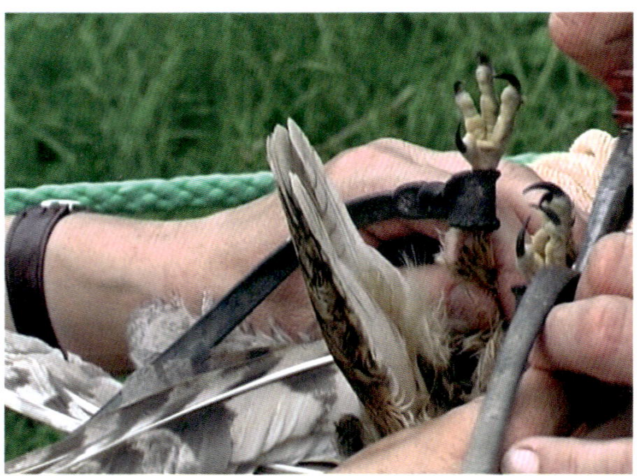

to IN A WORLD LIKE THIS (2006)—a series of double portraits of humans and birds occupying the same world, yet different.

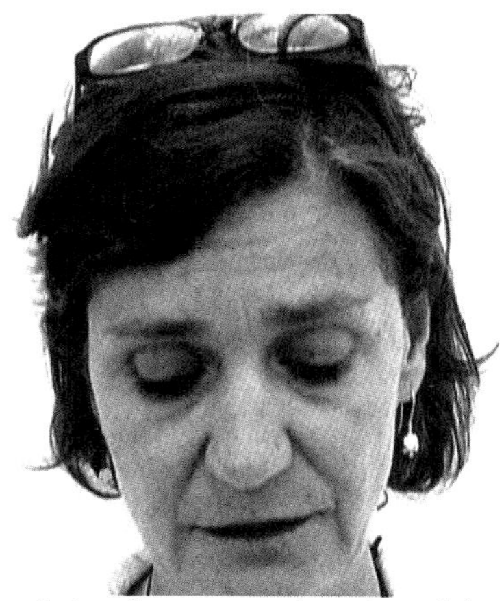

An explicit reference to the idea of the portrait occurs at the beginning of <u>TOWARDS A POLAR SEA</u> (2005), in which the director of the Frith Street

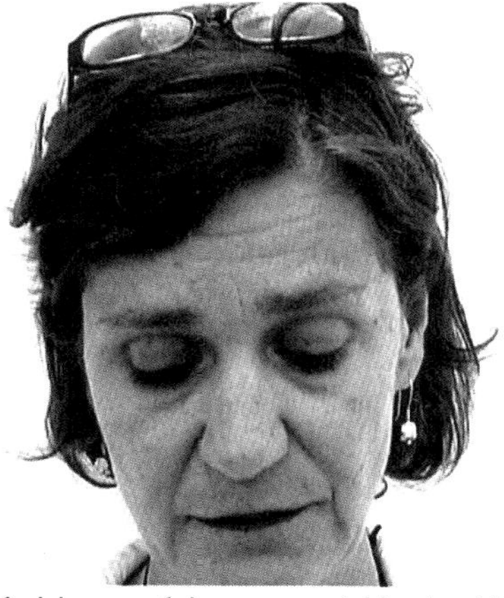

Horsfield one of the men said he had lived in that very house(at 59-60 Frith St.), and that the woman in the portrait had visited him there.

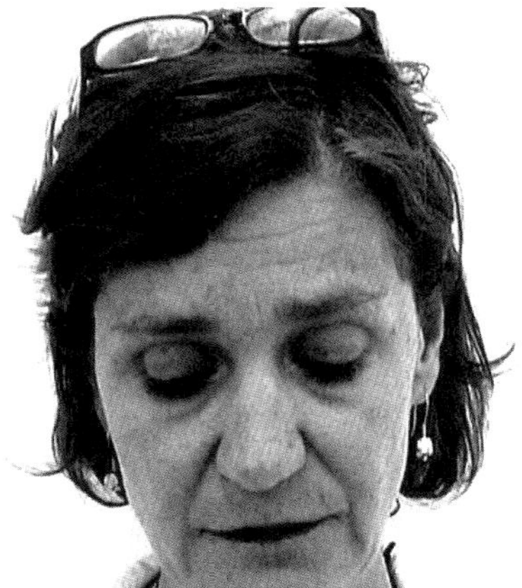

three-quarters profile, and looks down; she moves thus while in the voice-over simultaneously describes how a portrait became something real in the very

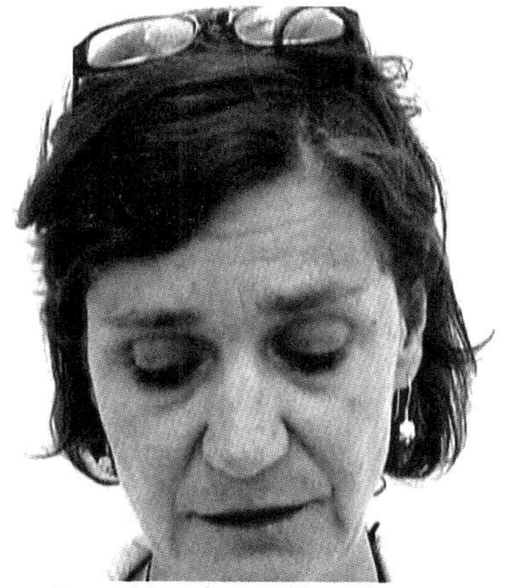

Gallery, Jane Hamlyn, offers the story of three men who once came into the gallery and on seeing a photographic portrait of a woman by the artist Craigie

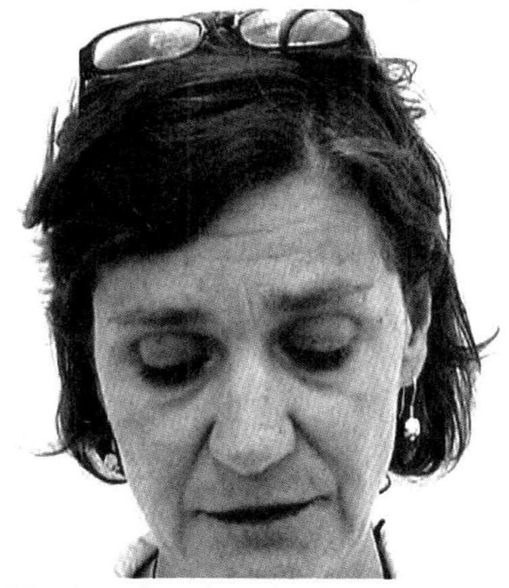

The film largely takes the form of a close-up representation of Hamlyn herself—in black and white, like Horsfield's photograph—as she turns her head to a

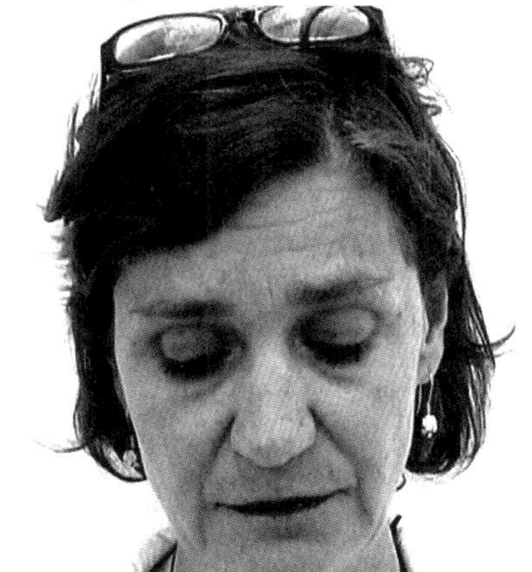

space where she sits.

PART III

Often, Irvine's work will combine the intense focus on a detail, to the point of fixation,

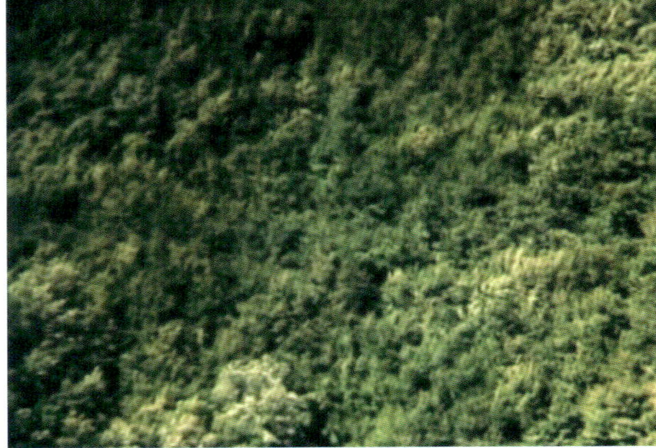

In <u>MOUNTAIN WIND</u> (2006), the screen is filled by a hillside of trees which undulate in waves as the wind blows through them.

with an expansion of the expression of passion outwards into the natural world.

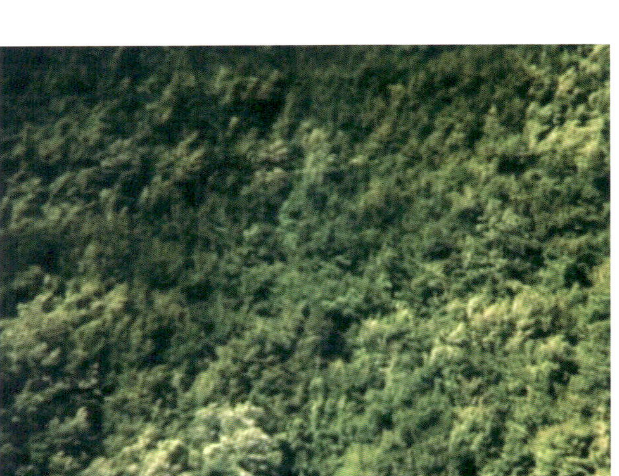

This is accompanied by a song in Italian in which a woman addresses a lover who is asleep, singing that she hates no one more than this person.

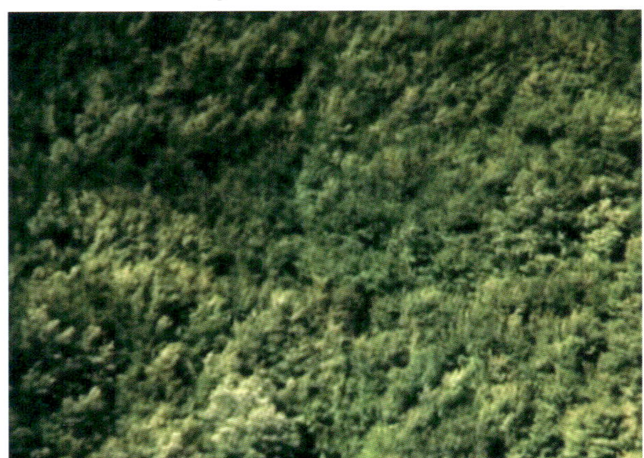

When the lover wakes up, she says, "I'm here/ my love, I love you".

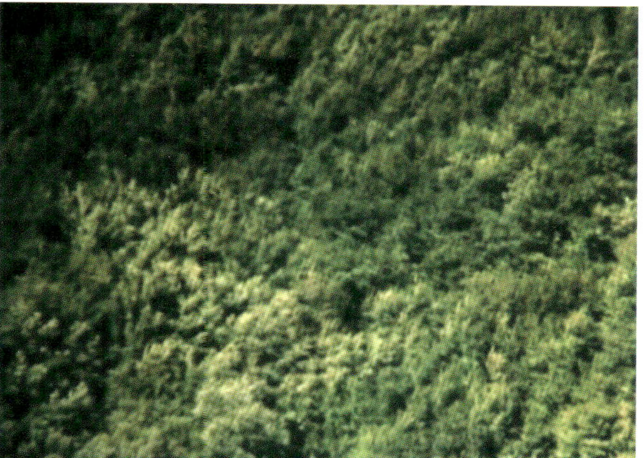

The song also inc udes the words

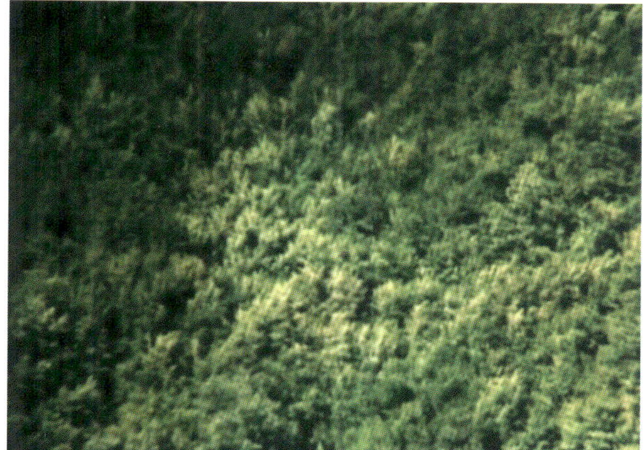

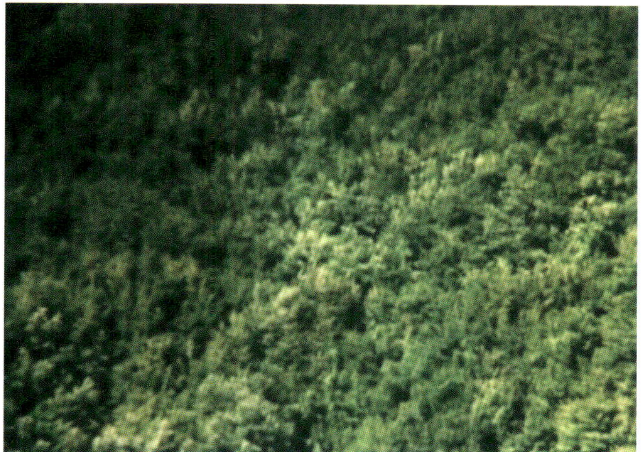

long eyelashes where

I found myself imprisoned. [5]

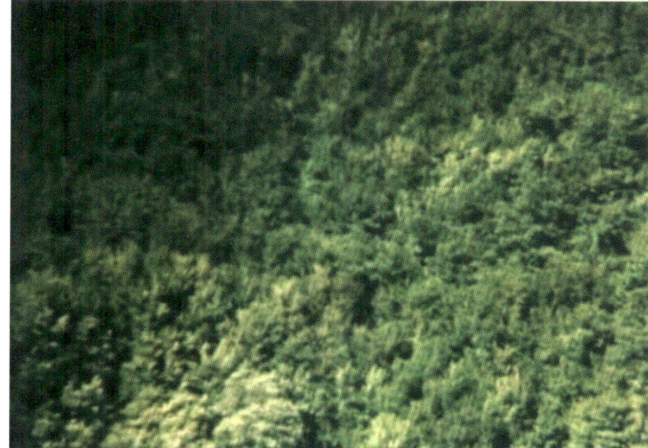

The lover is captivated in an ambivalent relationship with the other, mingling love and hate, reflected in the to-and-fro movement of the trees, which is the

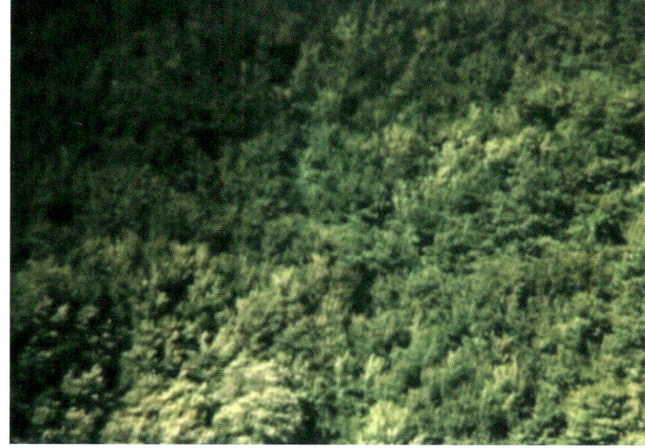

only indication of wind.

The film creates an equivalent for emotion and does so with a hint of exaggeration, so that the viewer is at once carried along

by this concurrence of image and soundtrack, and aware of the process.

Cliché is redeemed so that passion may be shared.

In the film <u>THREE FORMS OF SUDDEN DEATH</u> (2005), instead of song we hear the sound of the wind like whipping cloth.

Three giant Yorkshire rock formations—

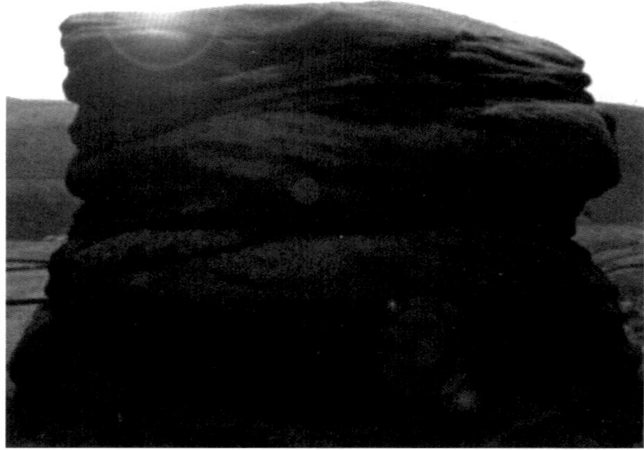

shot on black-and-white Super-8 film to convey in its slight juddering a sense of time—

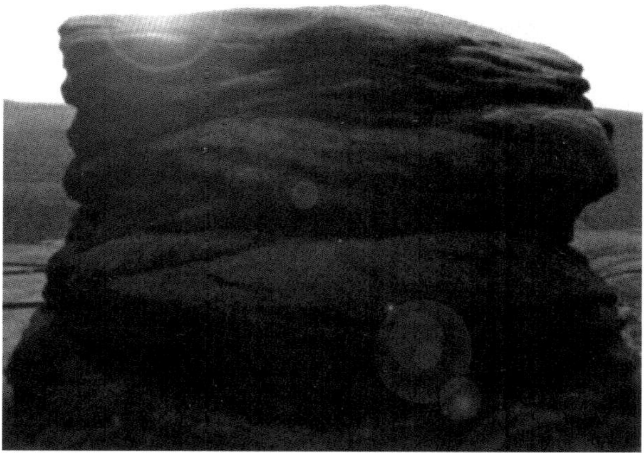

successively fill the field of vision.

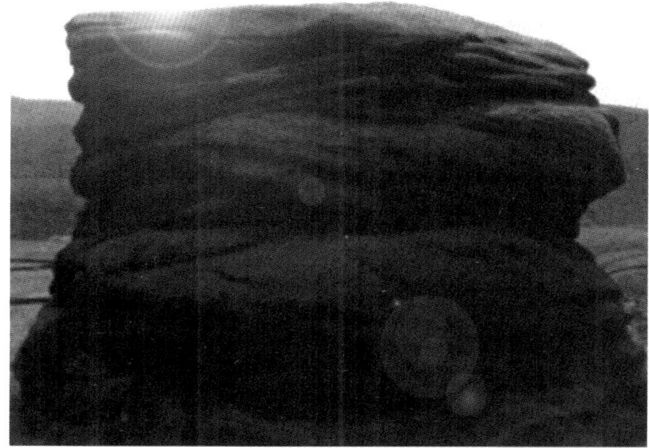

This work is accompanied by a text on *bezoars*,

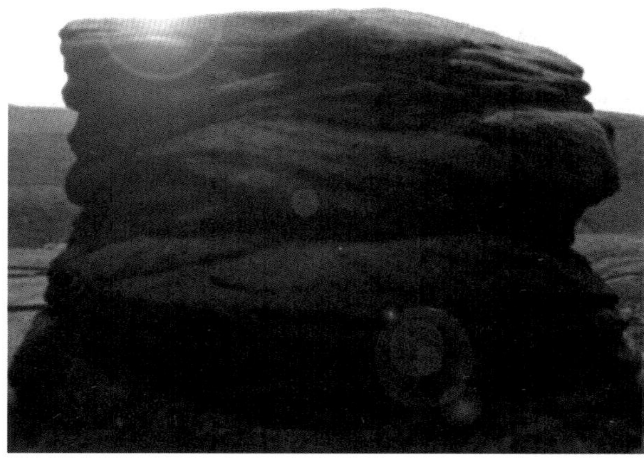

certain deer, when bitten by
venomous serpents, swam into
rivers and remained submerged

until they felt the effect of
the venom to subside.

At this point they shed a large
tear that solidified upon the
deer leaving the water. [6]

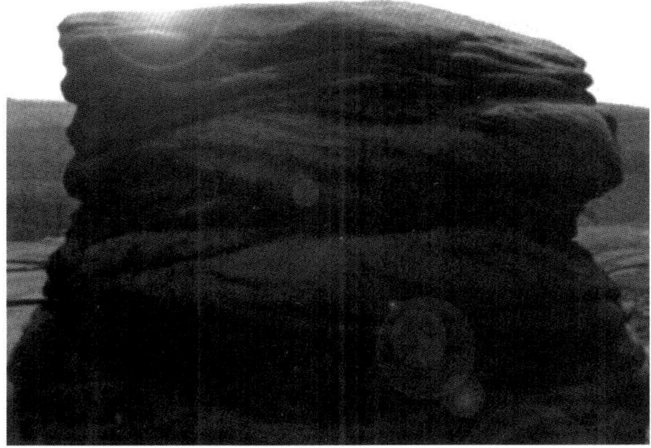

The term bezoar also applies to solid objects
found in the stomach, including accretions of hair that
has been compulsively swallowed,

to which some societies attribute curative properties.[7]

Body and soul are invaded by something alien, but the bezoar is the remains of a process of healing by externalization, an outside on the inside that is expelled.

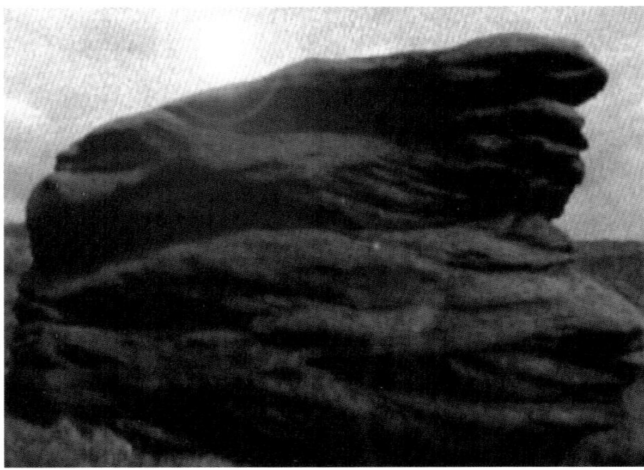

The "bezoar" is a *pharmakon*, the poison that is also a remedy.[8]

In <u>THREE FORMS OF SUDDEN DEATH</u>, the rocks confront the viewer with their massive indifference, the near-timelessness of which is emphasized

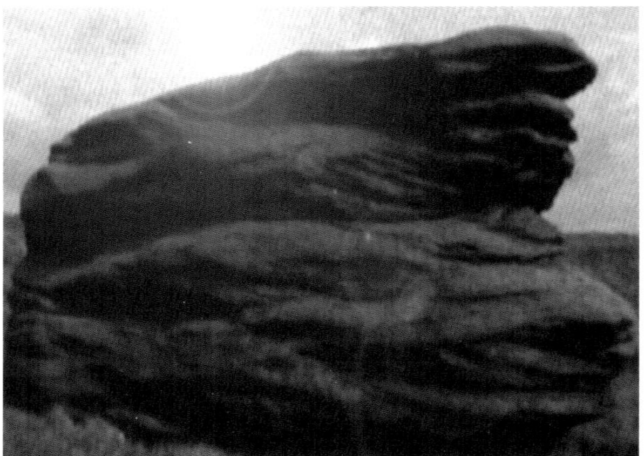

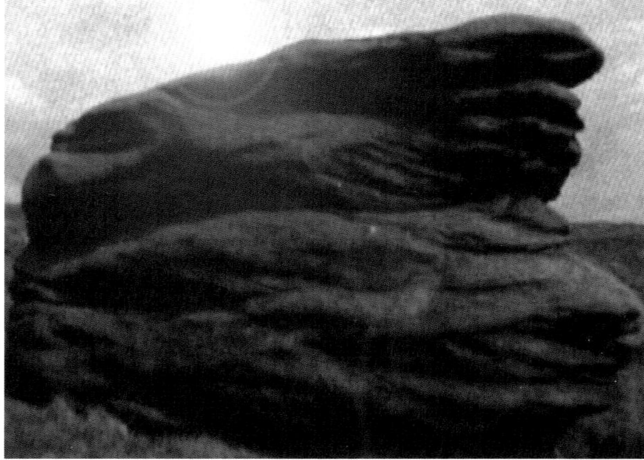

by the contrast with the jiggering movements of the film and the sound of the wind over the moor.

Just as when, having fallen in love, you are obsessed with someone, or mired in anguish at separation, and can think of nothing else, so these rocks fill the view-

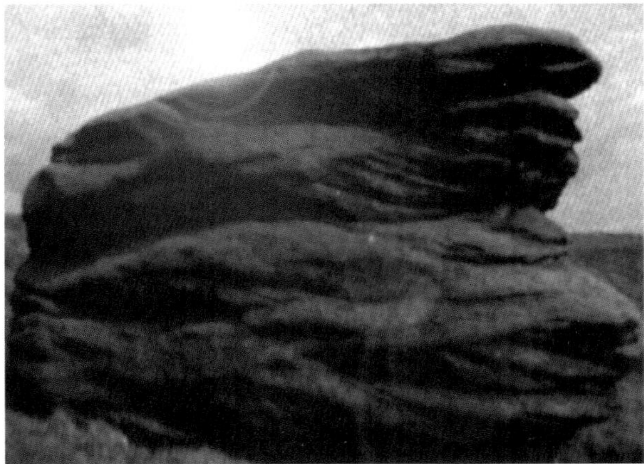

er's field of vision like a grief that blocks out the world.

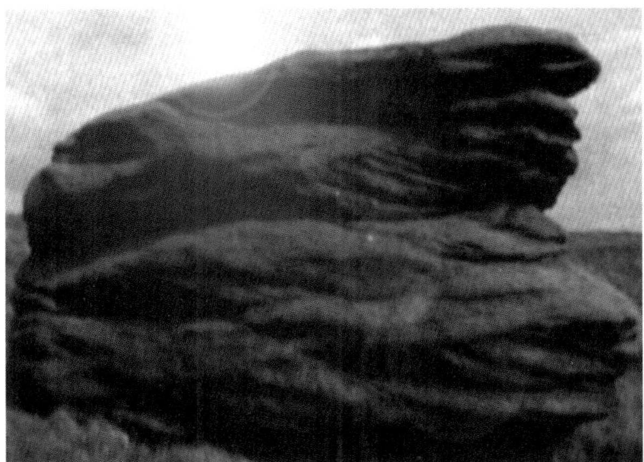

This blocking out of the world
by the giant rock formations

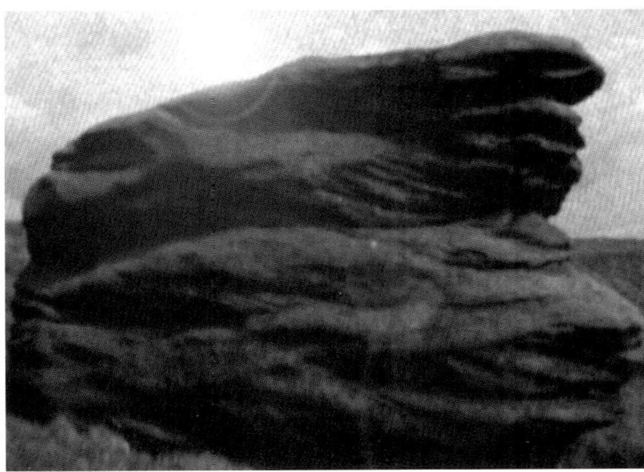

in THREE FORMS OF SUDDEN DEATH

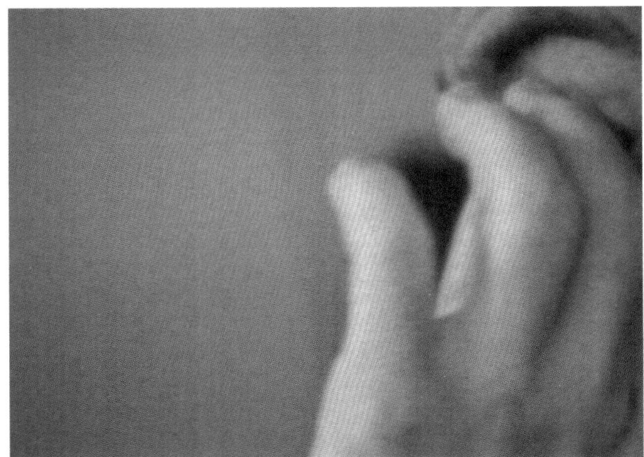

is reminiscent of the way the eyelashes take over the young man's imagination in EYELASHES, so that he gets stuck there.

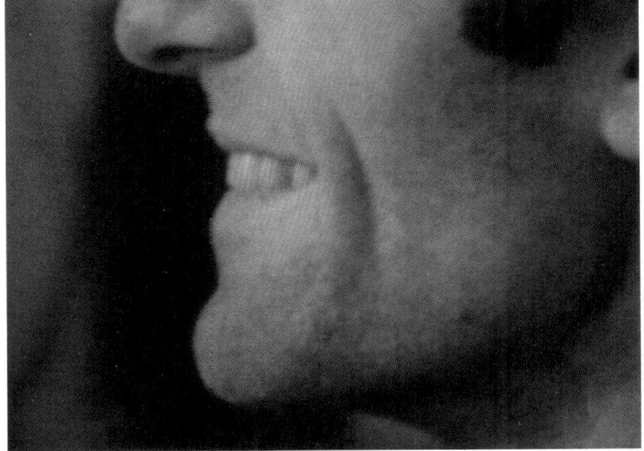

The voice-over, by a woman with a German accent, begins:

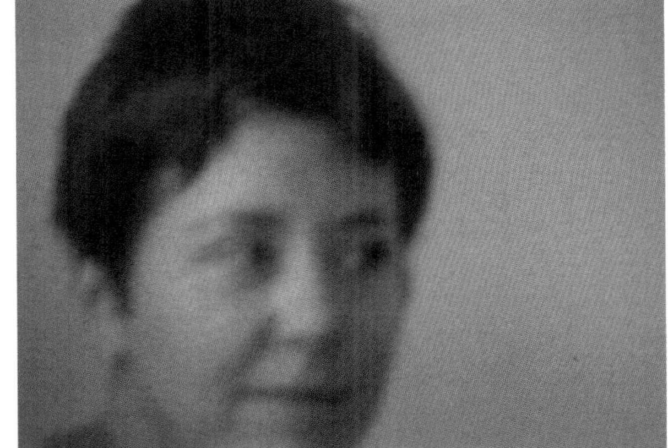

He was having difficulty with a woman…'It's her eyelashes', he said. .

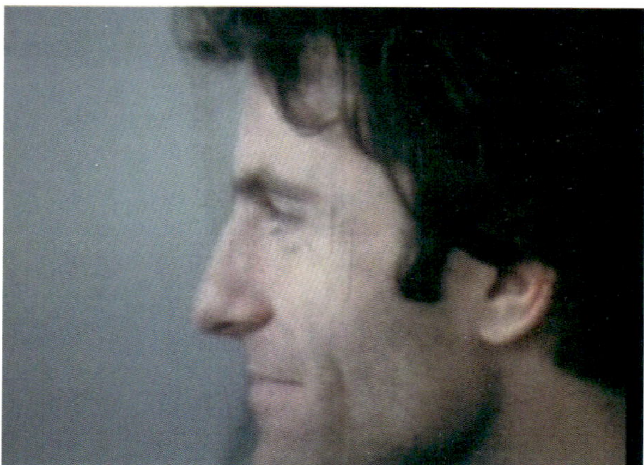

We are first shown his feet, in disintegrating woolly slippers, twitching, and then his smile,

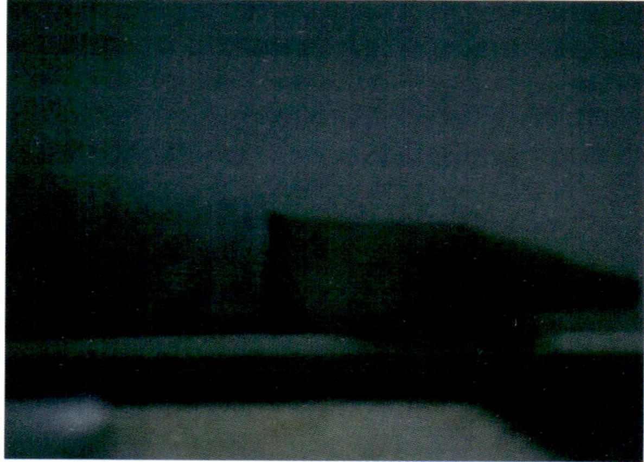

suggesting a discrepancy between his agitation and the way he shows himself to the woman across the table.

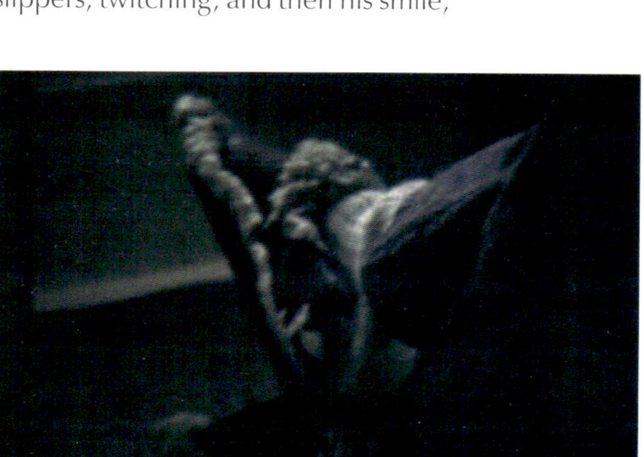

Is she a friend in whom he is confiding, or the woman to whom he refers?

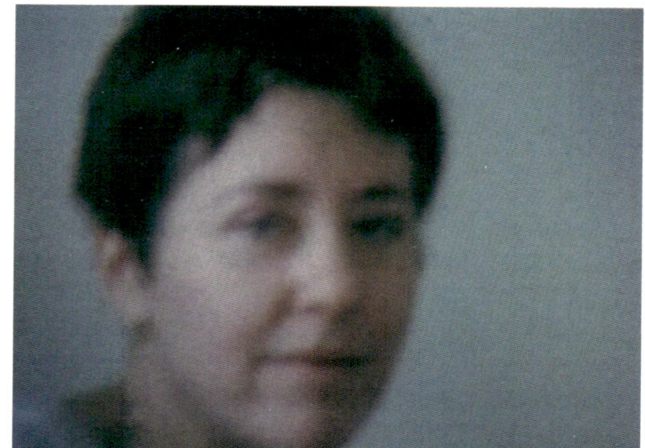

He is attractive, but so locked into his obsession that he appears narcissistic and self-absorbed.

His addressee seems a little skeptical and detached; her outstretched hand is shown tapping on a shelf and for a moment she smiles,

but is maybe a little irritated.

Because we only hear the third-person account of the voice-over,
not what the two are saying to each other,

we are left with a greater degree of uncertainty about their relationship.

The possible gap between what we see and what we hear opens up a space for interpretation,

and the viewer becomes conscious of his or her rôle in figuring out what is passing between the man and the woman.

What does it mean that the man is described as obsessed with the woman's eyelashes?

This fixation is reinforced by the repeating of sequences in the editing of the film.

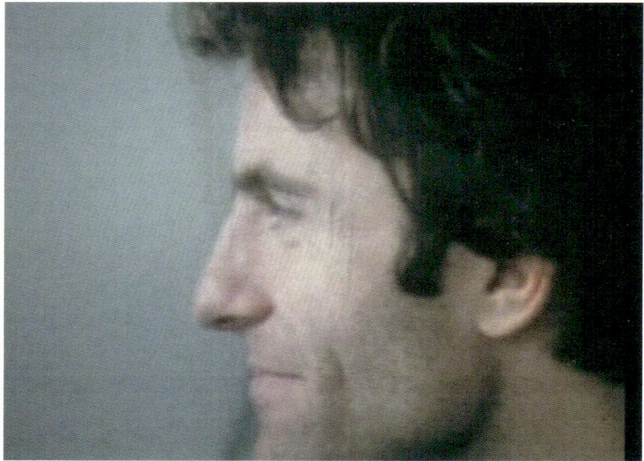

The eyelashes seem to become something like a gateway to her interiority or otherness that he can't get beyond, yet can't get away from either.

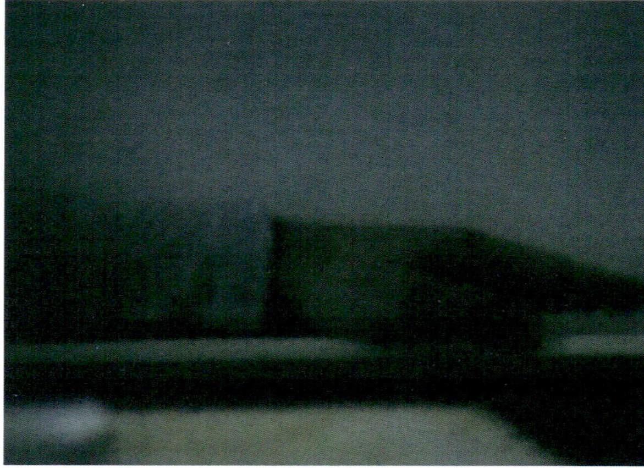

As that at which he halts in advance of the encounter with something that might threaten him as a subject—

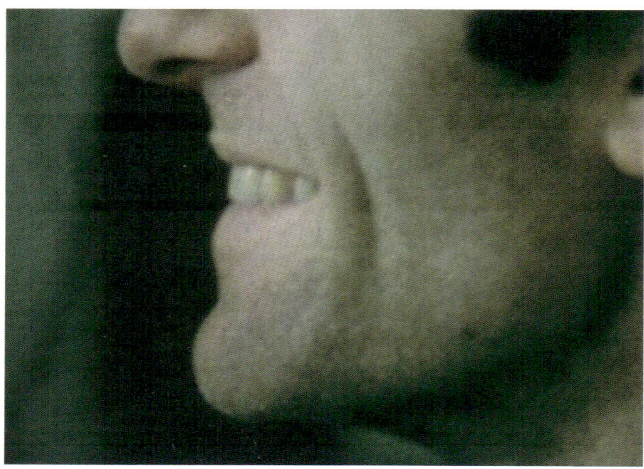

the return, perhaps, of the look (there is one moment when the woman in the film glances at the camera)—the eyelashes function like a fetish.

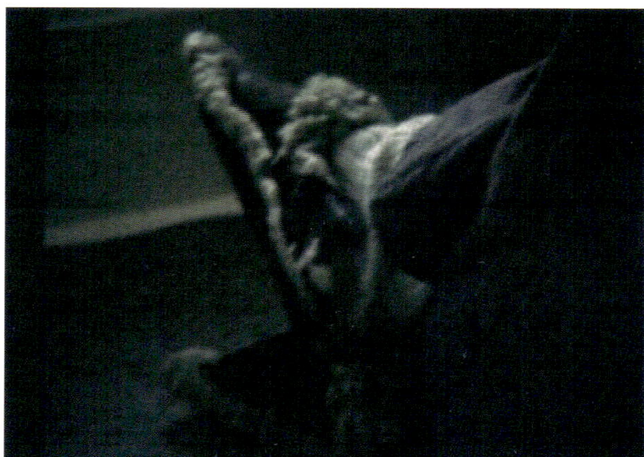

Impersonal, apt to detach themselves, they also have something of the abject about them. Elliptically, the film runs the gamut of love and obsession.

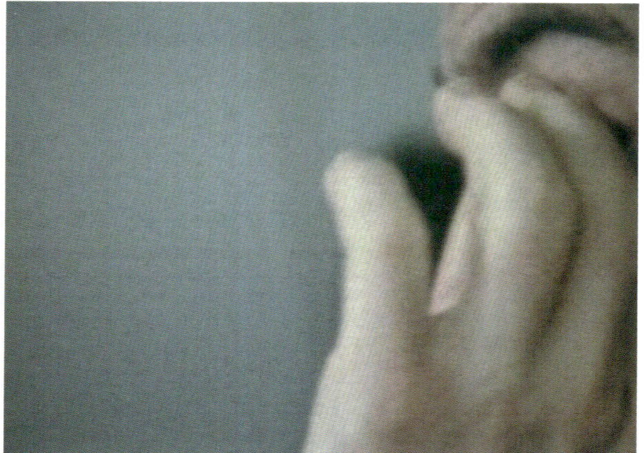

In the last shot in the room,
the two have moved closer to each other:
does this signal a change in their relationship?

Through his obsession the man has created
a solipsistic position for himself:
by fixating on a part of a woman—

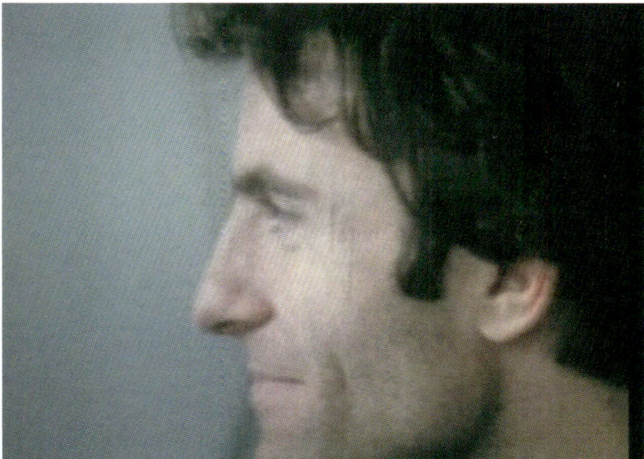

a part-object, a detachable excrescence—we could
say that he relieves himself of the obligation to
acknowledge her, to recognize that she exists as other,

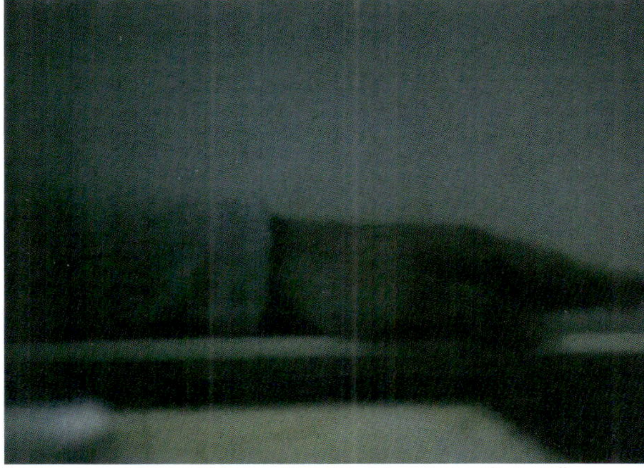

as unrelated to his point of view. This is also reflected
in the impression that he is talking *at* his confidant,
rather than conversing with her.

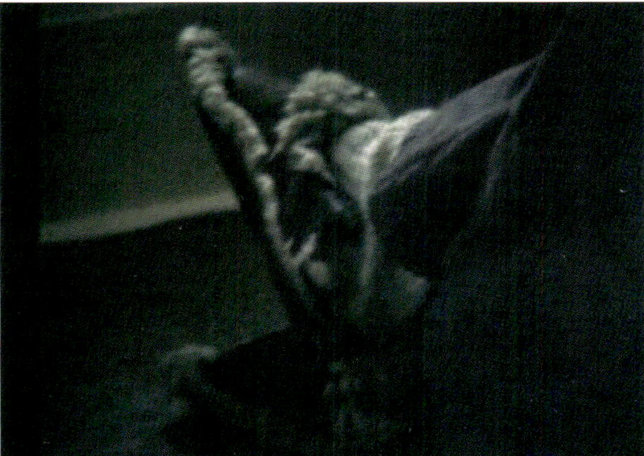

Finally, instead of facing each other, separated by the
table, they are standing beside each other, looking in
the same direction.

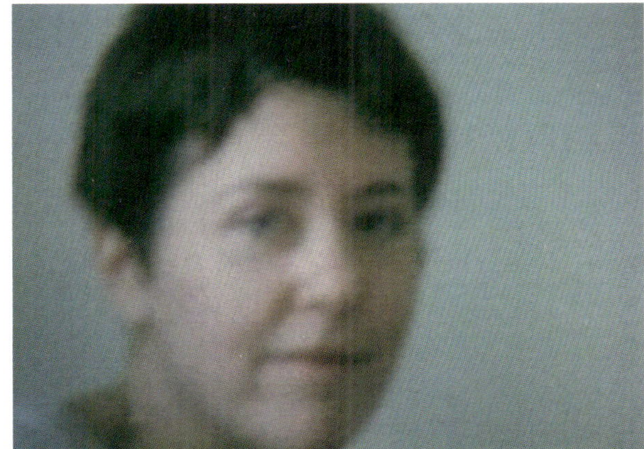

Does this hint at the possibility of acknowledgment
and a shared perspective?

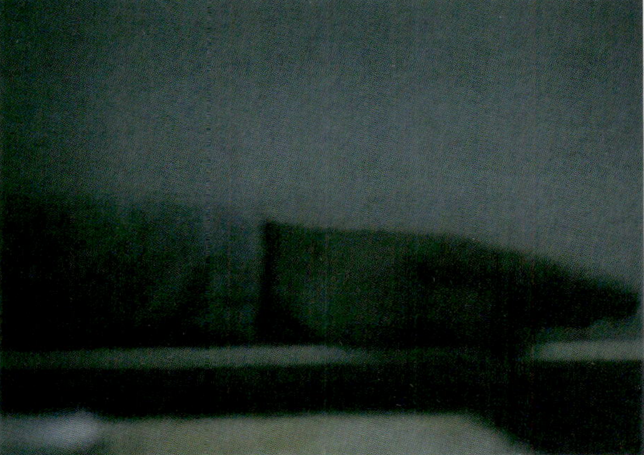

    The film ends as it began,
with a shot of the rooftop and the sun disappearing
behind passing clouds, with the heavy cello

of the string-quartet accompaniment:
two moments evoking the sublime frame the account
in the voiceover of the abject eyelashes.

Julia Kristeva writes that.

the abject is edged with the sublime

The abject is the pre-object that opens up the space of separation that is the condition for the subject to be,

as the sublime is the dissolution of the constituted subject in the vast or powerful: the two sides of over-whelming passion:[9]

The time of abjection is double: a time of oblivion and thunder, of veiled infinity and the moment when revelation bursts forth. Jouissance, in short… One does not know it, one does not desire it, one joys in it [on en jouit]. Violently and painfully. A passion.[10]

Equally, the movement of the camera to the exterior shot at the end of Irvine's film marks an expansion,

a shift from the interior and its micro-focus on the fix-
ations,

repetitions and misfirings of desire,

to the time of nature, the movement of the clouds,
the revolving of the planet as day turns to night.

This mundane domestic exchange, which is equally
a non-encounter between the man and the woman,
in which the man appears to be subject
to critical scrutiny by the camera as well as by the

woman in the film, takes place between the two limits
of the abject and the sublime.

If <u>EYELASHES</u> shows movement becoming repeti-
tion in the twitching gestures,

contains a hint that the very production
of a work about stasis reintroduces movement.

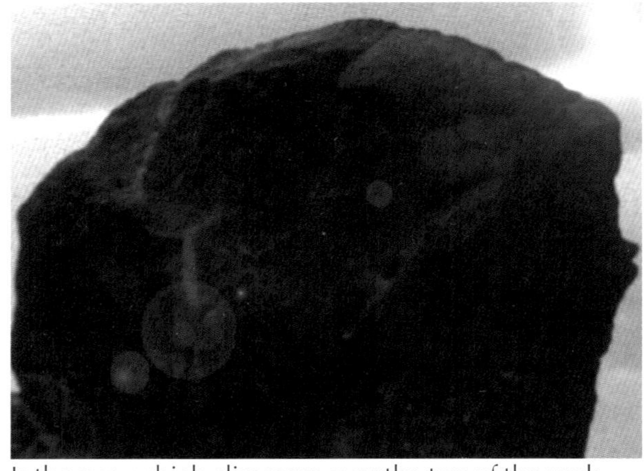

Is the sun, which glimmers over the top of the rock,
setting or rising?

The bezoar, solidified tear and accretion of grief,

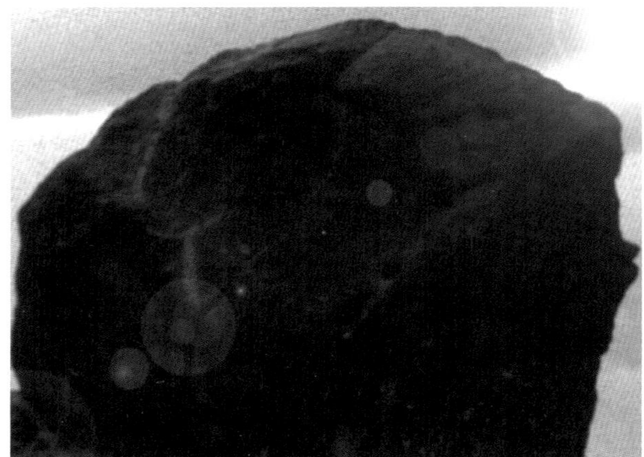

is also a metaphor for the work of art itself,

as a cure for the very malady that it expresses.

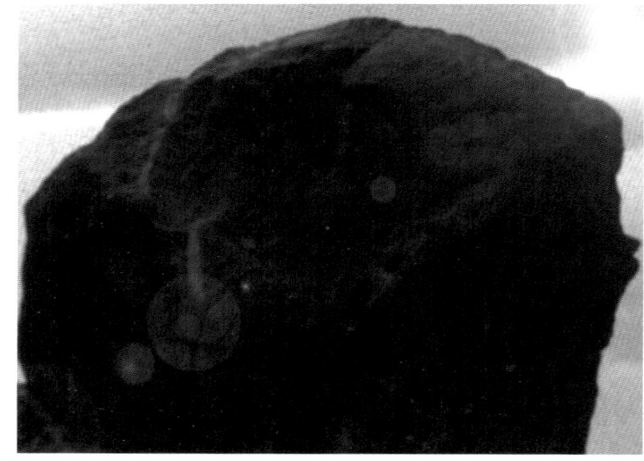

PART IV

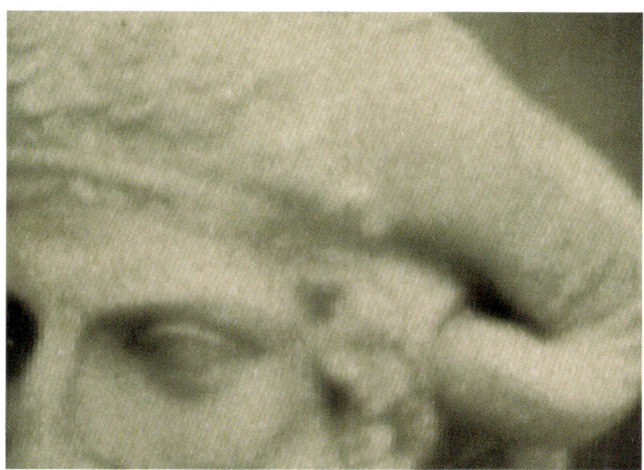

In <u>SWEETTOOTH</u>, as the camera wanders around
a stone-carver's yard full of fragments of sculpture,
a woman's voice speaks of loss

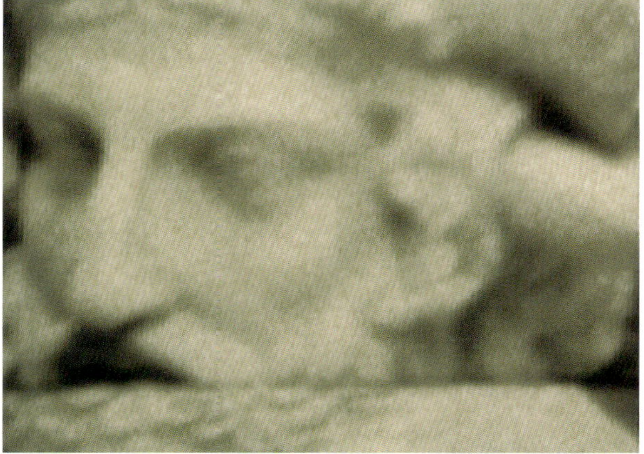

in a surprisingly chirpy way: a girl of nineteen had
`a serious sweet tooth` that led her to the
dentist `one sunny day`, where

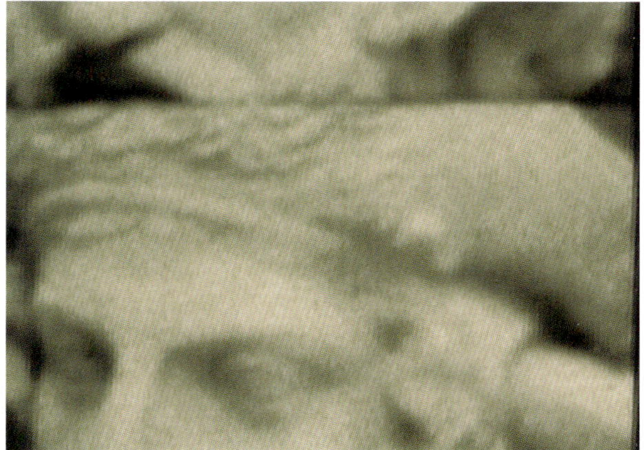

`all her teeth were pulled out.`[11]

She says she feels freer without them:

```
Then, whoever she was talking to would be slightly disturbed at
this, and she'd give them a big smile, the strangest smile a 19-
year-old girl had ever given them. But they wouldn't know how to
take that either, and would try to leave that smile just there,
exactly in the place where her teeth should have been.
```

Not to see the absence of the teeth for the smile
Is this a way of avoiding noticing absence,

to put something—even if as fleeting as a smile—in its
place? This description in the work also describes the
viewer's relation to it.

We don't know how to take this humour applied to loss. If the narrator is taken as a stand-in for the viewer, the girl could be a figure of the artist:

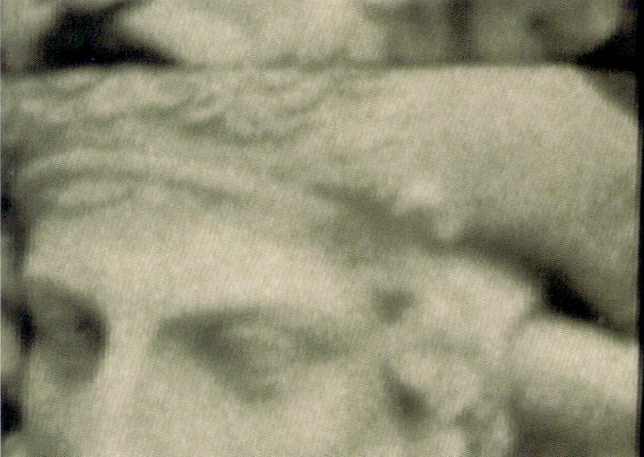

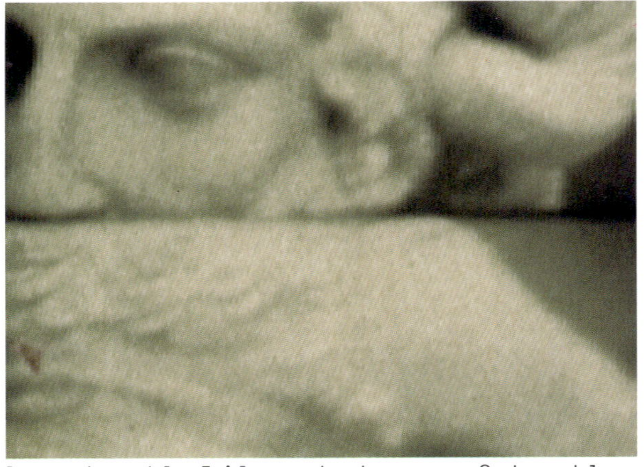

her teeth like statues of teeth,
like the dragon's teeth sewn by Cadmus,
mythic founder of Thebes,

took root and began to grow in my imagination.
The teeth blossom all the more effectively in their

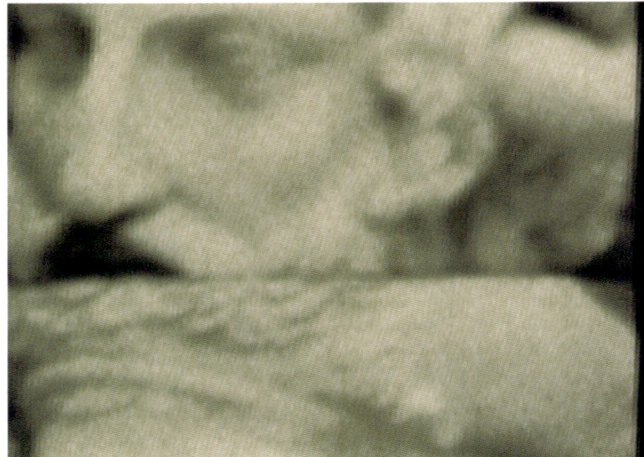

absence, as, according to Mallarmé, the word creates the oblivion of the disappearance of the thing, out of which arises

the very idea in its mellowness; in other words, what is absent from every bouquet.[12]

<u>THE HOTTEST SUN, THE DARKEST HOUR</u> enacts love and loss in five parts: meeting, ecstasy, otherness, departure, memory..

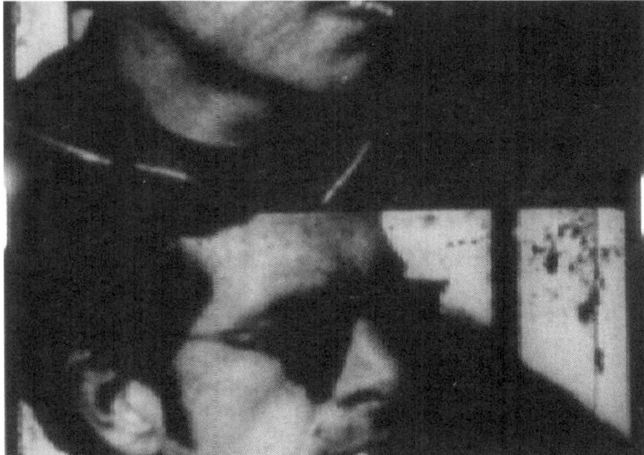

a woman sings in talian to a dog about the fear of being alone—in translation,

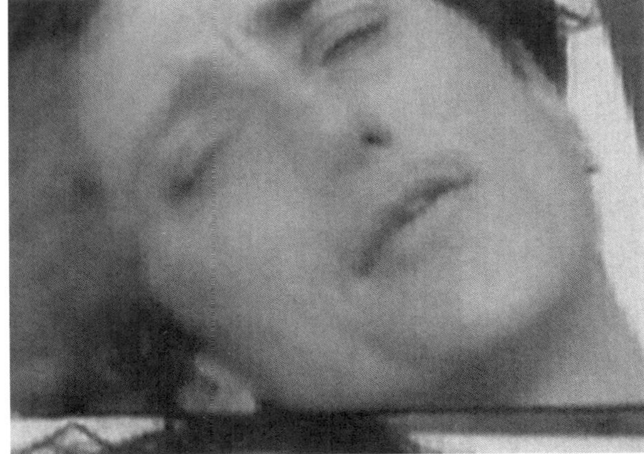

the view from the window of a plane taking off, set to a song titled I'll live without you;

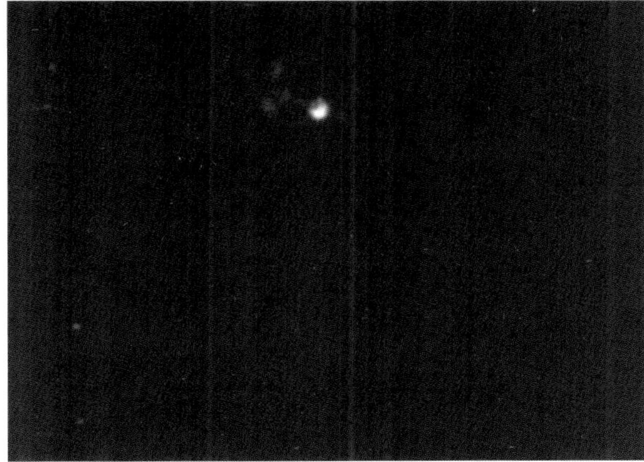

A man meets an older man who looks like him; a film of fireflies, as if an unrepresentable flash of ecstasy;

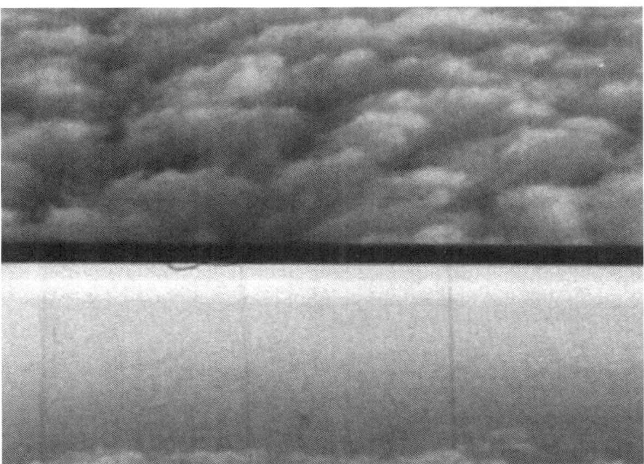

even when you are sleeping beside me, we don't dream the same dream;

then we look down towards the face of the woman, who smokes, makes kisses, and flirts with the camera.

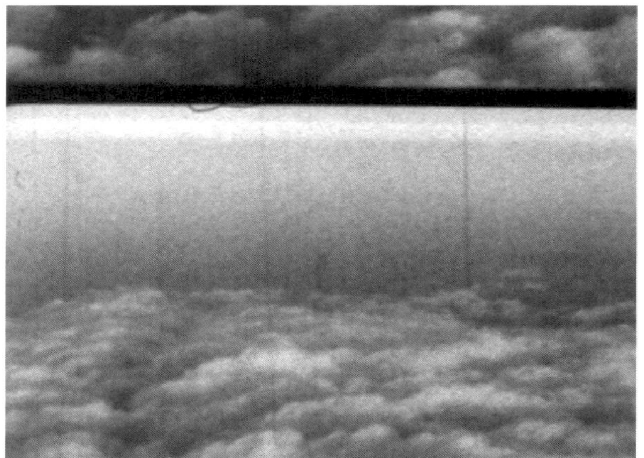 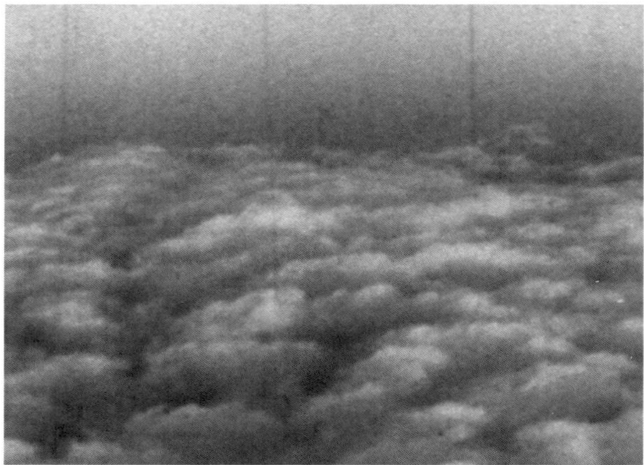

This scene has a retrospective feel,
as if the photograph's temporality of absent pastness

breaks through the flowing presence of the moving
image, and we are looking at an old movie remem-
bering how it was.

The title suggests the ambiguity of pleasure and pain:

the sun can warm but it can also burn,

the darkest hour can be a time of lassitude and
dreams, but it can also be a time of separation and
despair.

PART V

.

We tell stories to make the unbearable bearable.

And sometimes humour is a way of dealing with grief.

In the short story *The Facts behind the Helsinki Roccamatios* by Yann Martel, the narrator, inspired by Boccaccio's *Decameron*,

helps his friend Paul who is dying of AIDS
by playing a game in which they set out
to write a history of the 20th century

by each supplying a single episode
from alternate years.

The night before his death, Paul leaves behind
a fictional episode for the year 2001:

the writing of history as a sequence of stories
becomes a way of coping with the unbearable,
at once confronting and denying death.[13]

Does a story—or any work of art—have to do with
what it represents, whether fictional or true, or what it
enables us to endure?

Martel's novel the *Life of Pi*, is narrated from the
point of view of the son of a zoo-keeper from
Pondicherry, India,

who loses his parents in the wreck of the Japanese
cargo ship on which they are emigrating to Canada,
and ends up on a life-boat with a tiger

(tigers will feature in works by Irvine as well).

After he lands in Mexico, and the tiger has disappeared, Pi Patel offers the investigators from the
Japanese ministry of transport,

from Richard Brautigan's book *In Watermelon
Sugar* in which the narrator describes how tigers
killed and ate his parents.

who don't believe the story of the tiger, an alternative
story without animals, and says to them,

So tell me, since it makes no factual difference
to you and you can't prove the question either
way, which story do you prefer? Which is the
better story, the story with animals or the story
without animals?[14]

In <u>ANOTHER DIFFICULT SUNSET</u>
(1996) Irvine has a voice-over to a sequence of a man
in a London Underground train repeat the vignette

Interrupting their meal, this exchange takes place:

"We're just like you, " the other tiger said. "We speak the same language you do. We think the same thoughts, but we're tigers. "

"You could help me with my arithmetic. "
"What's that?" One of the tigers said.
"My arithmetic. "
"Oh, your arithmetic. "
"Yeah. "

"What do you want to know?" One of the tigers said.
"What's nine times nine?"
"Eighty- one. " The tiger said.

"What's eight times eight?"
"Fifty- six. " The tiger said.

Not only can tigers do their times tables, they make
mistakes too. They're just like us—but then they're
not. A little later,

They both went back to eating my parents.
I went outside and sat down by the river.

"I'm an orphan. " I said. [15]

Brautigan's tale appears to refute Ludwig
Wittgenstein's claim that

If a lion could talk,
we could not understand him.[16]

But does it? Stanley Cavell's gloss—
quoted by Irvine in ANOTHER DIFFICULT
SUNSET—on Wittgenstein's dictum goes as follows:

Whatever one may wish to imagine
about what a lion might, as it were, say if
he talked, I take Wittgenstein's statement
to mean that it is part of our understanding of
human beings that (without exception) they
talk and part of our understanding of lions that
(without exception) they do not, so that a lion's
talking rather than roaring would not clarify
for us, for example, why the lion is in discomfort.(It would, to say the least, perplex us in the
extreme; in any case it would prevent our car-
ing about his or her suffering then and there.)[17]

It's not just that a talking lion
would no longer be a lion.

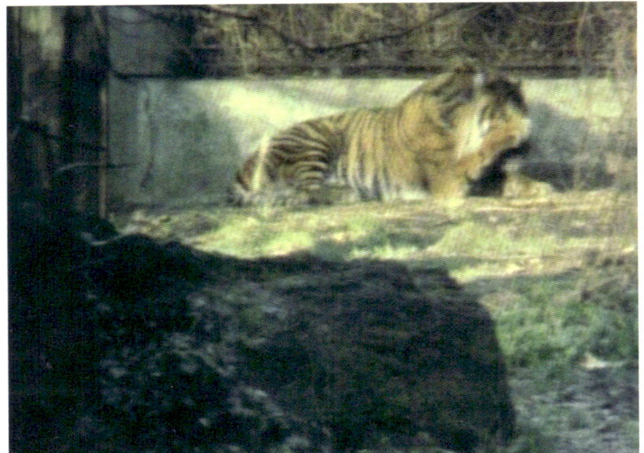

For a lion—or tiger—
to talk and for us to understand them

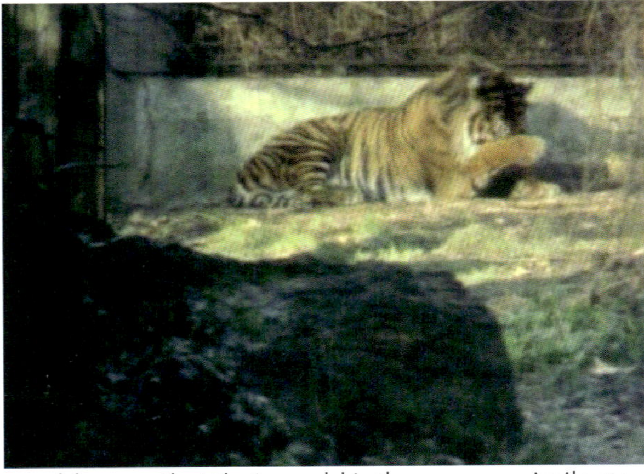

would mean that their world is the same or similar to ours.

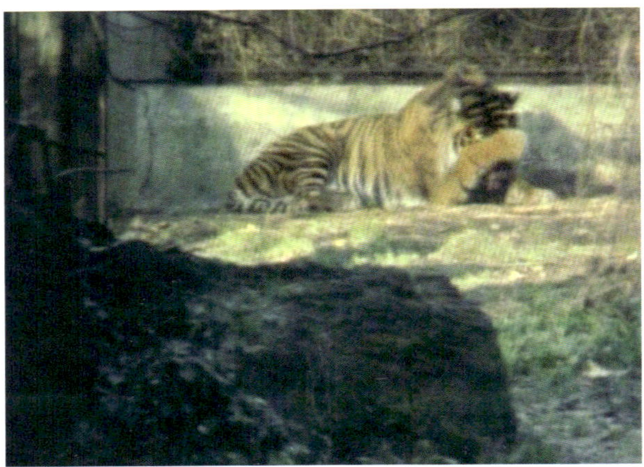

The point is not whether or not animals can talk, but rather, that if they did,

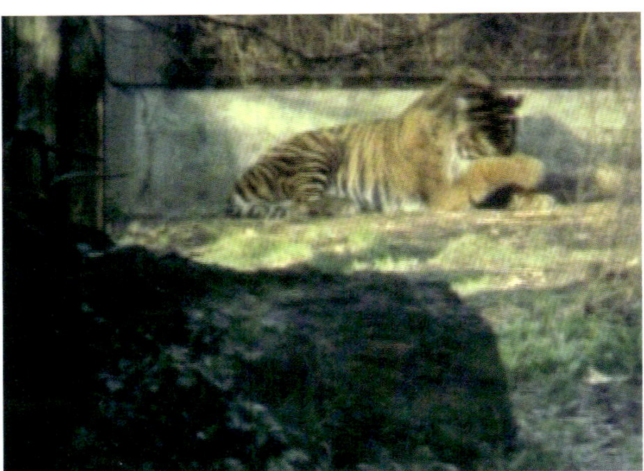

we wouldn't understand what they were saying.

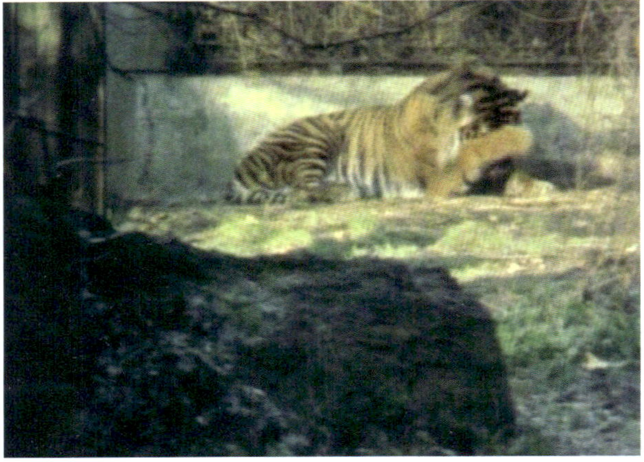

But, to a degree, is that not the case with any exchange of words?

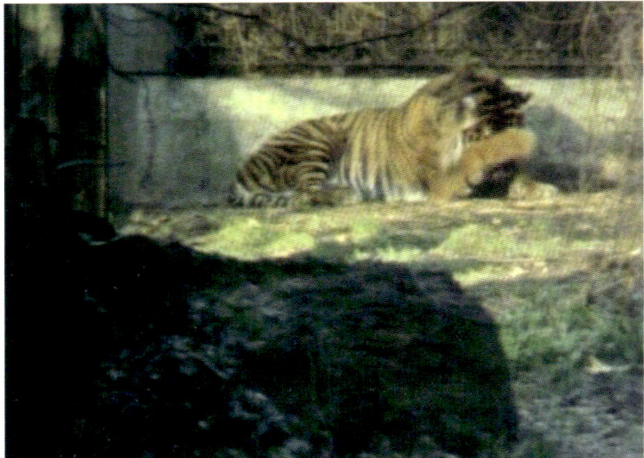

Isn't there always an irreducible element of opacity, or of worlds not shared even if we live together?

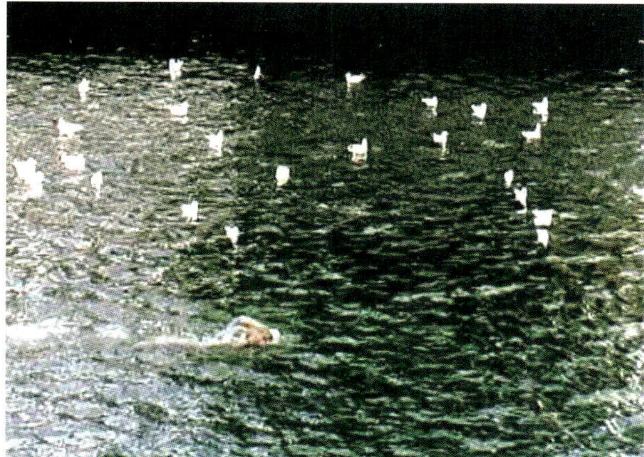

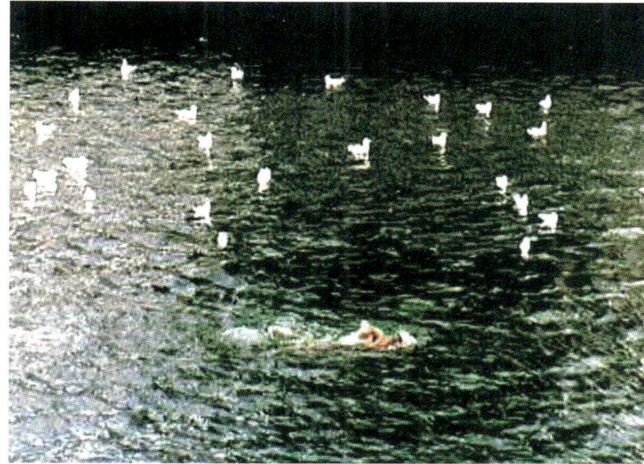

In Irvine's video <u>SWIMMERS AND SEAGULLS</u> (2003) footage of bathing-capped humans participating in the annual swim in Dublin's Liffey River

are superimposed with footage of seagulls landing, bobbing on the water, and taking off.

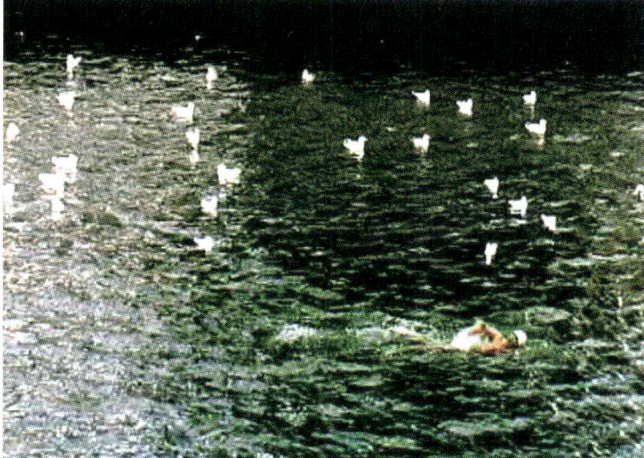

The water becomes the place where the birds who inhabit the air and the humans who walk on the land, meet,

and on this uncommon common ground it is the humans more than the birds who become strange creatures.

Irvine's work is about just that, the encroachments of strangeness.

Sometimes despite this a commonality is achieved, sometimes not.

PART VI

Anne Tallentire writes
of <u>ANOTHER DIFFICULT SUNSET</u> that

the clever logic of this work reveals itself
by drawing us towards a belief in that
which appears meaningful but which
at the same time dissolves into that
which is meaningless.[18]

What do we want from meaning?
What is at stake in meaninglessness?

How does this oscillation function in Irvine's work?

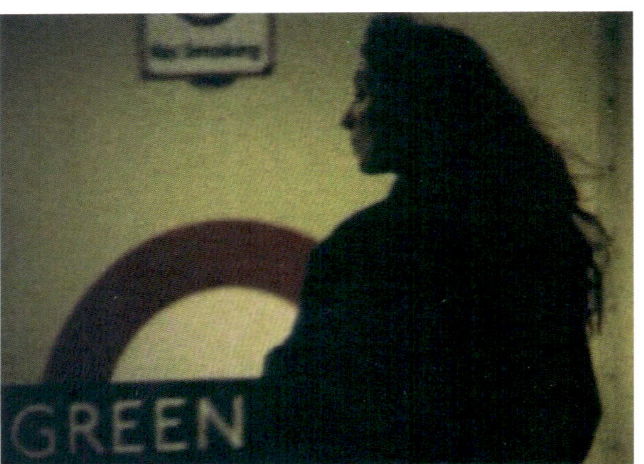

The various looped video sequences in
<u>ANOTHER DIFFICULT SUNSET</u> in which a
man and woman pass each other repeatedly without

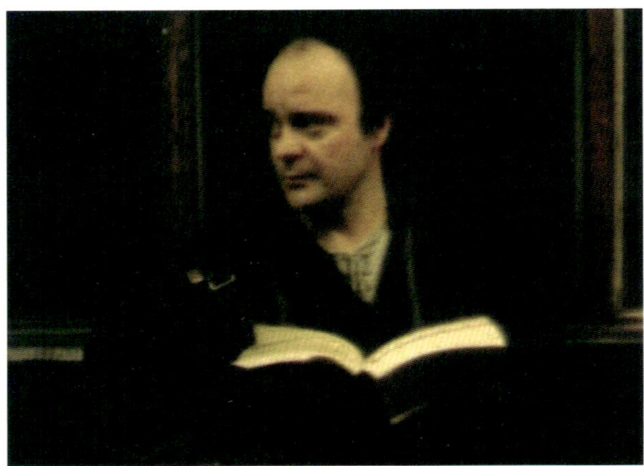

encountering each other are linked by references to
animals: a conversation about what would be the
case if lions could talk;

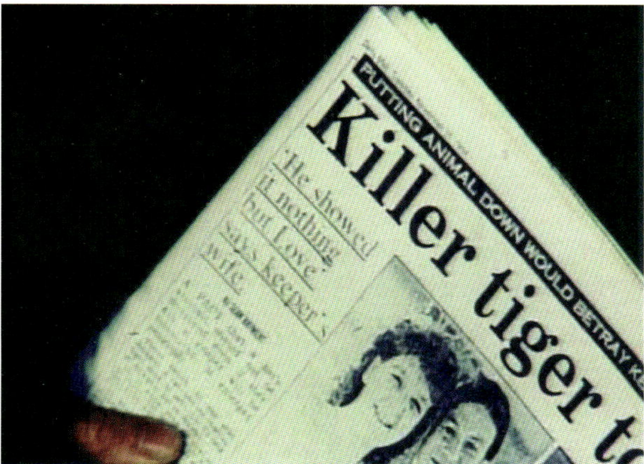

a newspaper story about a tiger that killed a keeper "who showed it nothing but love" at Aspinall's zoo;

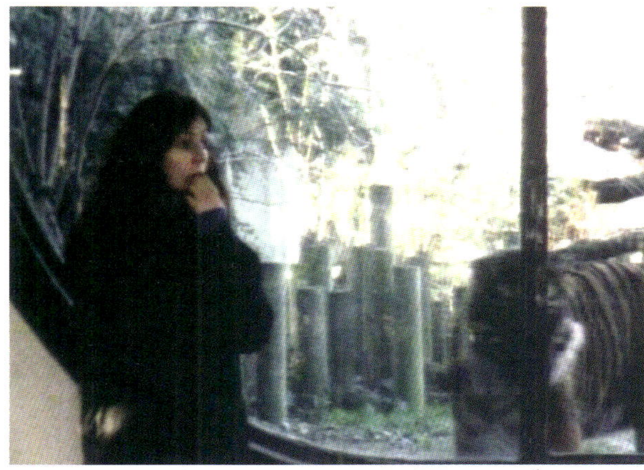

the tiger story from Brautigan's *In Watermelon Sugar* referred to above;

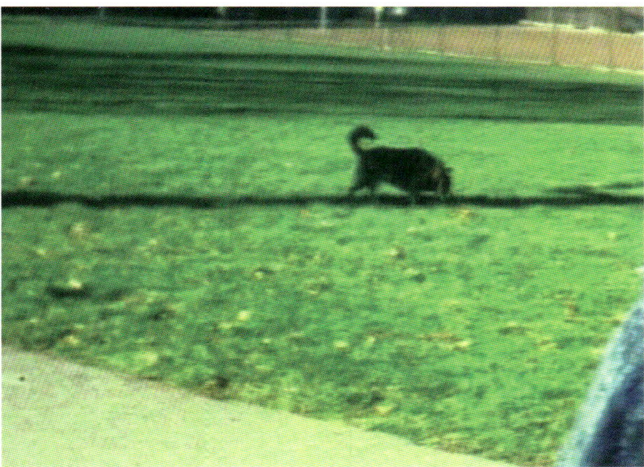

and sequences with a dog, and in front of the tiger enclosure at The _ondon Zoo.

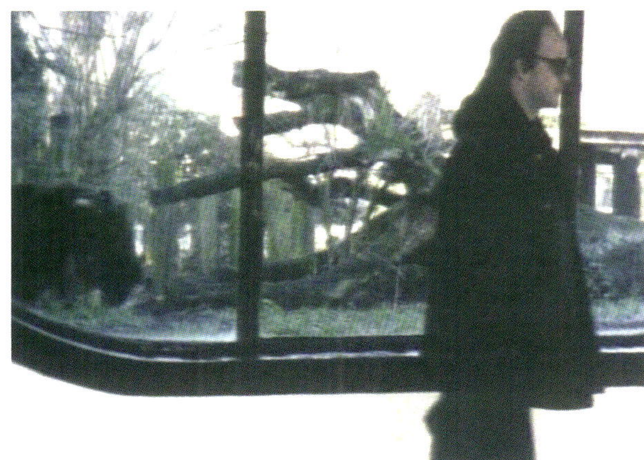

These repeated animal references, especially those to tigers, cause the world depicted to teeter into fable.

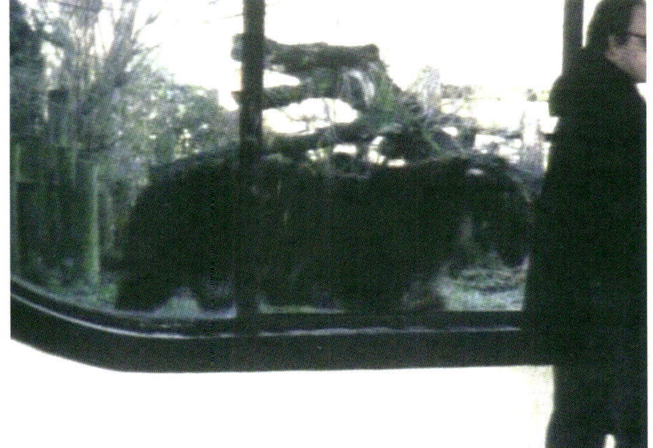

Instead of looking at the world, we start to look for meaning.

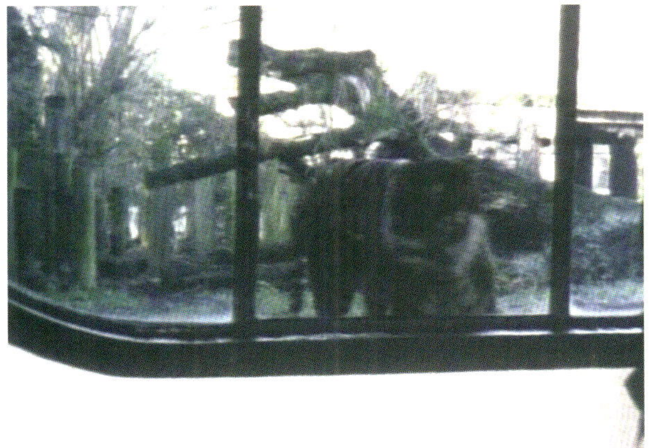

The seeding of the videos with animal and tiger references provokes us to look for connections: however.

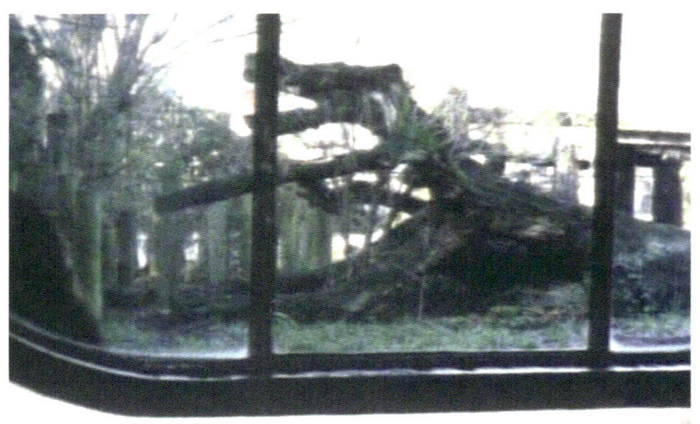 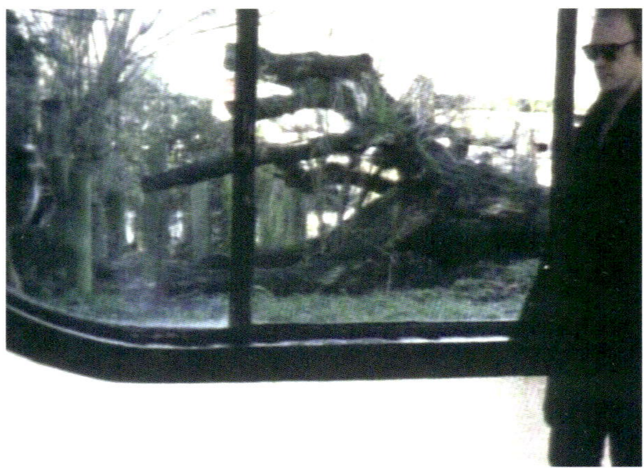

Meaning does not come as something that is present,
as fulfillment,
but rather the videos show *missed* encounters.

What is missed? Or, better, what is it to miss?

Stanislaw Lem's book *A Perfect Vacuum* is a collection of book reviews of nonexistent works of literature, one of which is titled *Rien du tout, or la*

conséquence [Nothing, or the Consequence] by Mme Solange Marriot—that her first name evokes the image of a fortune-teller is perhaps no coincidence.

According to the reviewer this—her first book—is also the first novel **ever to have reached the limit of what writing can do:**

It promised to communicate nothing,
to tell of nothing, to signify not a thing,
but merely to be, as a cloud is, a table, a tree.
Fine in theory. It failed, however [...].
What decides the defeat is the issue of
contexts: on them—on that which is
completely inexpressible—depends
the sense of what we say.[19]

A solution might be to write nothing:

It was necessary, then—and herein is
the consequence—to write nothing.
But can such a task make sense?
To write *nothing*—is it not the same
as to write *nothing*? What then?...[20]

How then to write *nothing* (italicized,
as if "nothing" can be substantive,
which of course it cannot) without writing nothing—

that is, without ceasing to write?
Would negation be a way?

The first sentence of *Rien du tout,
or la conséquence* reads, "The train did
not arrive"; in the next sentence we find
"He did not come."[21]

Although the sentence affirms nothing existentially,
for the reader,

there is conjured up involuntarily in his imagination a scene taking place at some railway station, a scene of waiting for someone who has
not arrived, and since he knows the sex of the
author (authoress), the waiting for the nonar-
rival immediately carries the anticipation of an
erotic encounter. What of this? Everything!
Because the whole responsibility for these conjectures, from the very first words, falls on the
reader.[22]
And the reviewer goes on:

The reader therefore is constantly thrown back
on himself, but that is the problem
of his own anticipations, conjectures,
his hypotheses ad hoc.[23]

The reader is no longer the one who "sees through"
the fiction as if it were illusion masking a reality,
since because of the negation nothing illusory is posited.

Rather, by being drawn into the interpretation
of *nothing*,

the basis of the illusoriness of fiction as such, the reader is exposed to his or her own nothingness.

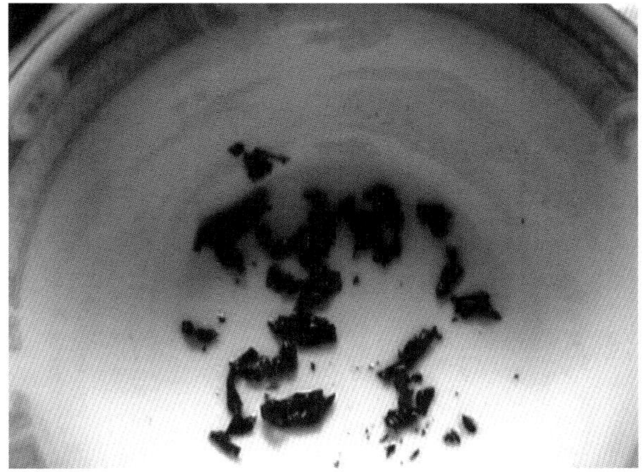

The train's not there... and
he hasn't arrived says the fortune teller in
IVANA'S ANSWERS,

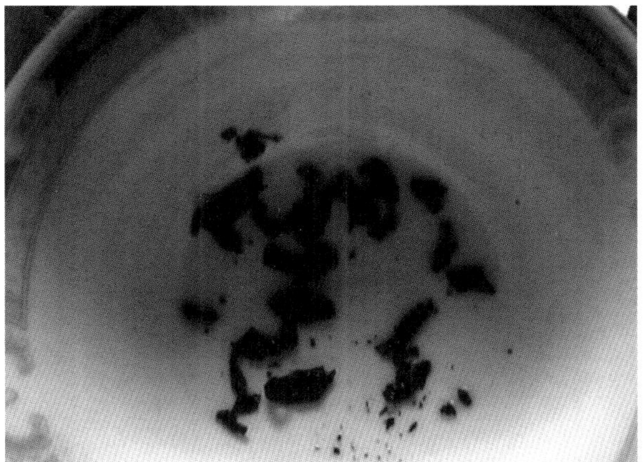

which begins with a shot of a train leaving a station at
night, and a woman's arms embracing a column of the
building—

evoking the cond tion Cyril Connolly called **angoisse
de gare**, also to be found in the nighttime station
paintings by the Belgian artist Paul Delvaux.

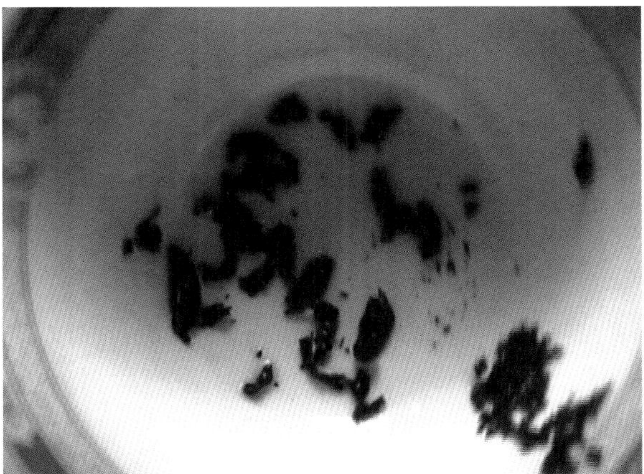

But, we will be induced to ask, when exactly does this
scene take place in relation to the other parts of the
work?

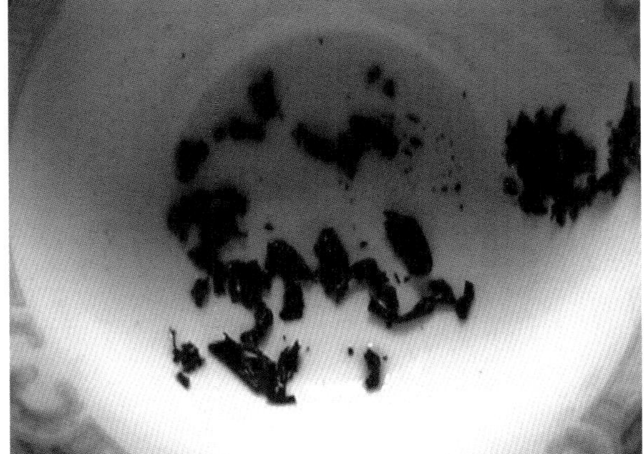

Indeed, does it take place at all?
The film cuts to the examination, through a loupe,
of insects,

followed by the interpretation of tea leaves in a cup—
a reflection of its own specular activity
and that of the viewer.

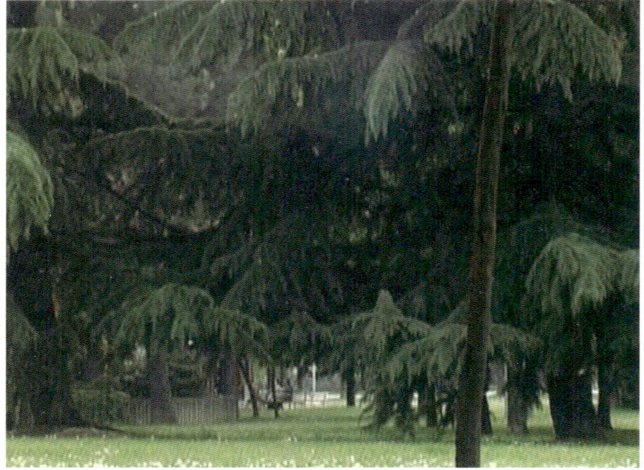

<u>IVANA'S ANSWERS</u> is a work about time,
about seeing and being seen,
interpreting the world and being a part of a story.

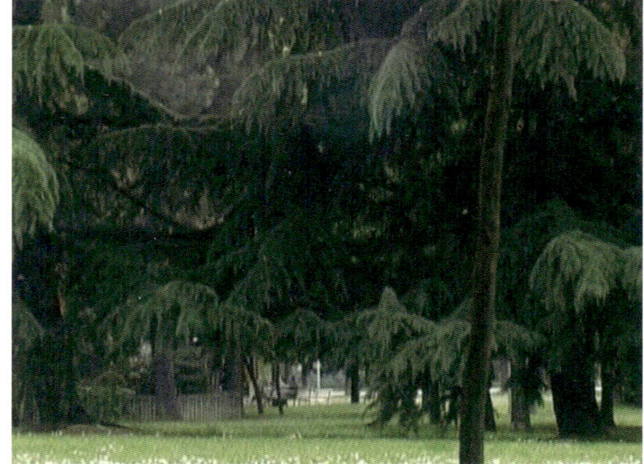

The magnifier through which the tendrils
on the insects leg are seen doubles the camera
as a viewing instrument,

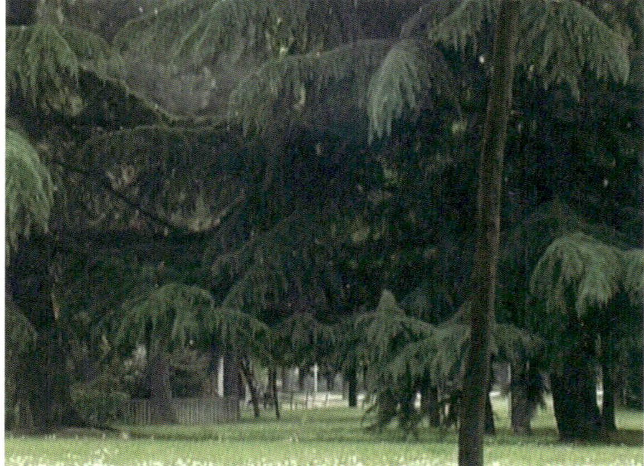

so when we then see Ivana looking at the insects
through a loupe, we are aware that she is also being
looked at by the camera.

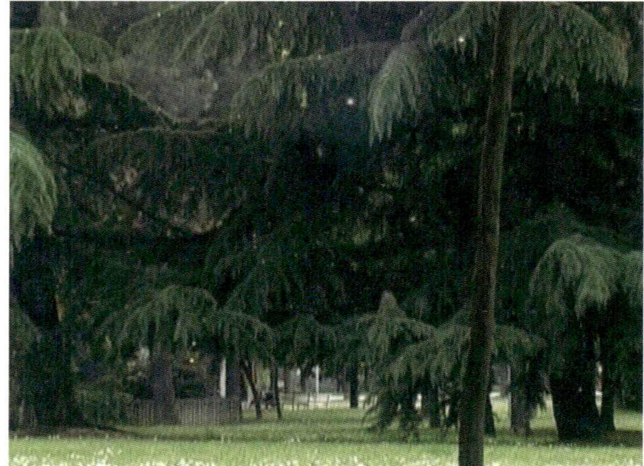

Mariela Tasseli, the reader, points out in the tea leaves
birds `sitting on a branch like
question marks` but then negates this—

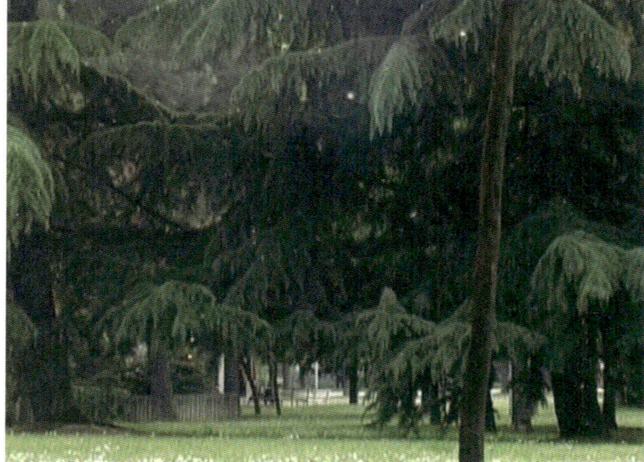

`"No sorry...I'm mistaken.`

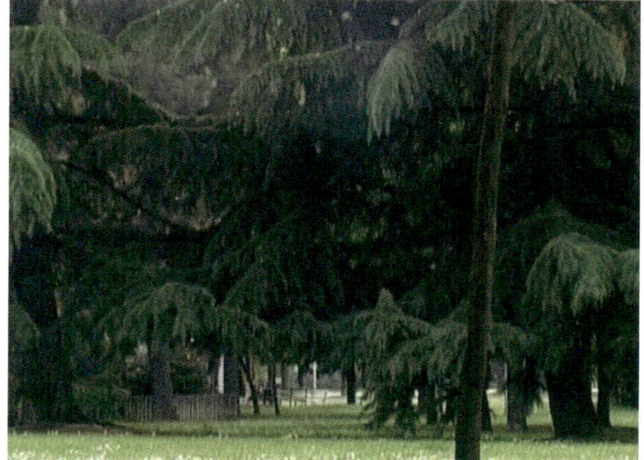

`They're not question marks,
they're answers...answers to
your questions.`

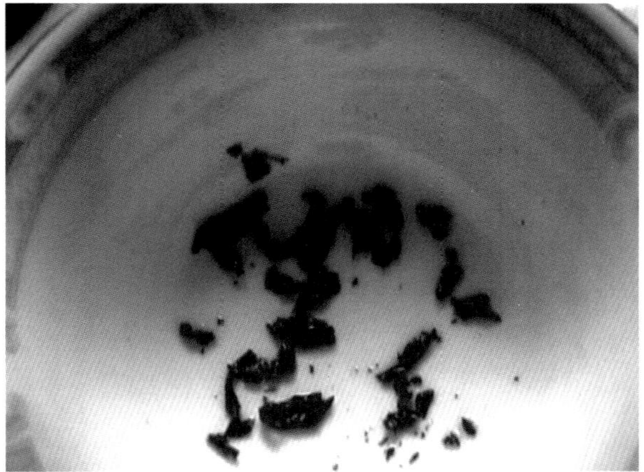

What questions? asks Ivana.

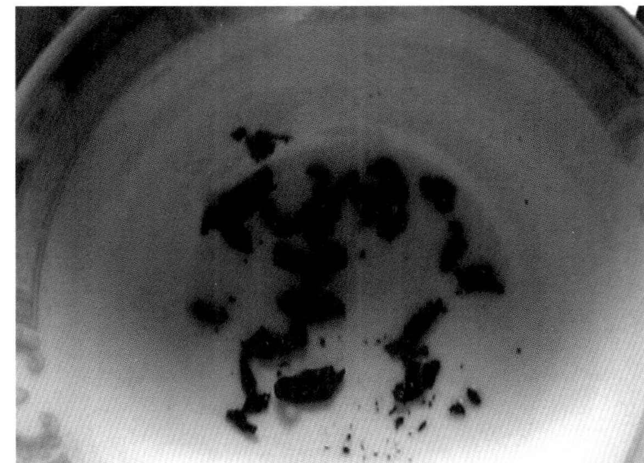

Exactly.. well done! says the reader.

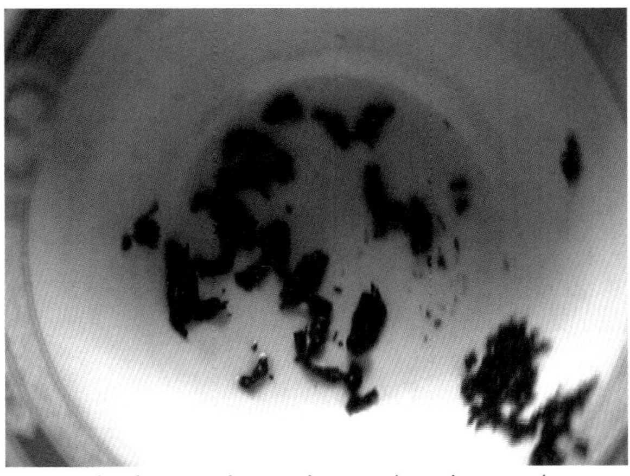

Ivana is looking at the tea leaves, but she needs to put herself in the picture—

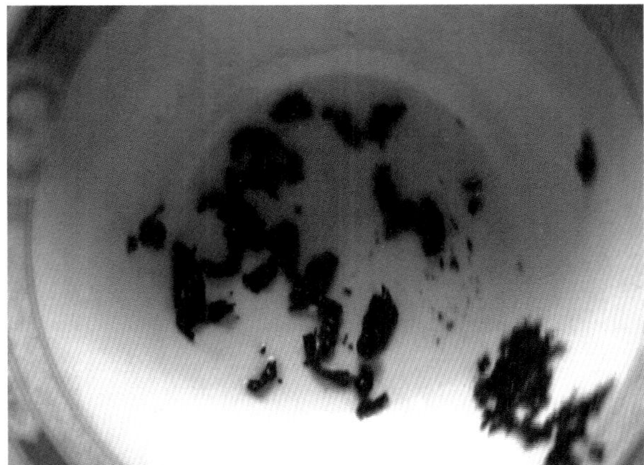

the tea leaves rhyme with the insects,

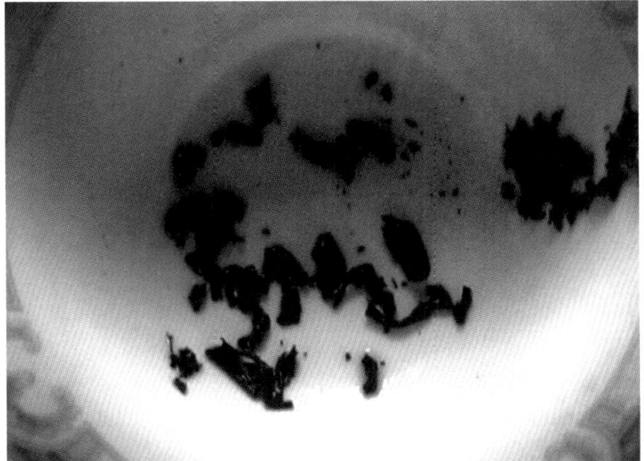

and we see a shot from above, with slides of insects all over the floor so that Ivana is surrounded by them.

This is followed by a shot of the tea-leaf reader, with a framed picture of a feather on the wall.

Later we will see Ivana watching birds in an aviary, but first the scene shifts to a view of a park, and while she says

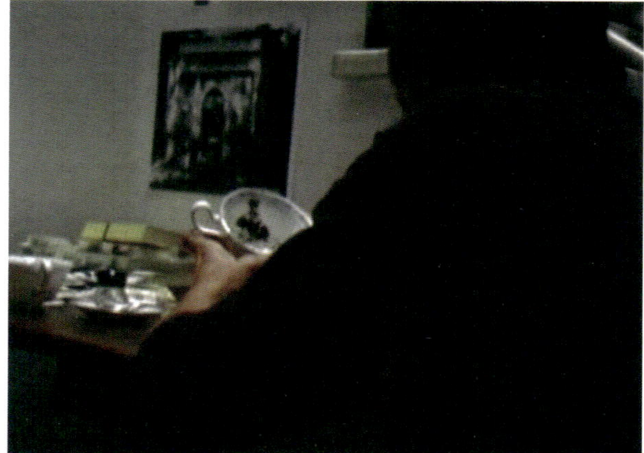

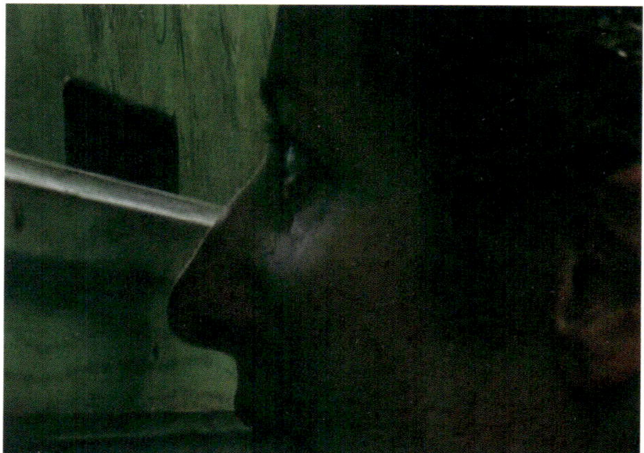

someone sitting on a bench just below the centre of the picture disappears—

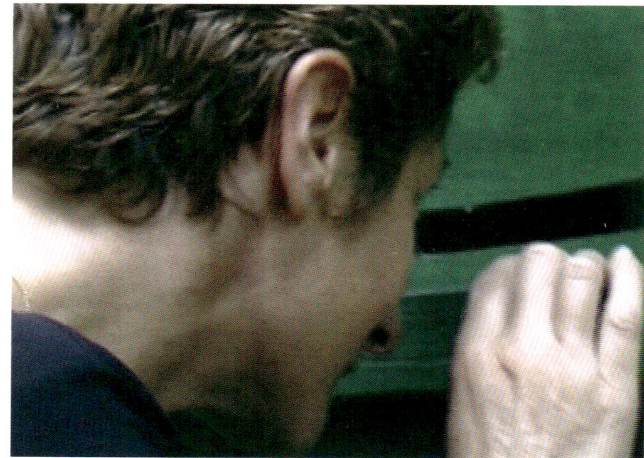

as if the world's holding together, indeed its very being, depends on her perception.

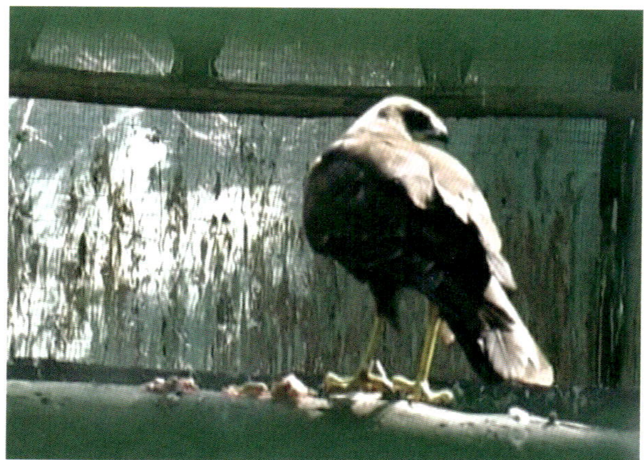

But is it her perception?
Shortly afterwards we see her looking into an aviary of falcons through a slot in the wall;

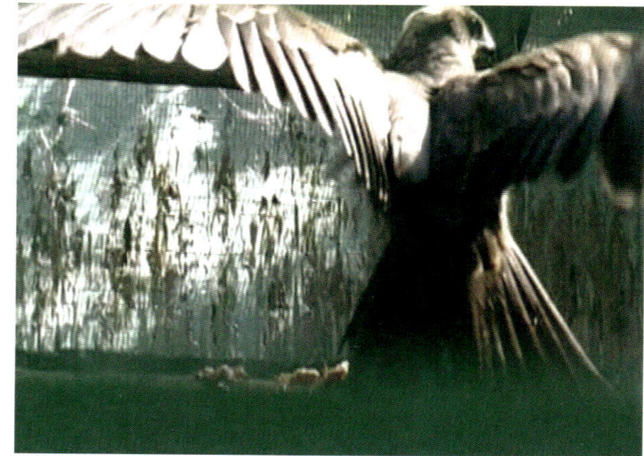

the camera observes the side of her face as she is doing this, and she appears unaware of it.

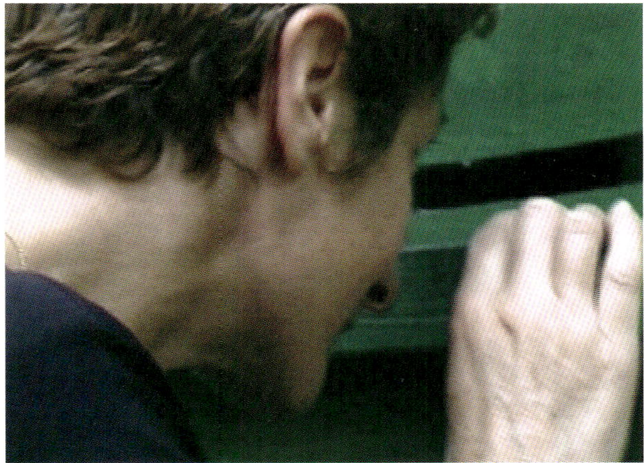

As she looks at the falcons, we look at her, but then
are we not also in her position,
looking while unaware of being looked at?

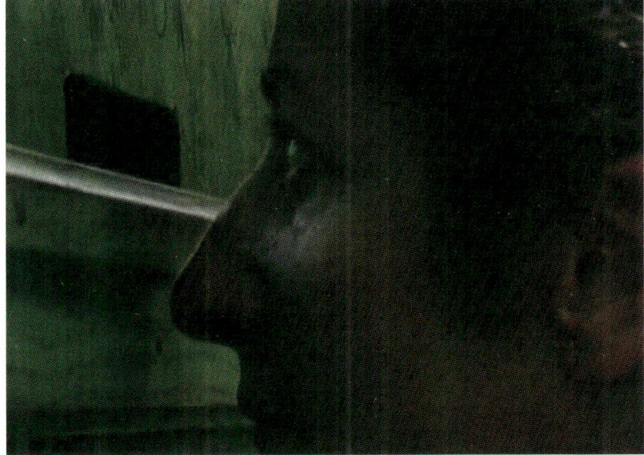

Isn't this an analog of cinema? So, if Ivana is being
watched by us, what gaze are we under?

In describing the gaze, the psychoanalyst
Jacques Lacan tells the story of a fishing expedition
he went on in Brittany,

a "romantic" spot where conditions were harsh
for the fisherman who lived there,
and many died of tuberculosis.

One of the fishermen on the boat, Petit-Jean
("Little John"),
who had already died of TB by the time of the telling,

points out to the young Parisian intellectual
a floating can,

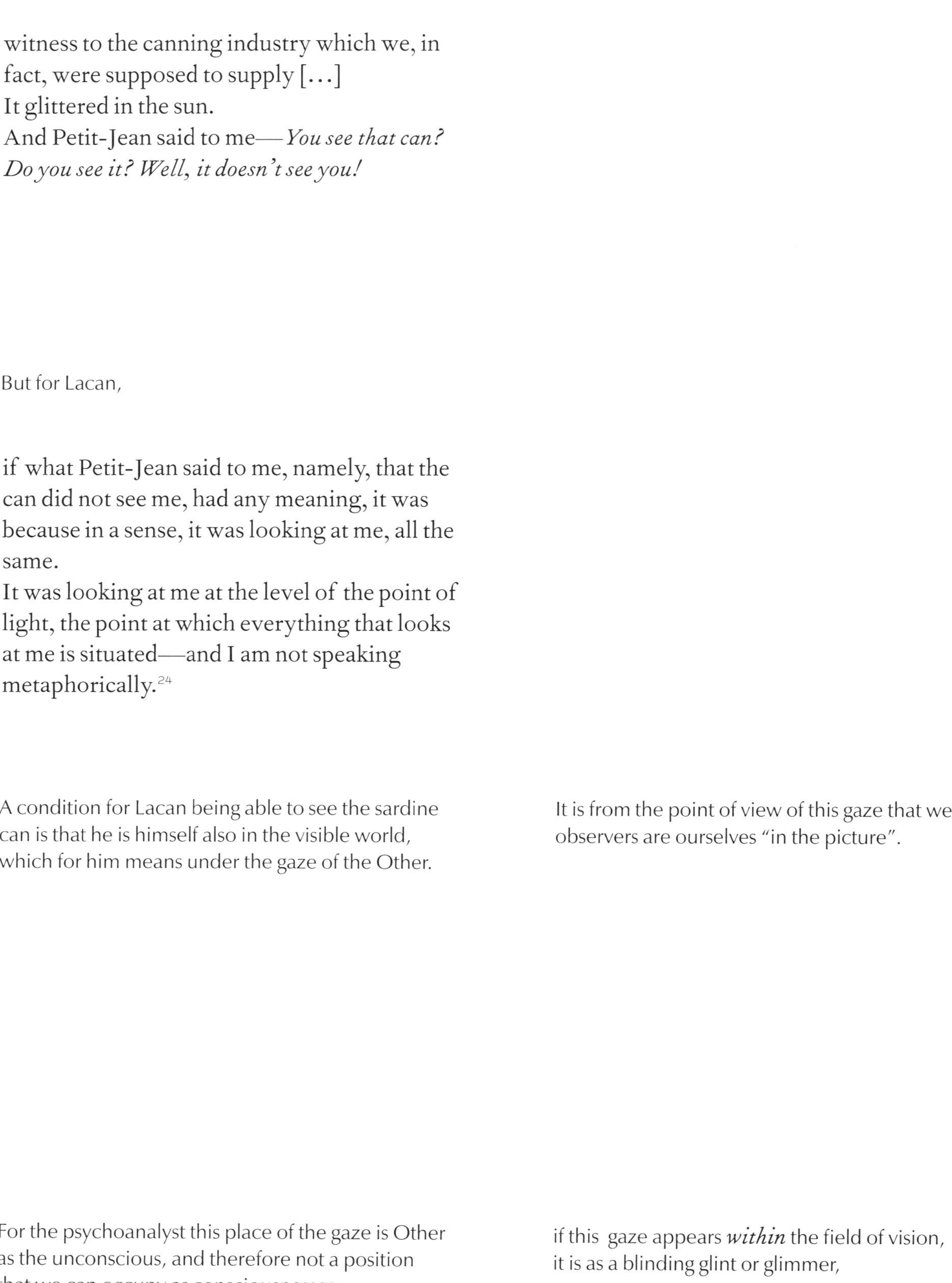

witness to the canning industry which we, in fact, were supposed to supply […]
It glittered in the sun.
And Petit-Jean said to me—*You see that can? Do you see it? Well, it doesn't see you!*

But for Lacan,

if what Petit-Jean said to me, namely, that the can did not see me, had any meaning, it was because in a sense, it was looking at me, all the same.
It was looking at me at the level of the point of light, the point at which everything that looks at me is situated—and I am not speaking metaphorically.[24]

A condition for Lacan being able to see the sardine can is that he is himself also in the visible world, which for him means under the gaze of the Other.

It is from the point of view of this gaze that we observers are ourselves "in the picture".

For the psychoanalyst this place of the gaze is Other as the unconscious, and therefore not a position that we can occupy as consciousnesses:

if this gaze appears *within* the field of vision, it is as a blinding glint or glimmer,

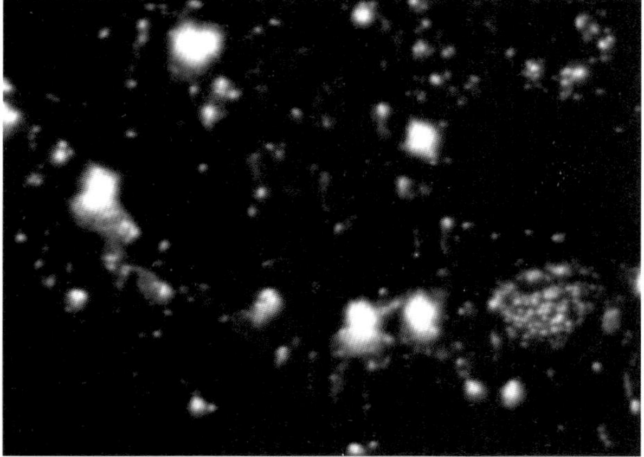

the flash of light emanating from the can
(it can also manifest as a stain, as Lacan describes in
his analysis of Holbein's painting *The Ambassadors*).

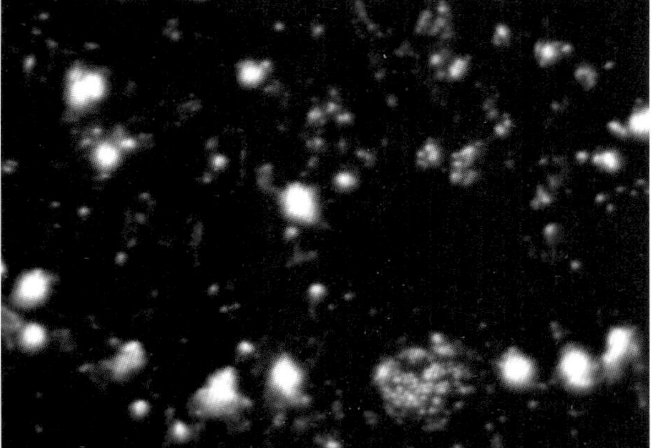

while the voice-over tells `a dry story`
`with a lot of vodka` about a man and
a drunk woman sitting at opposite sides of the bar.

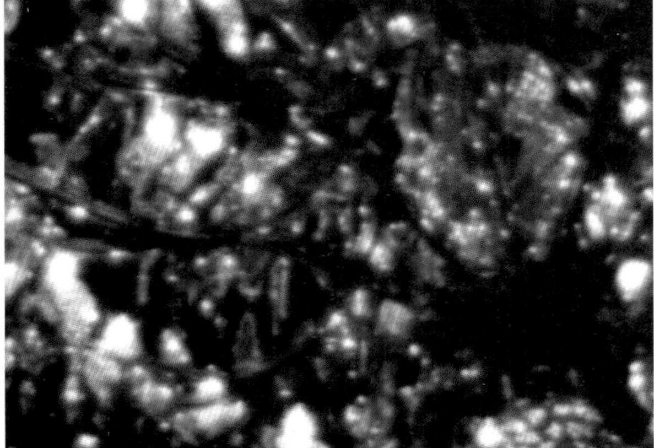

The scenario concerns the relation between distance
and desire (they sit at opposite sides of the bar).

Irvine's early work <u>STAR</u> presents this gaze
in a super-8 film that captures the glitter of light
emanating from the crystals of a chandelier,

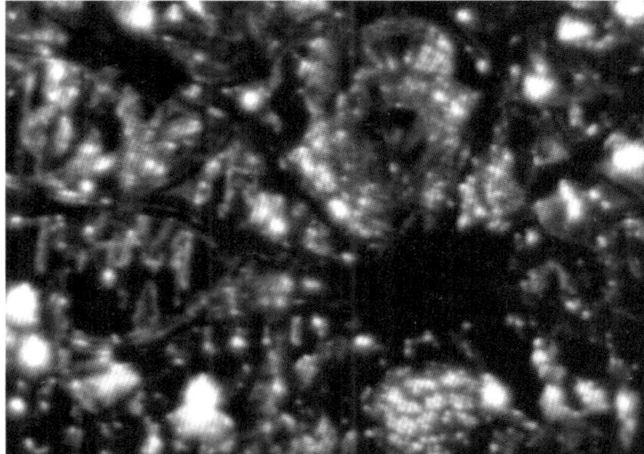

`Hey, handicap, would you like to`
`have another vodka?`
she repeats three times.

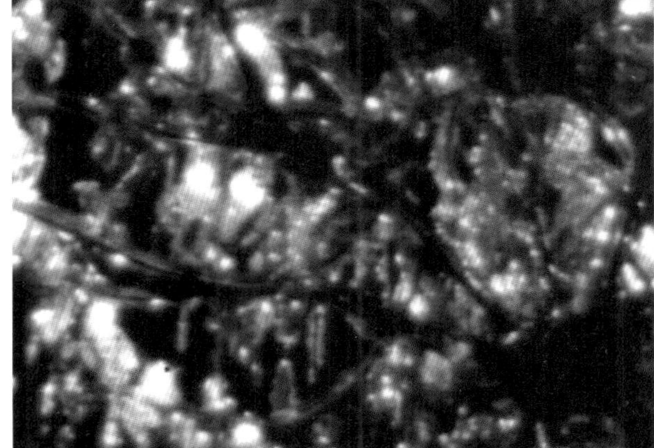

His refusal to join her is implied, and drunk,
she becomes a falling star.

We might also consider that what holds things together for Ivana is not, as she thinks,
her own consciousness as a centre of perception,

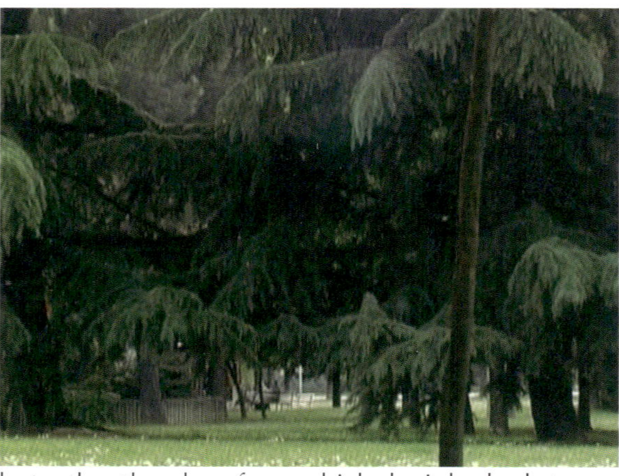

but rather the place from which she is looked at,
which is, in the end, not that of the viewer of the film,
but rather of the gaze, the `point of light`

from which everything is situated.
If this source of consistency is not thought of in solely
visual terms, other objects—

such as that button that `holds it all
together` in another work—
could also embody it.

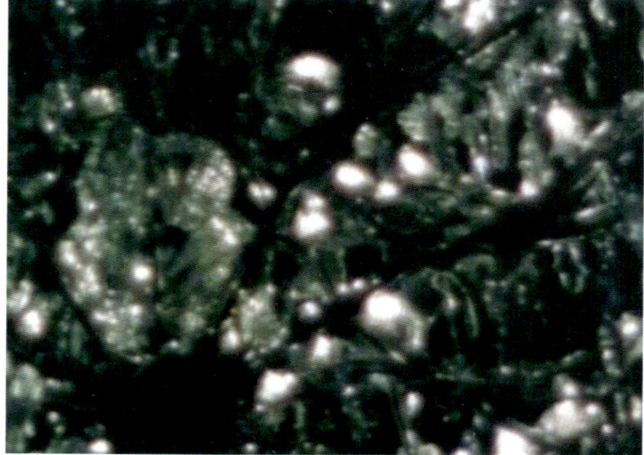

What we see is not a representation of the
story—not an illustration—

but something that broaches the limit of representation, like the glitter from a crystal chandelier.

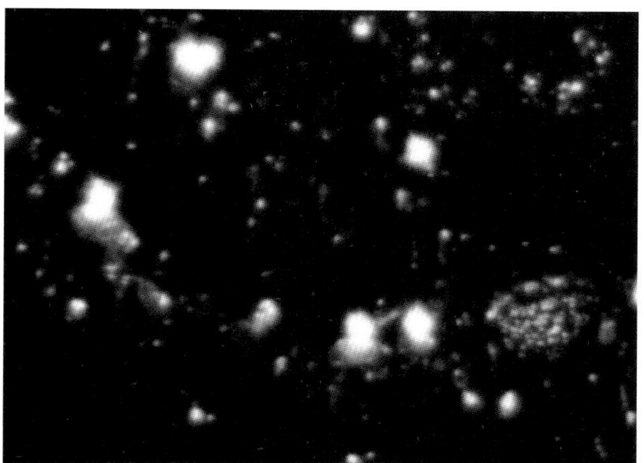

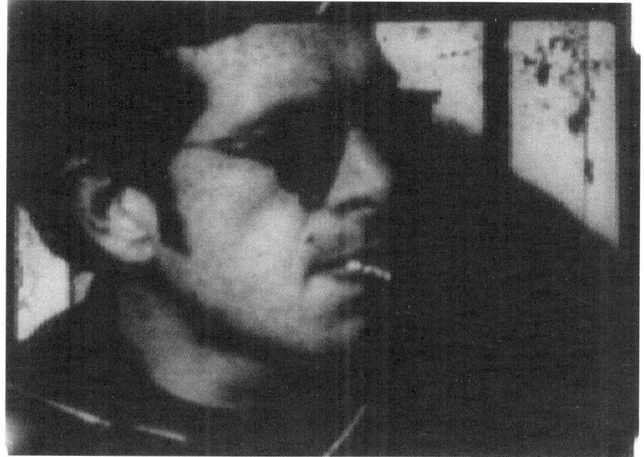

While Lacan tells a story that shows us something about the gaze, Irvine shows us something of the gaze that touches on that which is unnarratable in the story.

This also occurs in <u>THE HOTTEST SUN, THE DARKEST HOUR</u>, where the narration—

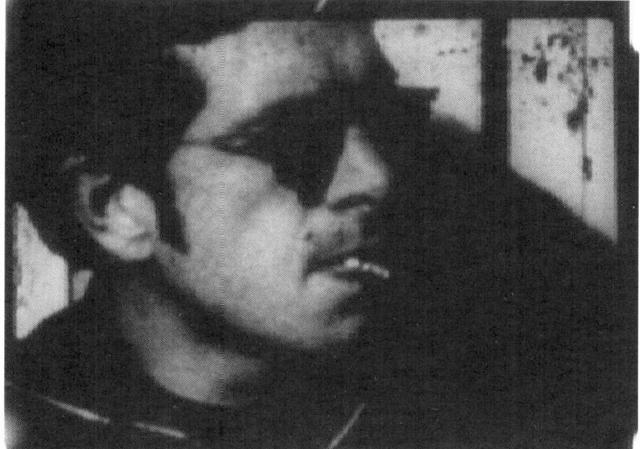

to a black and white 16mm film of a man sitting at a bar looking up and down a street in Rome—of the encounter of a young man

with an older one, is accompanied by another projection which comprises an almost unreadable film of fireflies, like scratches on the celluloid.

In <u>IVANA'S ANSWERS</u>, from a shot of live bluebottles, we return to the two women surrounded by specimens, looking into the tea cup.

Ivana asks, `Is there anything else?`

Yes, there's a bat, the reader replies,
but that's got nothing to do
with you.

Bats will appear in another work,
but in the meantime,
the sense we take away from this remark

is that neither Ivana nor the viewer
is the centre of the world—
it is not her consciousness that holds the world together.

Fortune-telling reveals coincidences
and connections that are beyond intentionality.

The references to another work of literature, and to
other works by Irvine, suggest that for the artist art-
works themselves do something rather like that.

Insofar as these works use the mediums of film and video,
the events they stage are also non-events; arrivals,
watched again and again, are equally departures.

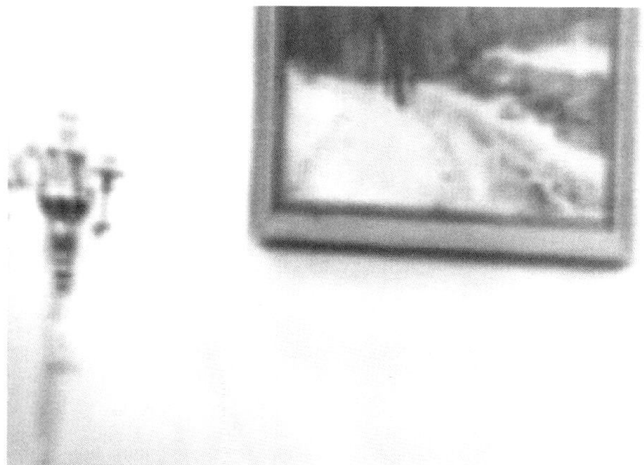

In the installation <u>LOSING DORIS</u> (1996)
we are shown two separate life-size projections of
images together with a single voice-over told by a

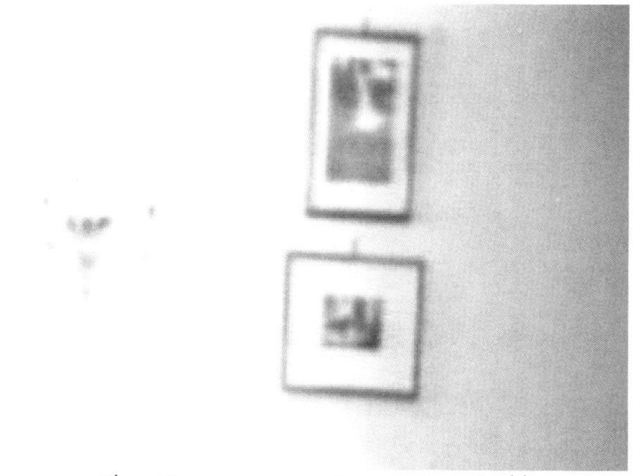

woman with a German accent accompanied by
music: one projection is of a woman in an armchair
in a sitting room; the other is of a woman outdoors.

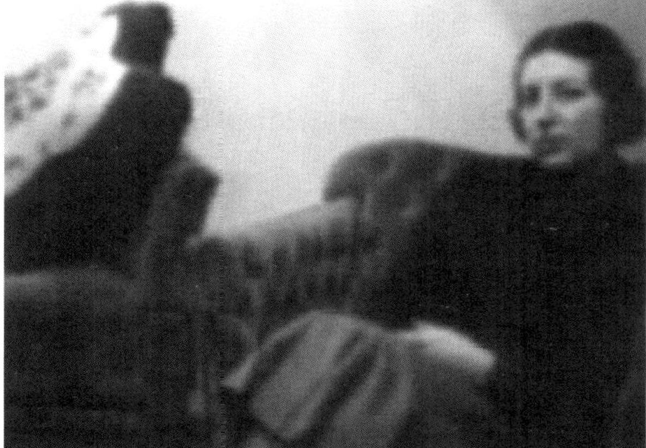

She recounts a meeting between a young man and
woman. She is telling him about fish swimming
around in a cave who have lost their sight

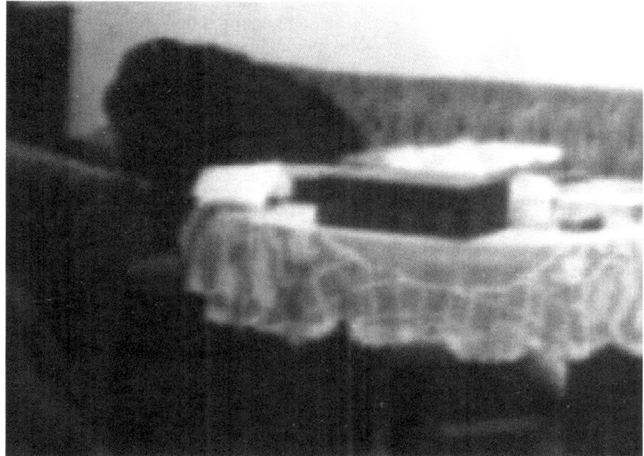

and wondering how it happened:
He blinks and blinks and tries
to smile.

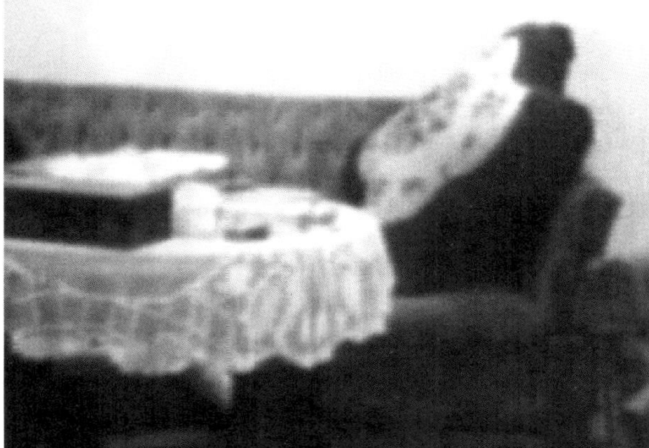

The woman looks very far away
and strange to him, as his hands
move about, restless.

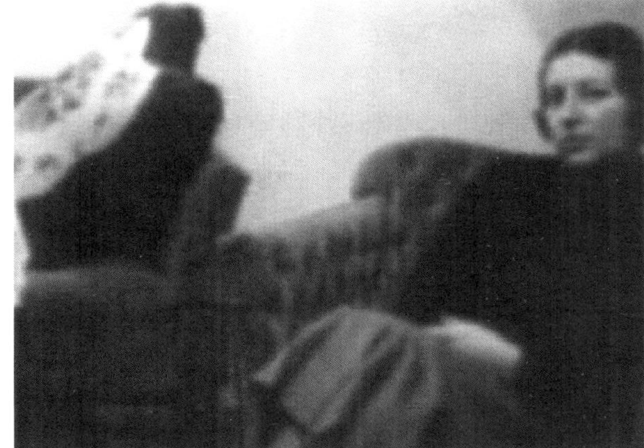

In one of the projections, she moves her head, and
blinks.

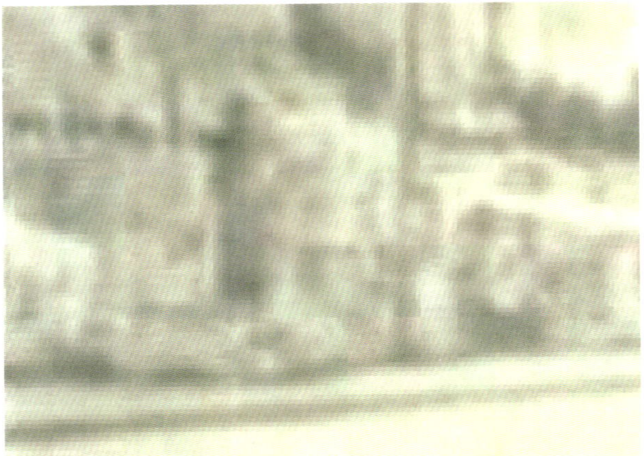

The other screen shows a picture of a woman in a street; she is holding out a hat in her hand, which becomes like a strange blob or stain.

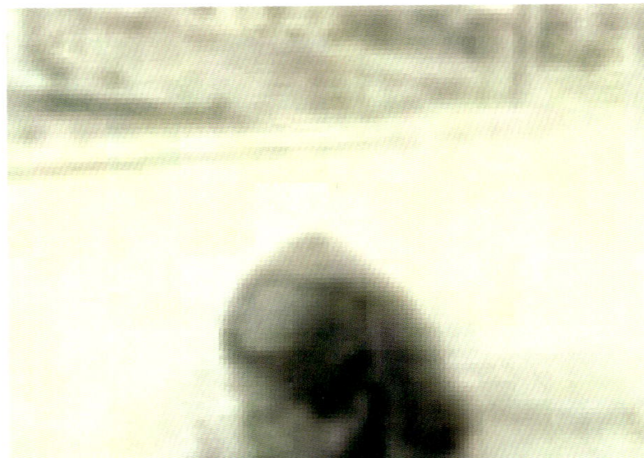

The voice-over describes, a man who stares at a glass with two ice cubes inside melting,

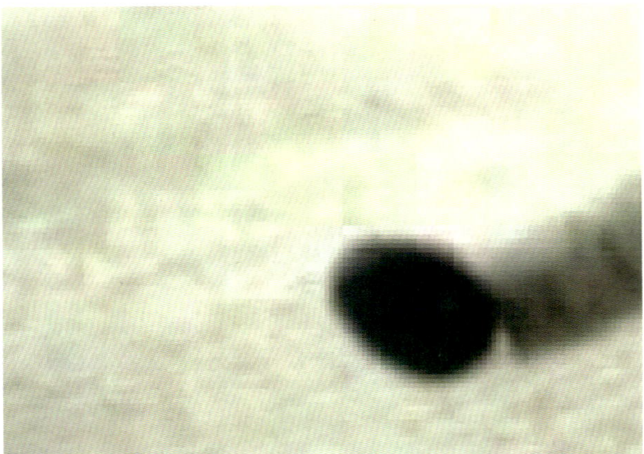

and then is distracted by a `small empty space a few feet away from him` which had once belonged to a young woman.

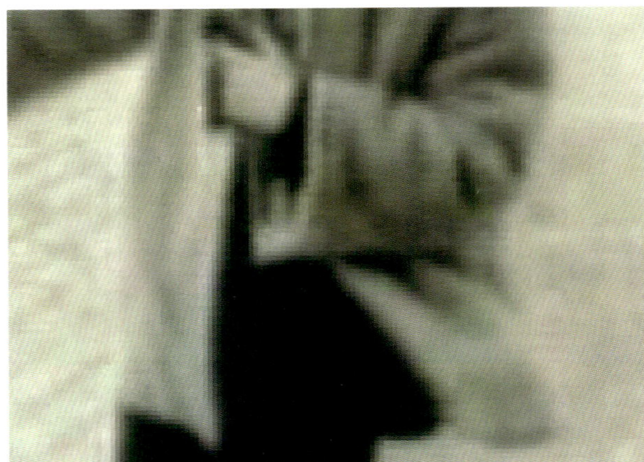

He addresses the space—in other words, he addresses an absence—which begins to become a presence: `It moved a little closer and`

`began to look vaguely familiar.`

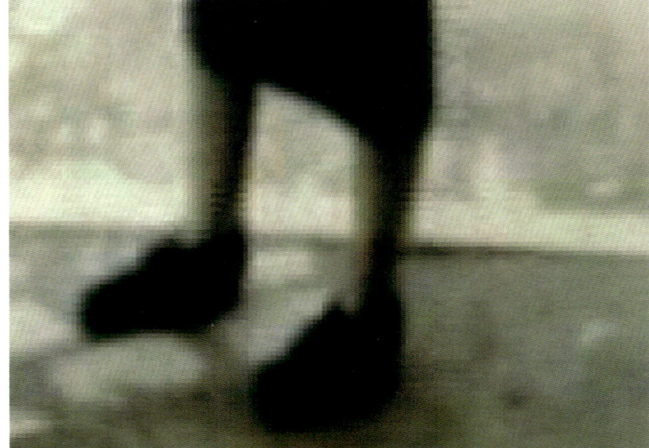

`He smiled.` In relation to the sensation of being trapped, absence and loss, here, could also be the conditions for freedom.

PART VII

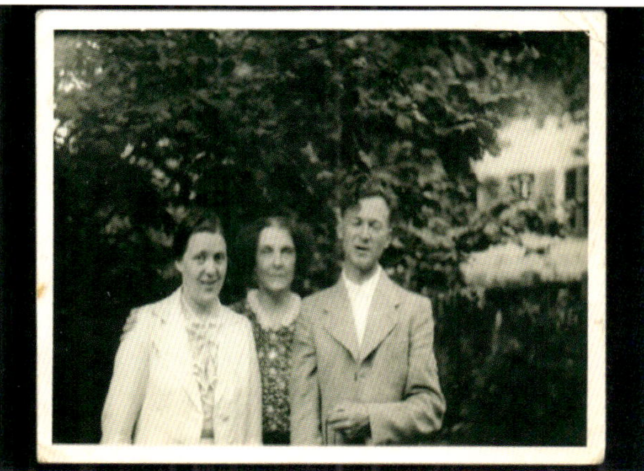

To a piano and violin accompaniment,
the film <u>HOLDING IT ALL TOGETHER</u> (2002)
begins by showing a photograph of a man

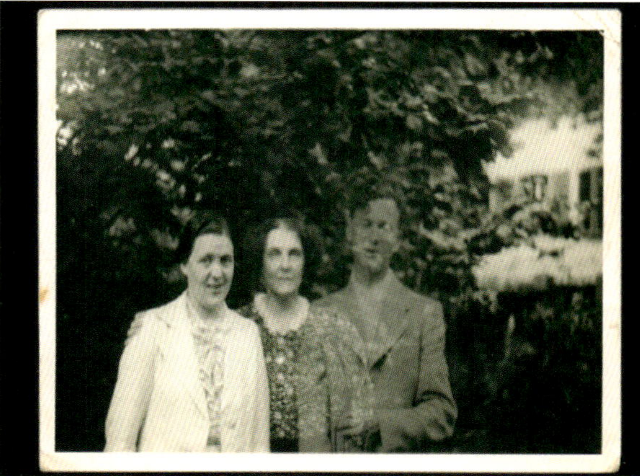

and a woman on each side of an older woman.
Maybe from the 1930s or 40s? They could be a family.

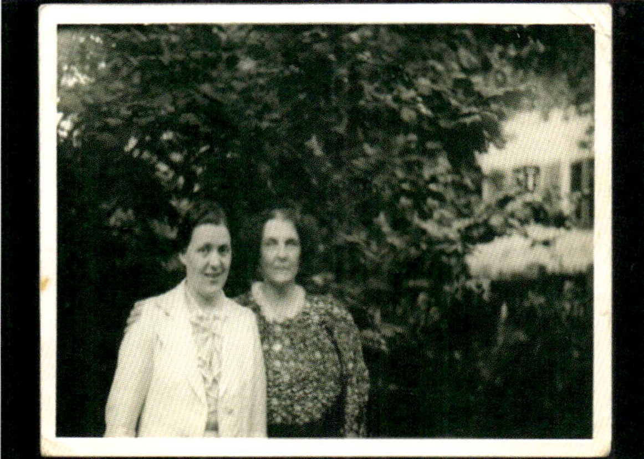

The man has his eyes closed;
the women are both looking at the camera.

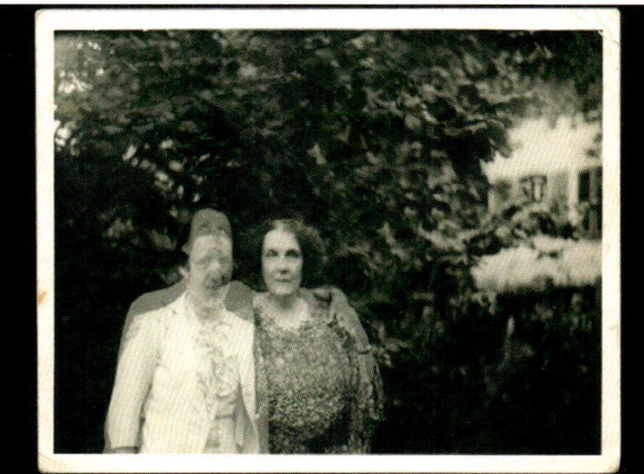

Then the man fades, leaving the older woman looking
at the camera and the younger one looking up at the
sky.

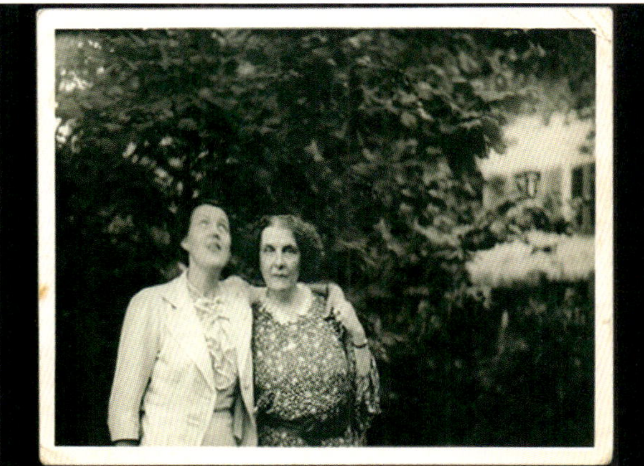

The younger one's arm is over the shoulder of the
older woman, who holds her hand.

Irvine uses the photograph, either made to move or with the illusion of movement, to explore loss and the abyss that opens up when things fall apart, as well as ways of holding the world together through its inter-penetration by memory, and certain otherwise insignificant objects that take on a special rôle.

Then he disappears from the picture.

```
He's got both hands stuffed
inside the pockets of his pin-
stripe jacket...It's raining
heavy wet stuff...Standing
there, soaking wet, staring at
something in his head, one but-
ton holds it all together.
```

The voiceover doesn't quite match the image—it is not a description of what we are seeing—and this opens up a gap.

The suggestion is that the disappearance of the man `staring at something in his head` is connected with the loss of the button.

Sometimes something can be so used and worn,
so threadbare, that there is only one little thing
that stops if from falling apart.

But the rôle of the button here seems to be connected
not just with the jacket, but with the consistency and
coherence of the world as such.

Whether the sense of holding it all together relates to
his experience, or ours as viewers, is ambiguous.

He disappears for the viewer,
but maybe it is also the case that his existence
for himself is linked to his relation to the button,

that it is the object that for him holds it all together,
that keeps him from "fading", as he does in the film.

The situation is analogous to the moment in
<u>IVANA'S ANSWERS</u> when Ivana says
`I have the sensation`

`that if I'm distracted for`
`a second things fall apart`
and in the film the person on the bench disappears.

Many of Irvine's works pose the question of what it is
that holds the world together, and what does it mean
for this "thing" to be lost.

Again and again her works pose themselves on that
edge between consistency and disintegration.

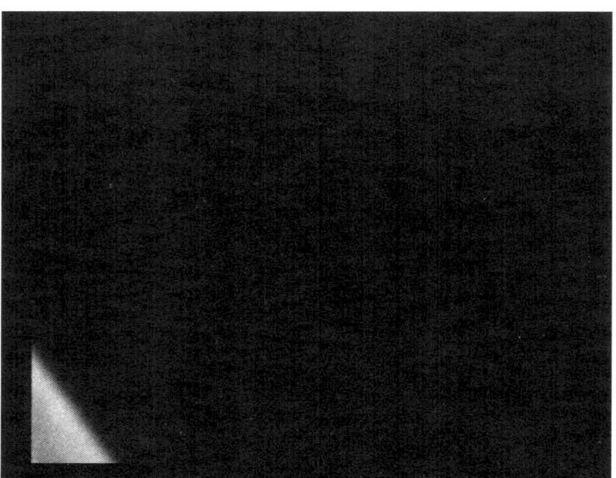

Disappearance is also enacted in
<u>FOR ALL THE LIVES</u>
<u>WE'LL NEVER LIVE</u> (2004).

At the archive of the Henry Moore Institute in Leeds,
Irvine found photographs of a woman doctor who
was a friend of the sculptor Betty Rea (1904-65).

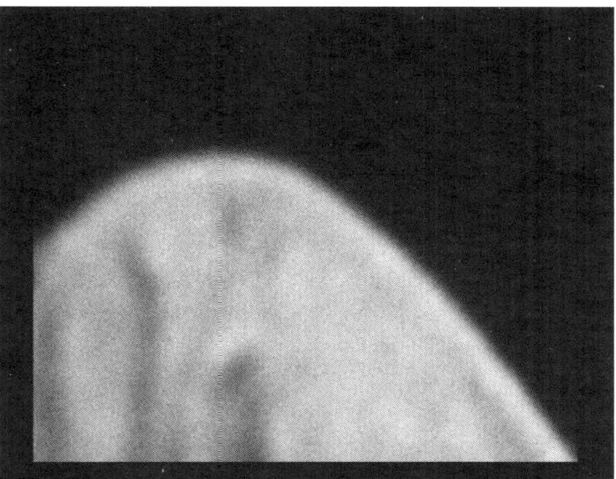

To the music of *Adagio for Strings* by Barber,
the image draws back from a grainy detail,
which seems to resemble a skull, to reveal the face

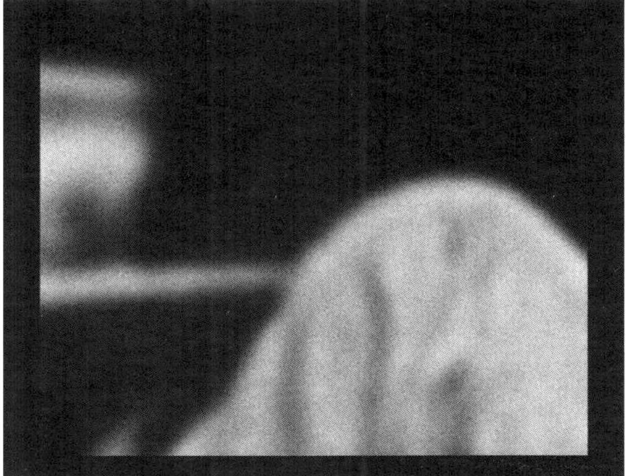

and then body the trousered woman
sitting in a window, holding a china cup of tea,
looking towards the camera. In a second image

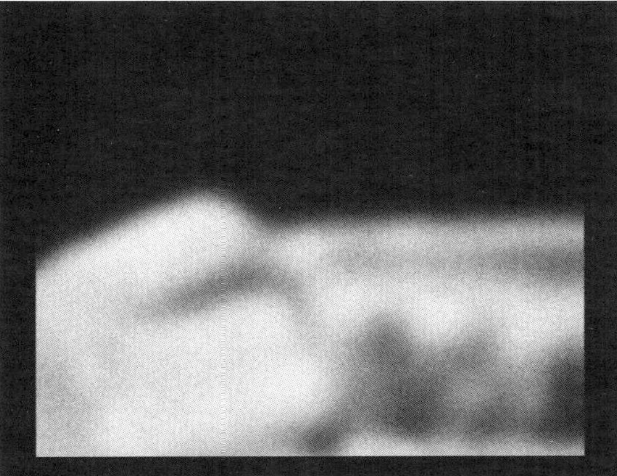

she turns her head away, then fades, leaving only a
curtain, which disappears in its turn.
It is as if Irvine wants to resurrect this woman

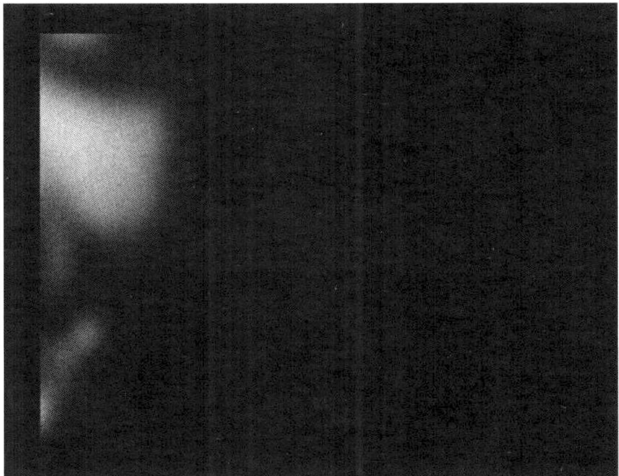

by animating the photograph, but she cannot
be brought back, and we are reminded
that her's was a life we cannot share.

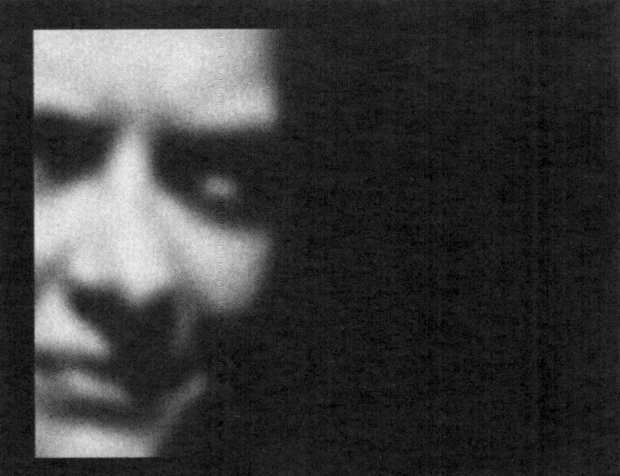

This interplay between still and moving image,
between photograph and film, between return and
loss, is reminiscent of Chris Marker's *La Jetée* (1962),

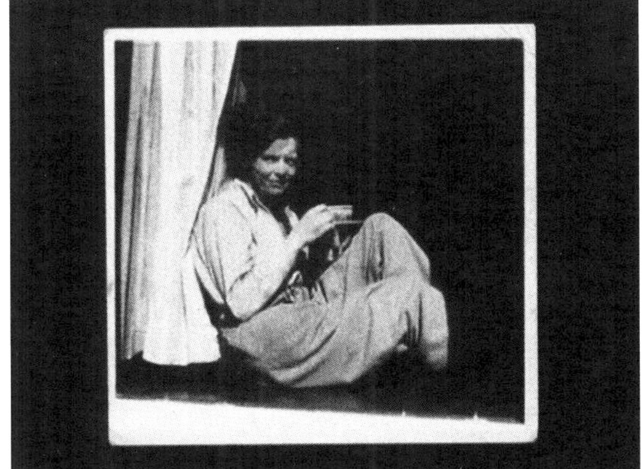

where the protagonist returns to the past through his
memory to find a woman who, in the only moving
sequence of this film of stills, blinks as she awakens.

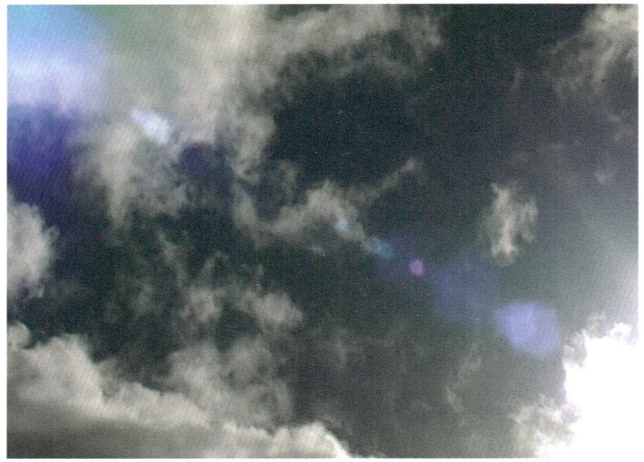

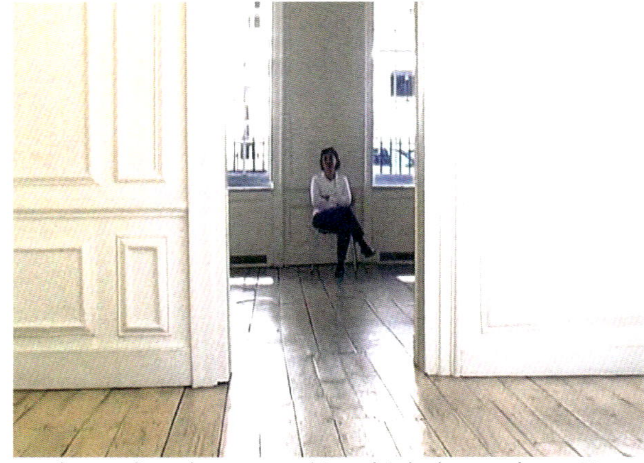

Another work dealing with loss, <u>TOWARDS A POLAR SEA,</u> takes as its starting point the memory of a building, the house in Frith Street in which the work was first shown, and in which the explorer Sir John Franklin lived for a time before he disappeared on his final polar exploration.

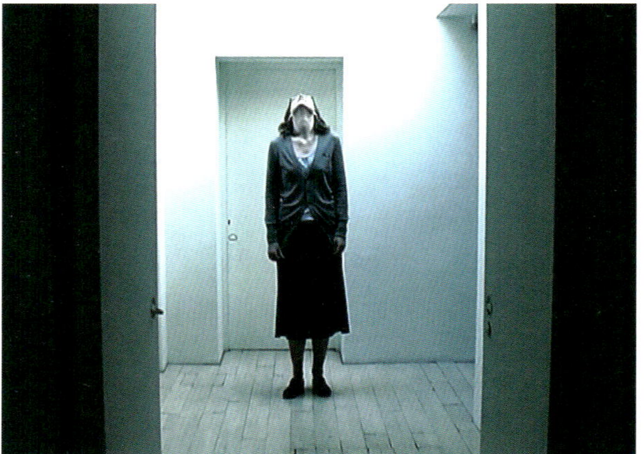

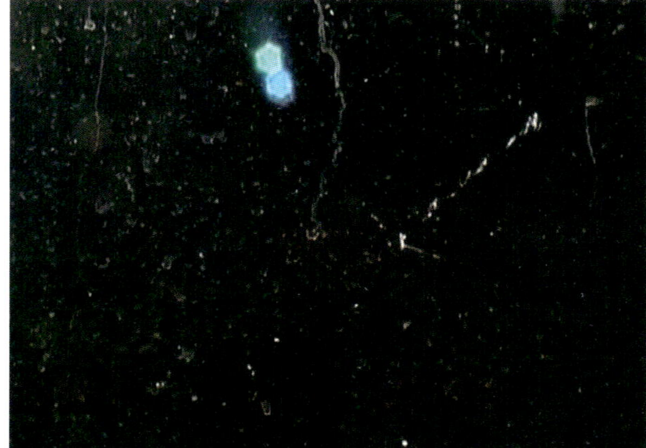

The voiceovers are spoken by the people who work in the gallery. The ghosts of the past haunt the present, traces of absence.

The participants become fictions of themselves who live a private fantasy within the reality of their semi-public workspace, in which, through Irvine's film,

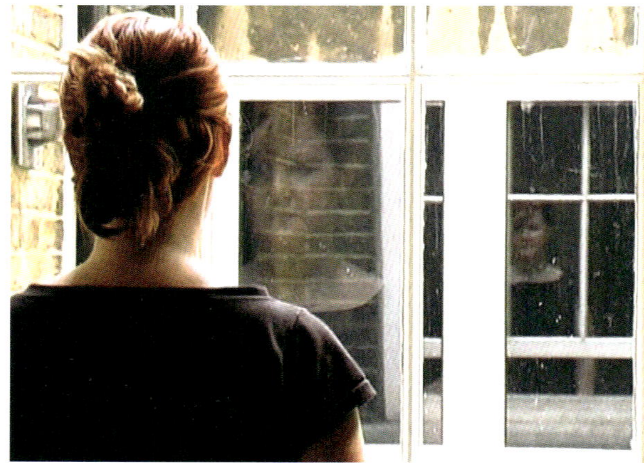

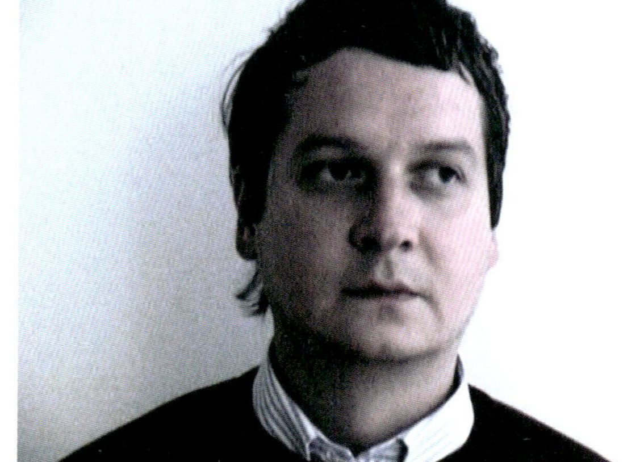

they may see themselves acting—acting themselves, as well as the figures in the narrative of Franklin's disappearance.

So in expressing their feelings about his absence, they are also leading a double life, as private and public figures, speaking of the absence of their own intimacy.

PART VIII

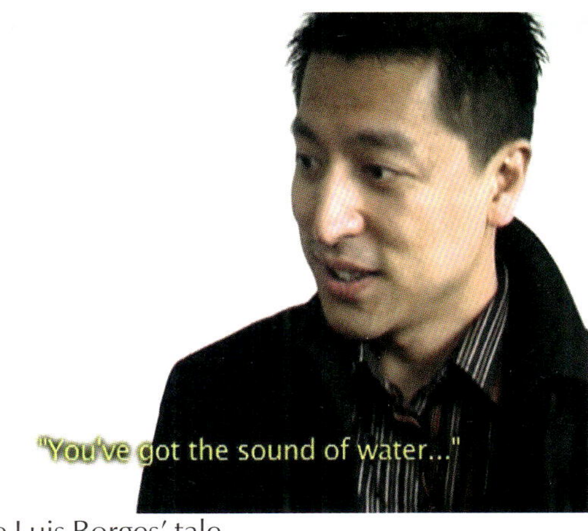

In Jorge Luis Borges' tale
The Garden of the Forking Paths,
a Chinese spy for Germany during the First World War,

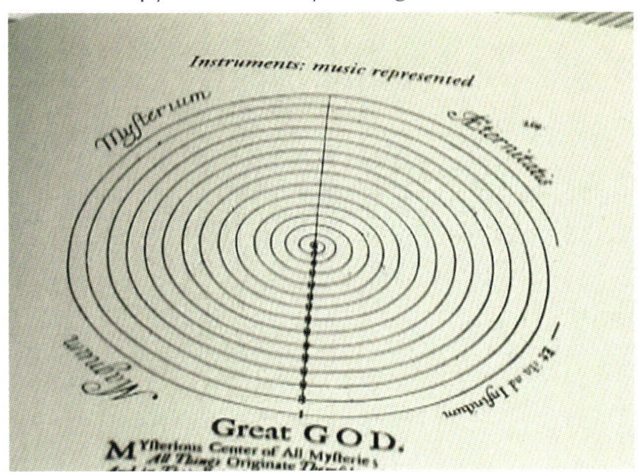

finds a way to make known from England
to his boss in Berlin, where the new British artillery park
has been established.

This spy has an ancestor, Ts'ui Pên, who wrote a mysterious novel, and was supposed to have built a labyrinth, only no-one had ever found it.

He visits a sinologist, Stephen Albert, and learns that the key to the labyrinth is the only word prohibited in the novel—"time":

He believed in an infinite series of times, in a dizzily growing, ever spreading network of diverging, converging and parallel times. This web of time—the strands of which approach one another, bifurcate, intersect or ignore each other through the centuries—embraces every possibility.
We do not exist in most of them. In some you exist and not I, while in others I do, and you do not, and in yet others both of us exist.[25]

Time itself is the labyrinth, and the latter is the key to the structure of time.

Borges is echoing the philosopher Leibniz's idea that there are an infinite number of possible individuals, and that each possible individual,

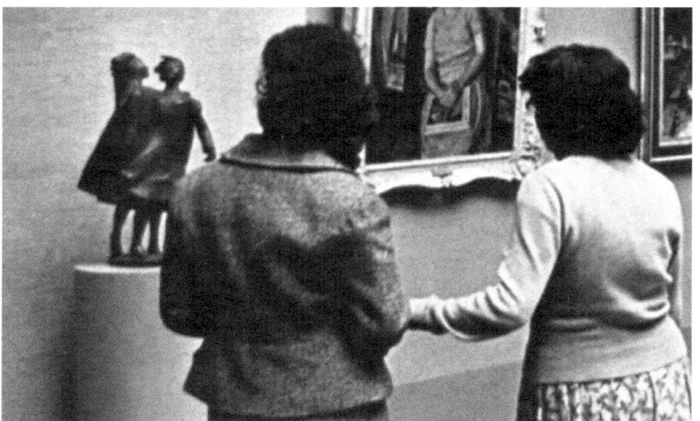

including those that never existed and never will, is part of a possible world and mirrors that world.

How can something both occur and not occur, such that incompatible events may coincide?

Would that not be to deny truth, a condition for which is non-contradiction?

Leibniz avoids contradiction by saying that these contrary possibilities occupy worlds that are **incompossible**.

Deleuze refers to Borges' story
to argue
that the labyrinth of time is
the line which forks and keeps on forking,
passing through *incompossible presents*,
returning to *not-necessarily true pasts*.

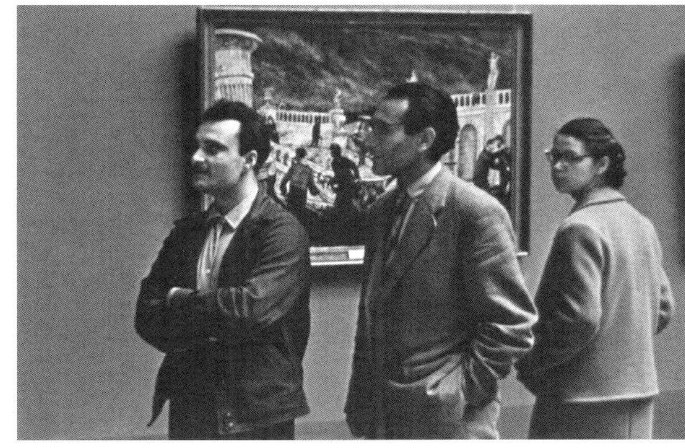

If truth requires non-contradiction,
then the condition
for the
simultaneity of incompossible presents, or the
co-existence of non-necessarily true pasts is the
power of the false

that is inherent in cinematic time
of the **time-image**.[26]

Cinematic time—as a form of virtual memory—
allows for the co-existence of the incompossible,
the paths not taken with the one taken,

all equally real even if only one becomes actual.
In this way, revisiting the past may open up
the present itself to heterogenous futures.

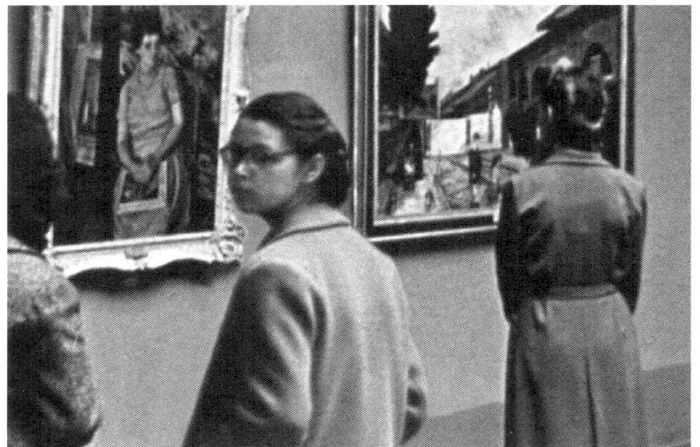

In <u>EXHIBITION OF 1957 RE-VISITED</u>
(2004) Irvine takes two photographs from
the *Looking at People* exhibition at the Pushkin Museum, Moscow—they are again
from the Betty Rea archive and include a sculpture by
her—and manipulates them by moving people and

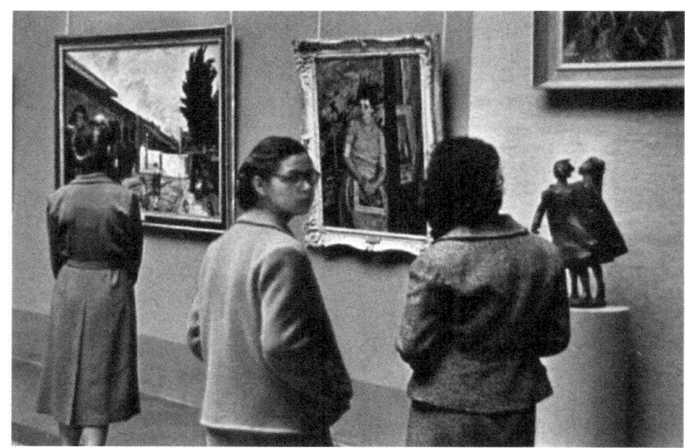

objects around to make nine images.
Irvine thus creates paths which may or may not have
been followed; connections between people that may or may not have been made;
and, when we see that one image is a "flipped"
version of another, spaces that are "impossible",

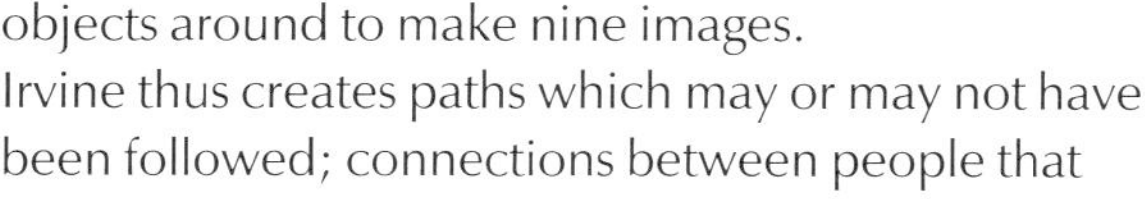

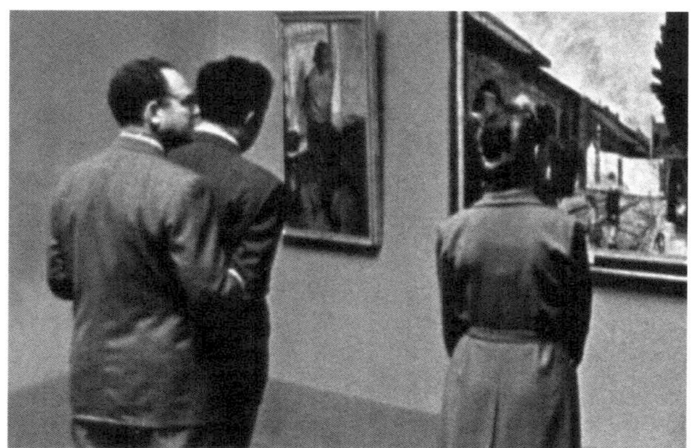

incompatible with one another—incompossible.
Of the two men and three women,
we follow in particular a woman with glasses, because she is looking away from the works of art,
suggesting that the exhibition space is one
full of erotic possibility.

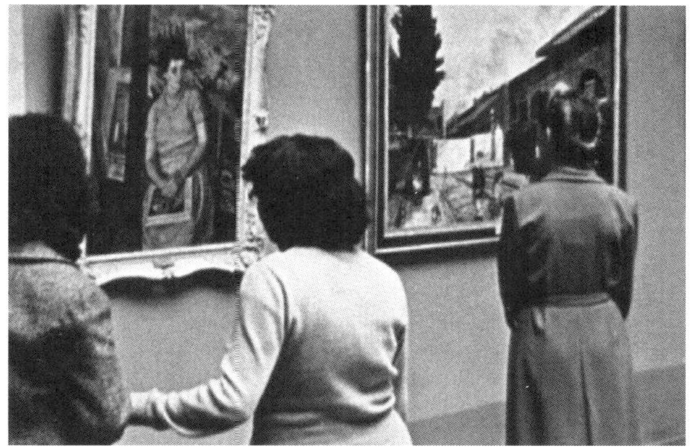

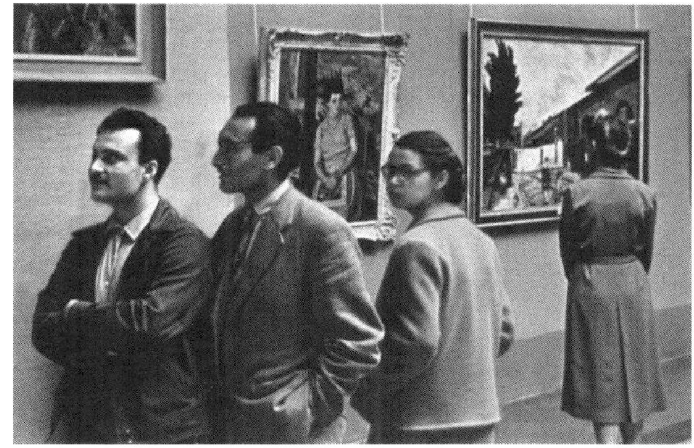

The very act of revisiting makes it otherwise, opening virtual paths and connections between people that are created by trying to re-enter a space that no longer exists.

Subject to the "power of the false", the archive is turned into a place not just of recollection but also of rearrangement and potential.

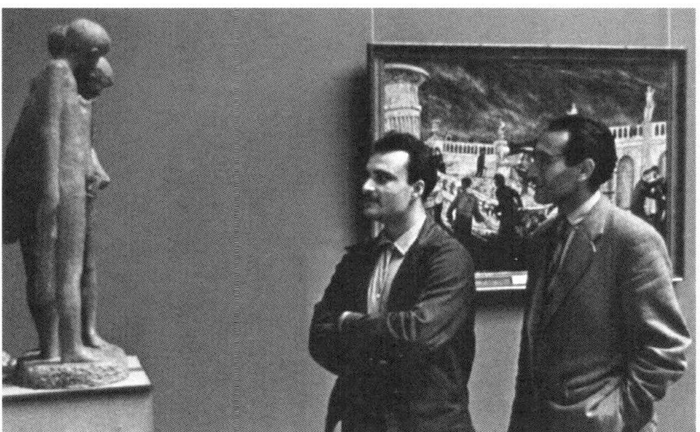

Elsewhere Borges writes of his mythic land Tlön, which has its own philosophy, language, geometry and literature, that all things both duplicate themselves and tend to become effaced and lose their details when they are forgotten. A classic example is the doorway which survived so long as it was visited by a beggar and disappeared at his death. At times some birds, a horse, have saved the ruins of an amphitheatre.[27]

In Irvine's video NIGHTINGALE (2004), as if produced by the song of a bird, parts of a folly from the Villa Borghese in Rome emerge out of the blackness.

If the bird sings the building into being,
so the appearing and disappearing of the folly seems
like a materialization of the song.[28]

The appearance is momentary,
and we never see the whole thing at once.

We are reminded that disappearance is intrinsic
to manifestation, and that the being of the world
is not only for us,

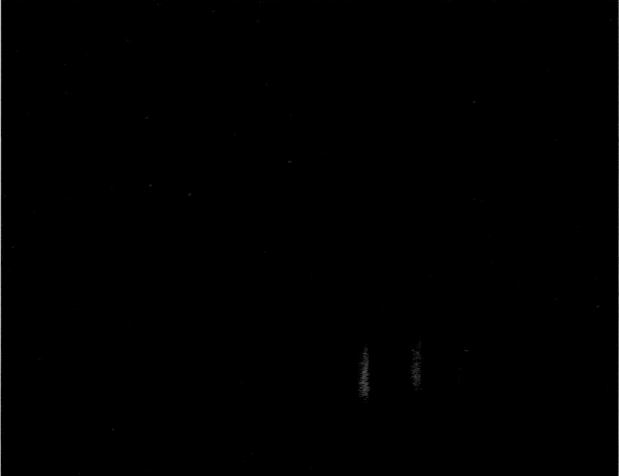

not something that we humans control exclusively,
but is conjured up by many different beings,
including animals.

The world is the co-existence of incompossibles,
the different worlds of humans and animals
conjured in time,

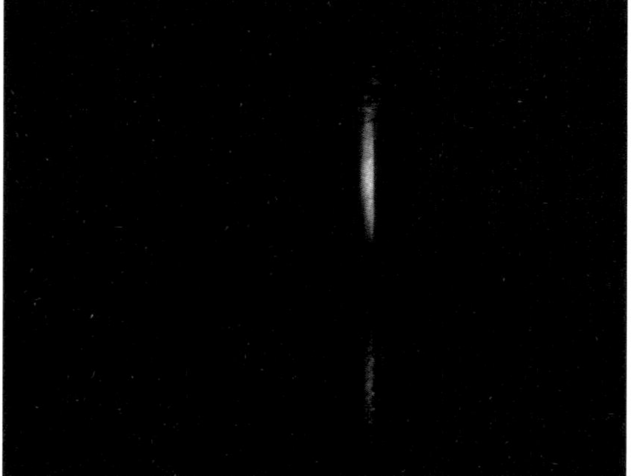

as well as the coincidence of different times in space.

PART IX

<u>THE SILVER BRIDGE</u> (2003) begins
with starlings swarming to the sound of their
shrill cries against the blue sky,

at first separate then flocking together
like a single being.

As we stare at them,
they become increasingly alien and a little sinister.

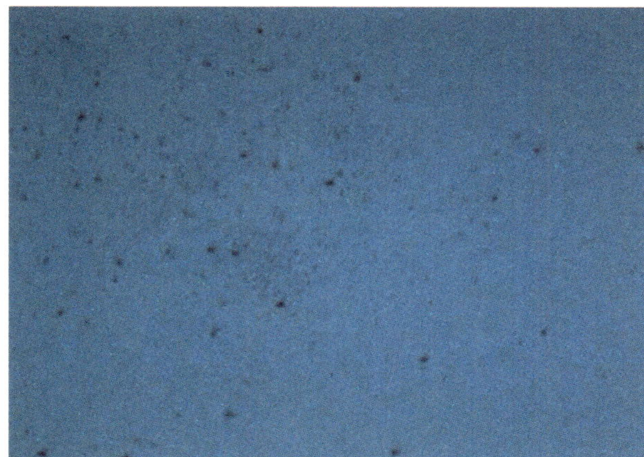

In another video we see a man pacing in a field
as if he is waiting for someone;
he eventually sits down under a tree

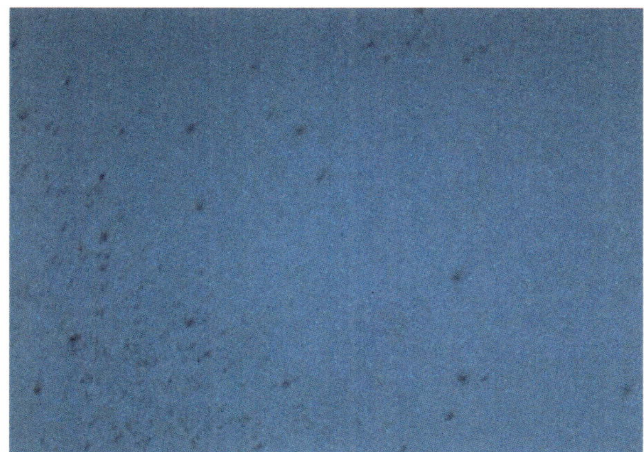

that has been blown into a sideways curve
by the wind.

The viewpoint is quite low, from the bushes—
is it a human, or an animal, that is watching him?

Another film shows a forest in which stags walk
and graze between freestanding white doors—

in a gesture towards an episode from the Irish tale
The Pursuit of Diarmuid and Grainne.

The white doors create the effect of something at
once surreal and staged.

In a fourth film a woman enters the bat house
of a zoo, and becomes an onlooker to a diorama
recreation of the bats' world—

we see a close-up of two bats interacting.

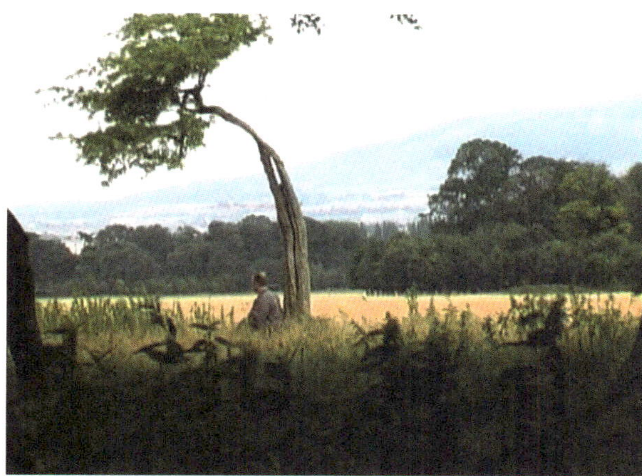

After a while, a man, who looks like the man who was
waiting by the tree but is coming from the opposite
direction looks at her in passing, and leaves.

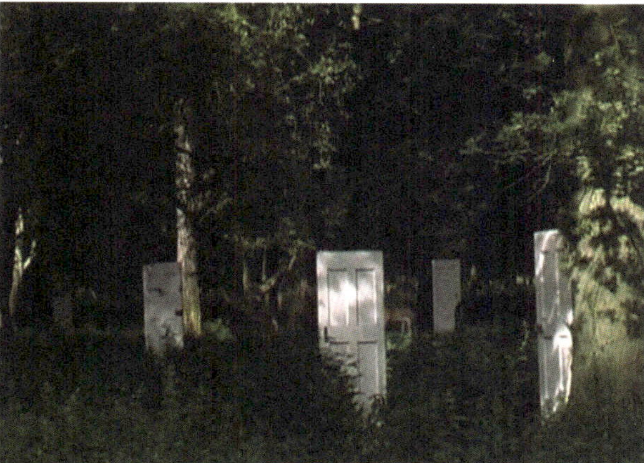

Another film of the bats shows them hanging
from a wire ceiling, flying,
and stretching their membranaceous wings.

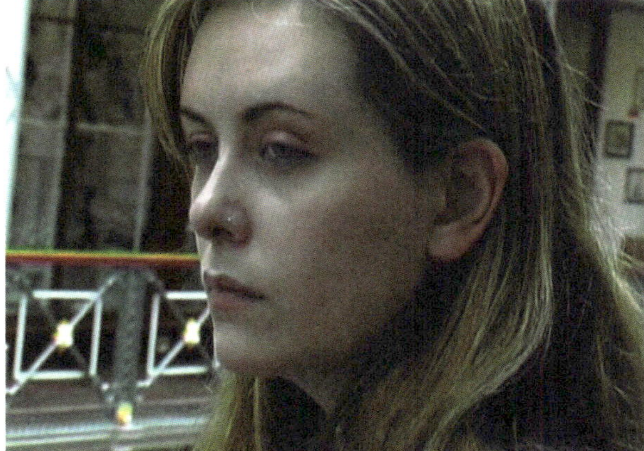

filmed using a slow motion technique familiar
to nature films, to show what animals are really doing;
but the mode of observation changes the observed,

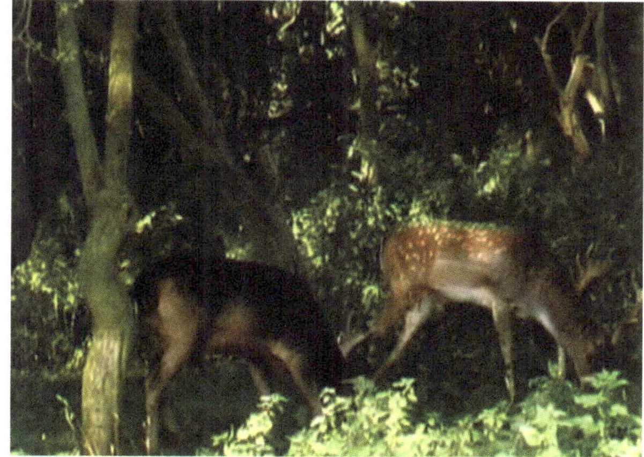

One of the bats follows the other,
and is pushed away—it is as if the bats express
what doesn't happen between the humans.

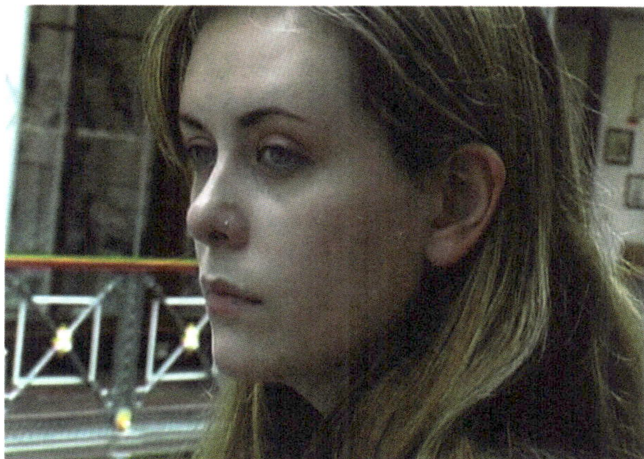

In a sixth film, we see a woman in a natural history
museum slowly blinking her heavily made up eyes,
like the specimens around her,

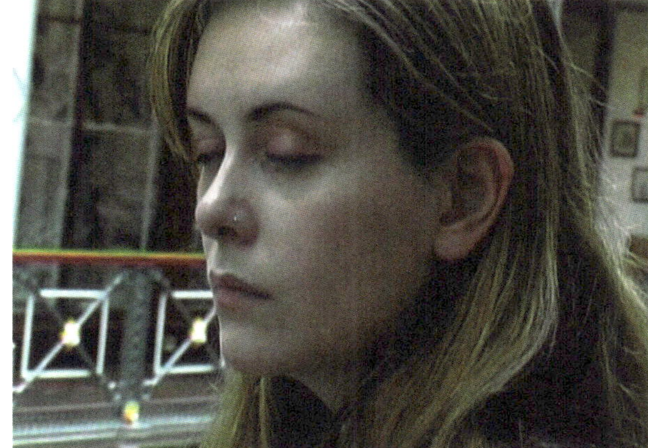

and, slowed down, her eyelids seem to grow heavier,
harder to lift, a metamorphosis accompanied
by the cries of seagulls.

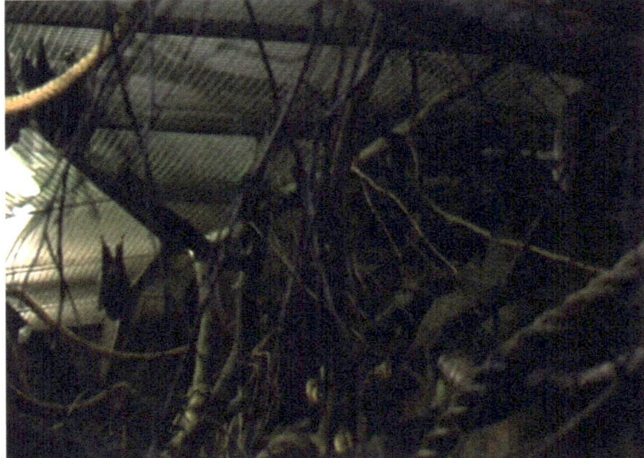

We also see her from above,
amid the display of taxidermied and skeletal animals
—we are reminded of the relation of humans,

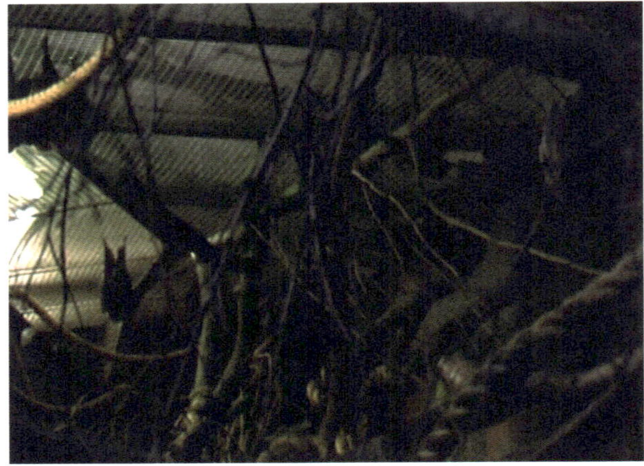

via primaeval life forms,
to the starlings flocking in the first film.

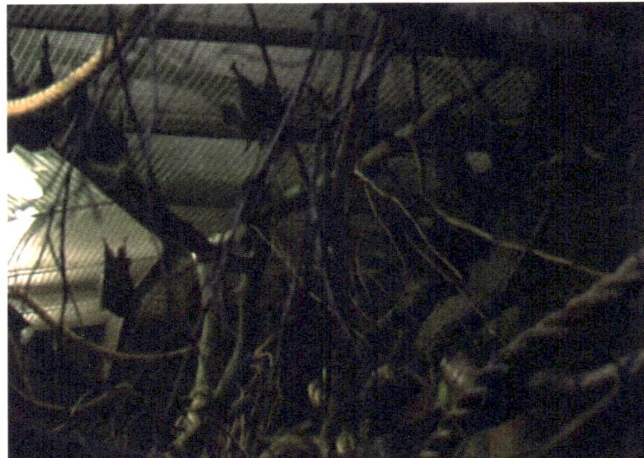

The cast-iron walkways of the natural history museum,
as well as the skeleton hanging from its ceiling,
are recalled by the skeleton of the bridge in the next

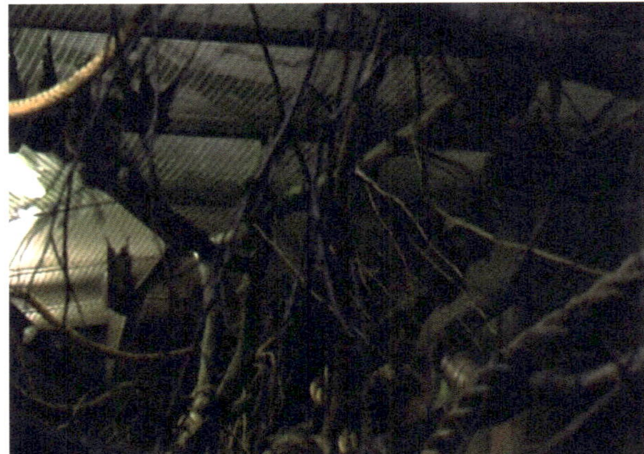

film, across which a woman crawls on her stomach
away from us towards an arched doorway,
accompanied by loud bird sounds—

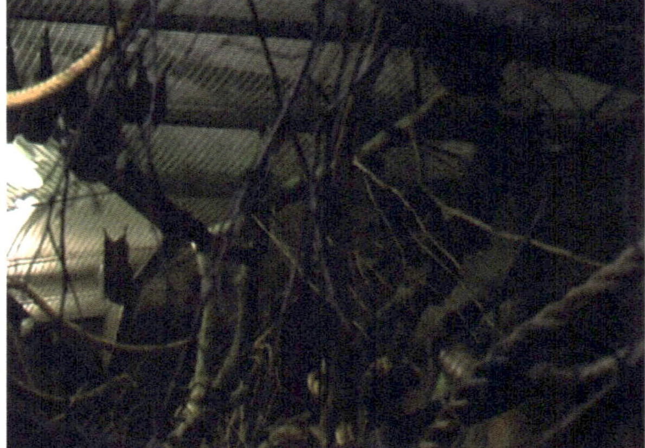

rather than walking,
she is forced by the structure of the bridge
to revert to a form of locomotion, crawling,

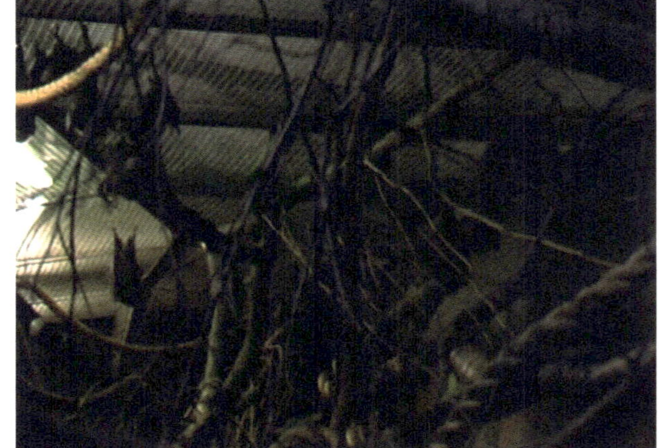

reminiscent of a reptile,
as if in a regression to an earlier evolutionary stage.

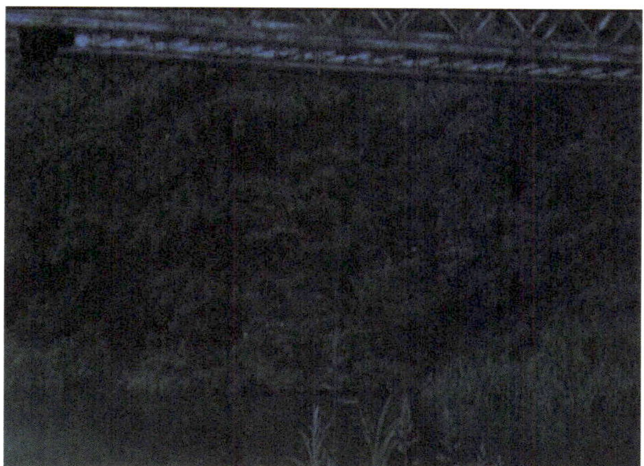

But the fact that she gets nowhere throws such notions of progress into question,
as well as the idea of the human as a separate and

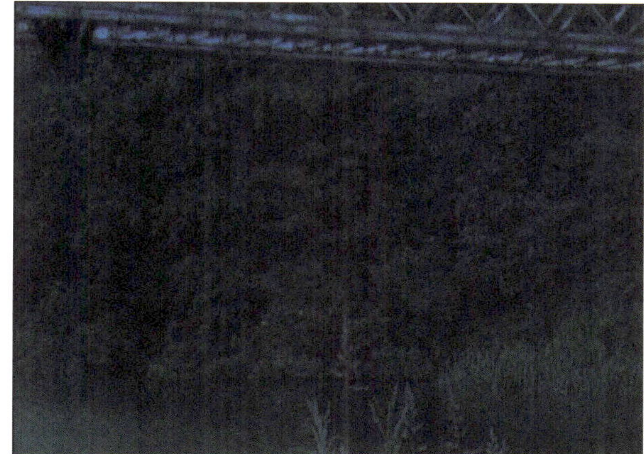

"higher" life form—the birds seem far away and strange, but we are related to them.

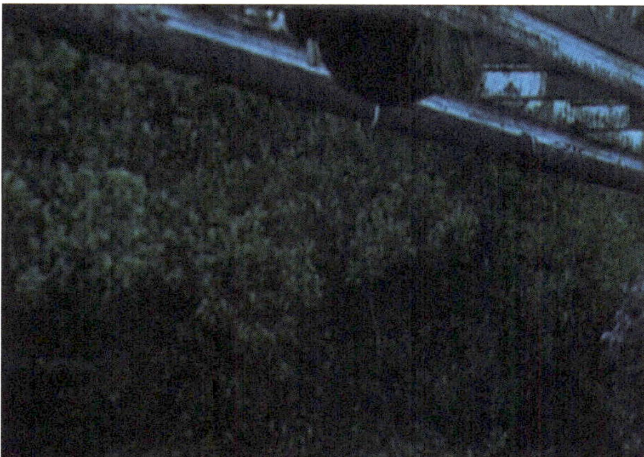

Finally, we see two women hanging from a disused bridge by their feet—like bats—performing acrobatics together, embracing each other, over water, their long

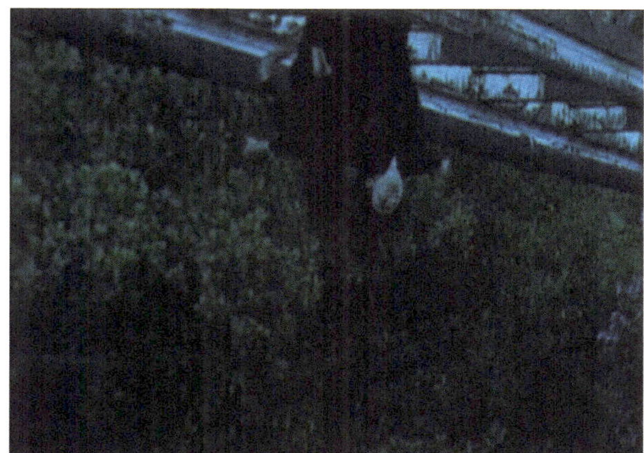

hair and identical clothing making them look almost like doubles, until one drops down, leaving the other, legs folded, hanging by one hand from the bridge.

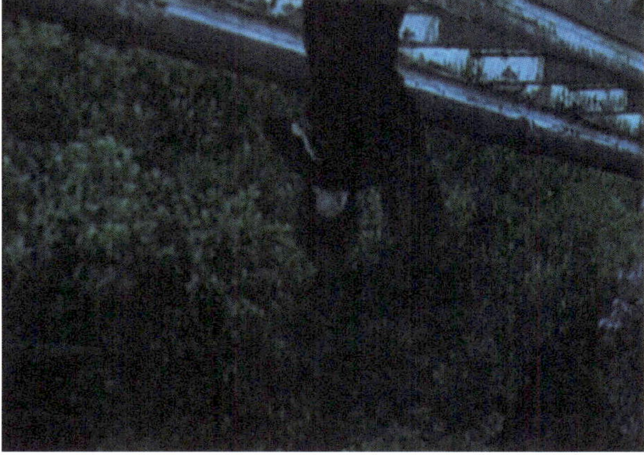

Why, in <u>THE SILVER BRIDGE</u>, is it specifically bats that reappear, and seem to provide the model for the relationship between the two

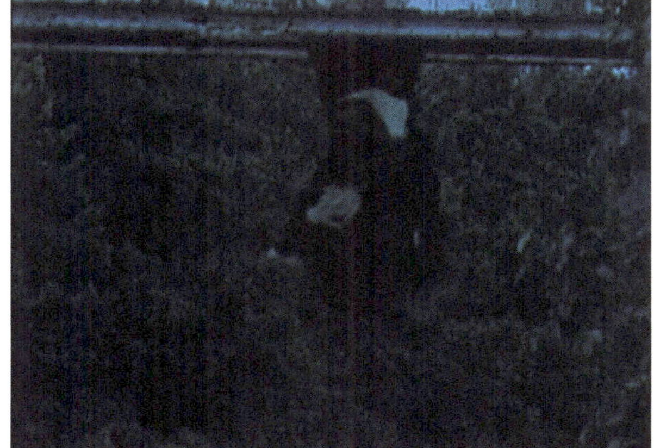

women at the end? Humans behaving like bats inevitably recall the figure of the vampire.

The vampire reproduces as a species not by giving birth,
but by infecting human beings to whom he—
or she—is drawn.

another girl is left to recover from a carriage accident
outside the feudal house
to which her father had retired.

The narrator in J.Sheridan LeFanu's *Carmilla*,
originally published as a short story in 1872,
tells of what happened when, as a girl,

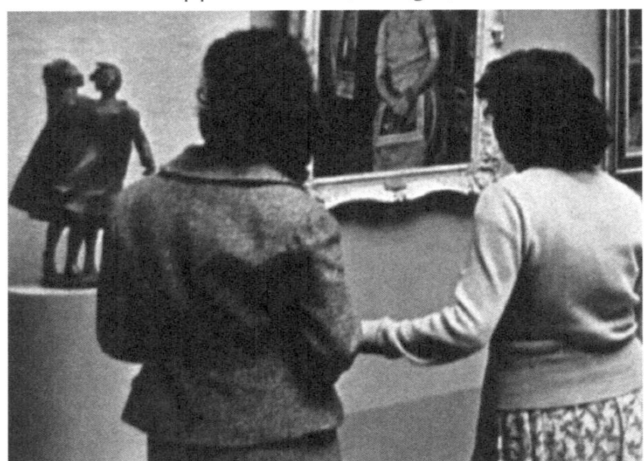

This languid girl, who disappears from her room
at night, and exactly resembles a girl in a painting
from 1698, seems to draw the narrator to her:
Her soft cheek was glowing against mine.
'Darling, darling,' she murmured, 'I live in
you; and you would die for me, I love you so.'
I started from her.
She was gazing on me with eyes from which
all fire, all meaning had flown, and a face
colorless and apathetic.[29]

The vampire crosses not only the boundaries
between human and animal, but also
between love for the other sex and love for the same.

The vampire is prone to be fascinated with an
engrossing vehemence, resembling the passion
of love, by particular persons and in certain cases

seems to yearn for something like sympathy
and consent.

It multiplies itself outside the lines
of filiation of the patriarchal law:

It is the nature of vampires to increase
and multiply, but according to an ascertained
and ghostly law.[30]

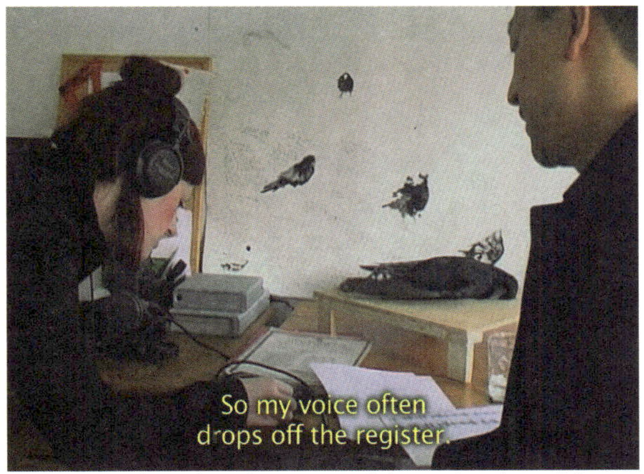

Irvine matches the alienness of the animal world
with the strangeness of others.

Others, and animals, are not entirely inaccessible to
us, in so far as we recognize that we are strangers to
ourselves.

Henceforth, we know that we are foreigners
to ourselves, and it is with the help of that sole
support that we can attempt to live with others.

writes Julia Kristeva.[31]

Or, as Giorgio Agamben puts it,
what makes it possible for us to relate to what
is other than the human is the division of life within us:

The division of life into vegetal and relational,
organic and animal, animal and human, therefore passes first of all as a mobile border within
living man, and without this intimate caesura
the very decision of what is human and what is
not would probably not be possible. It is possible to oppose man to other living things, and at
the same time to organize the complex—and
not always edifying—economy of relations
between men and animals, only because something like an animal life has been separated
within man, only because his distance and
proximity to the animal have been measured
and recognized first of all in the closest and
most intimate place.[32]

Only insofar as we recognize that we are other
to ourselves are we able to acknowledge the other,
the stranger.

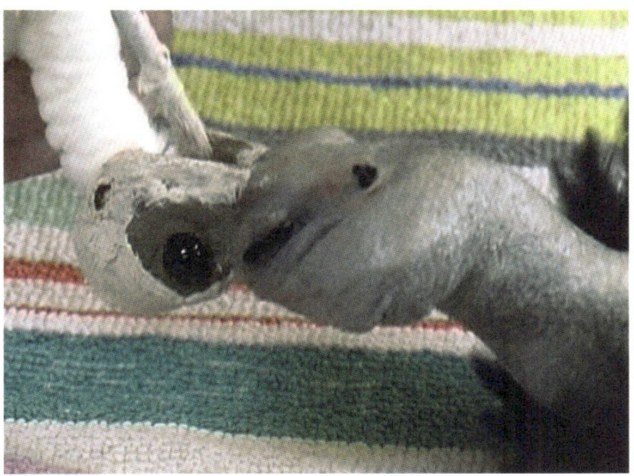

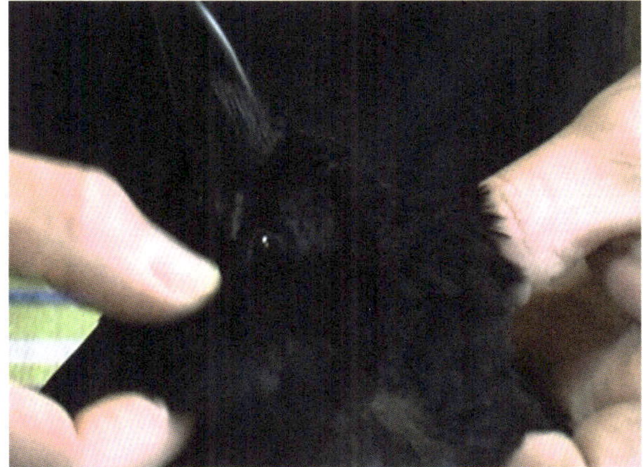

And only out of our intimacy
with the caesura
within us between the human and the non-human

are we are able to relate to the worlds of other beings.

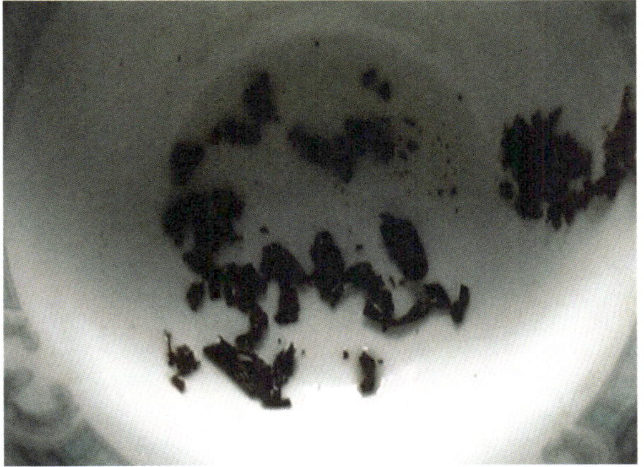

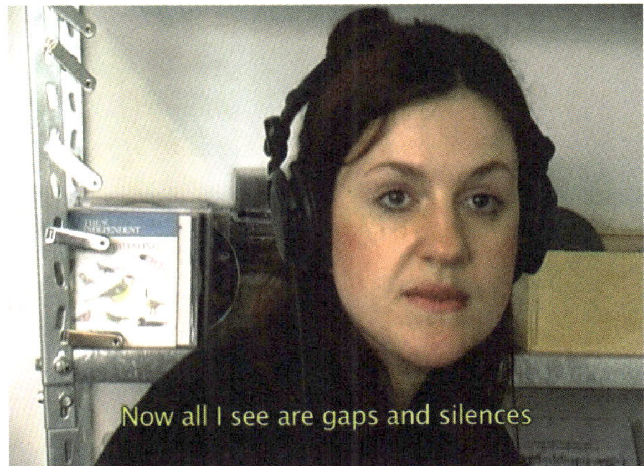

As Irvine shows so well in her work, the world of the other
and other worlds are not to be encompassed by coloniz-
ing them, or making them conform with our desires.

Rather, among the missed encounters and failed
connections, there is a hint that some kind of co-
existence with others might be attained

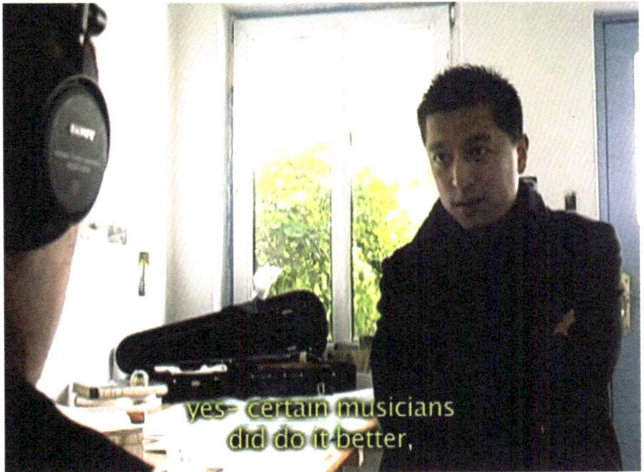

through the acknowledgment of differences
across an abyss of ignorance,
the recognition of worlds we may share

with other people,
and with animals,
without really ever knowing them.

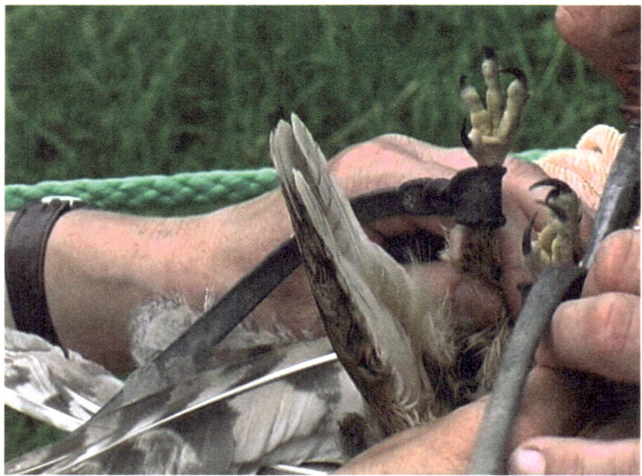

<u>IN A WORLD LIKE THIS</u> (2006)
recreates a space within the world where the world
of the human family meets that of the birds, and,

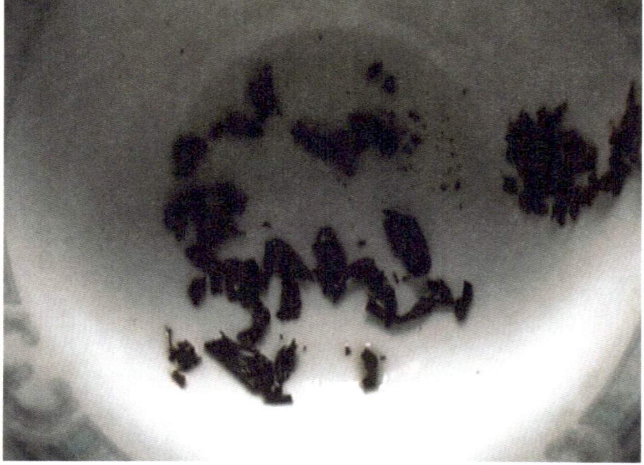

This coming together of the human and the bird is
anticipated in <u>IVANA'S ANSWERS</u>, although
there Ivana watched falcons in an aviary through a slit,

The position of the later work is indicated by two
words of the title, <u>IN</u> and <u>THIS</u> : humans and animals are *in* a world together, a garden or sanctuary,

despite their utter difference, these creatures come to
resemble one another.

separated from them not only by the wall but also by
seeing her world in terms of perception, with her as
the centre and perceiver.

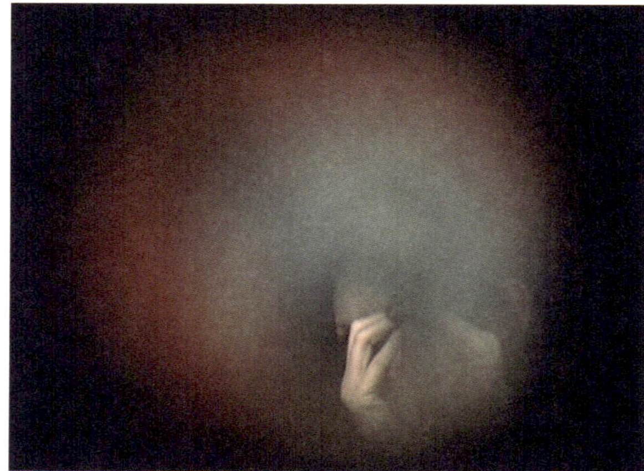

and the world shown is *this* world—
at once this-worldly and a world in a world,
almost utopian, yet not nowhere but somewhere.

In <u>IVANA'S ANSWERS</u>
the reader sees in the tea-leaves
someone whose body is made up of falcons.

    They're sitting on a branch like question marks,
    and you're there too.

The same could apply to the viewer
of Jaki Irvine's works.

END

(The [subtitled] *stills on pps 131, 143, 145–6
are from* Room Acoustics Revisited *(2008)
a work not directly mentioned by this essay)*

Notes:

1. Stanley Cavell, "The Avoidance of Love" in *Must we mean what we say?*, Cambridge, Cambridge University Press, 1976 (1st ed. 1969), p.276.

2. Cavell, *Must we mean what we say?*, op.cit., pp. 277-8.

3. Cavell, *Must we mean what we say?*, op.cit., p. 286.

4. Irvine's THE ACTRESS could in part be considered as a reworking of Jacques Lacan's account of the "mirror stage", where the infant identifies with its image in a mirror, which goes on to form the ideal with which, as a body in bits and pieces, it does not correspond (see Jacques Lacan, "The mirror stage as formative of the function of the I as revealed through psycho-analytic experience", in *Écrits: A Selection*, trans. Alan Sheridan, New York: W. W. Norton, 1977, pp. 1–7), with regard to the woman's agency as an actress, at once performing and detached from the performance (for this aspect of acting, see Denis Diderot, *The Paradox of Acting*, New York: Hill and Wang, 1957).

5. "Thoughtless Liar" from Mina, *Minantologia*, 1969.

6. Quoted from F. Gonzalez-Crussi, *Three Forms of Sudden Death and other reflections on the grandeur and misery of the body*, London, Pan, 1987, p. 199, note 4, in Jaki Irvine, *Plans for Forgotten Works*, ex. cat., Leeds, Henry Moore Institute, 2005, p. 25, and as a text on a photo-graph, p. 26.

7. See Gonzalez-Crussi, op.cit., p.91-2

8. See Jacques Derrida, "Plato's Pharmacy" in *Dissemination*, trans. Barbara Johnson, Chicago: University of Chicago Press, 1981, pp.63-171, esp. Pp.71-2.

9. Julia Kristeva, *Powers of Horror: An Essay on Abjection*, New York: Columbia University Press, 1982.

10. Kristeva, *Powers of Horror*, p.9.

11. People who could not afford dental treatment would have all their teeth extracted and replaced with dentures.

12. Stéphane Mallarmé, "Crisis of Verse" in *Divi-gations*, trans. Barbara Johnson, Cambridge, Mass. and London: Harvard University Press, p.210.

13. Yann Martel, *The Facts behind the Helsinki Roccamatios*, Toronto, Vintage, 2003 (orig. publ. 1993), pp.3-72.

14. Yann Martel, *Life of Pi*, Canada, Vintage, 2002, p. 352.

15. Richard Brautigan, *In Watermelon Sugar*, Boston, Houghton Mifflin/ Seymour Lawrence, 1989 (originally published 1969), p. 34.

16. *Philosophical Investigations*, trans. G.E.M. Anscombe, Oxford: Blackwell, second edition (1958)., II, xi., p. 223.

17. *In Quest of the Ordinary: Lines of Skepticism and Romanticism*, Chicago and London: University of Chicago Press, 1988, p.69.

18. "The Trouble with Speaking" in *Art from Ireland: Jaki Irvine/Alistair MacLennan* (ex.cat. The Venice Biennale, The Cultural Relations Committee of Ireland, 1997), n.p.

19. Stanislaw Lem, *A Perfect Vacuum*, trans Michael Kandel, Chicago, Northwestern University Press, 1999, p. 70.

20. Lem, *A Perfect Vacuum*, op. cit., p. 71.

21. Lem, *A Perfect Vacuum*, op. cit. p.75.

22. Lem, *A Perfect Vacuum*, op. cit. p. 75.

23. Lem, *A Perfect Vacuum*, op. cit. p. 76.

24. Jacques Lacan, *The Four Fundamental Concepts of Psycho-Analysis*, London, Penguin, 1977, p. 95

25. Jorge Luis Borges, *Fictions*, trans. Anthony Kerrigan, London, Calder, 1985, p.91.

26. Gilles Deleuze, *Cinema 2: The Time-Image*, London: The Athlone Press, 1989, p.131.

27. Jorge Luis Borges, "Tlön, Uqbar, Orbis Tertius" in *Labyrinths*, Harmondsworth, Middlesex, Penguin Books, 1970, p. 39.

28. NIGHTINGALE is produced using a computer program that layers black over the image, and allows the user to "rub out" the blackness.

29. J. Sheridan LeFanu, *Carmilla*, Aegypan Press, p. 60.

30. LeFanu, *Carmilla*, op. cit., p. 145, 147.

31. Julia Kristeva, *Strangers to Ourselves, Strangers to Ourselves*, New York, Columbia University Press, 1991, p. 170.

32. Giorgio Agamben, *The Open: Man and Animal*, Stanford, Cal., Stanford University Press, 2004, pp. 15-16.

Michael Newman teaches in the Department of Art History, Theory, and Criticism at the School of the Art Institute of Chicago and is Professor of Art Writing at Goldsmiths College in the University of London. He holds degrees in Literature and Art History, and a doctorate in Philosophy from the Katholeike Universiteit Leuven, Belgium. He has written extensively on contemporary art, including essays on James Coleman, Jeff Wall, Alfred Jensen, Hanne Darboven and Joëlle Tuerlinckx. He has curated several exhibitions, including *Tacita Dean* at the Art Gallery of York University, Toronto (2000), on whom his essays have been published by Tate Britain (2001) and Musée d'Art Moderne de la Ville de Paris (2003). His book *Richard Prince: Untitled (couple)* (Afterall and MIT) was published in 2006 and his monograph *Jeff Wall* (Poligrafia) in 2007. He is co-editor of *Re-Writing Conceptual Art* (London, Reaktion Books, 1999). In philosophy he has published essays on Kant, Nietzsche, Derrida, Levinas, and Blanchot, and is currently writing a book on the trace in art and philosophy.

Born in Dublin (1966), where she continues to live and work, Jaki Irvine's career spans time spent in London and Italy, and she has exhibited extensively internationally. Though spending a large amount of time living and working away from Ireland, her work has always been central to contemporary practice in Ireland.

Solo Exhibitions

2008
Room Acoustics Revisited, Kerlin Gallery, Dublin
. . . . p.131, 143, 145–6

2006-7
In A World Like This, Model Arts and Niland Gallery, Sligo and Chisenhale Gallery, London
. . . . p.5–37

2006
Smart Project Space, Amsterdam

2005-6
The Silver Bridge, Irish Museum of Modern Art, Dublin p.137–41

2005
Plans for Forgotten Works, Henry Moore Sculpture Foundation, Leeds. p.123–5, 128, 134

Towards a Polar Sea, Frith St. Gallery, London
. . . .
p.83, 130

"Nightingale" in *Paradise*, Douglas Hyde Gallery, Dublin. p.135-6

2004
Solo Screenings, Kerlin Gallery, Dublin
Things Changed, Galleria Alessandro de March, Milan

2001
Ivana's Answers, Delfina, London . . p.113–17, 121

1999
The Hottest Sun, The Darkest Hour, Douglas Hyde Gallery, Dublin and Frith St. Gallery, London p.73, 99, 121

1998
"Fledermaus she said....", Staatliche Kunsthalle, Baden-Baden, Germany

1997
Another Difficult Sunset, Frith St. Gallery, London
and Irish Pavillion, Venice Biennale, Italy
. . . . p.103–110

1996
Eyelashes, Project Arts Centre, Dublin
. . . . p.74–5, 89–93, 95

1994
Margaret Again, Anthony Wilkinson Fine Art,
London

<u>Selected Group Exhibitions</u>

2008
Machinic Alliances, Danielle Arnaud Gallery,
London

2007
Screening curated by Polly Staple and LUX at
Whitechapel Gallery, London
Screening curated by Vaari Calffey and Isabel
Nolan at Kerlin Gallery

2006
Hugh Lane Municipal Gallery, Dublin
*A la recherché d'une beaute perdue: homage to
Luchino Visconti*, Galleria Comunale
d'Arte Contemporanea di Monfalcone,
Italy
Cooling Out: On the Paradox of Feminism,
Glucksman Gallery, Cork, Ireland
The Square Root of Drawing, Temple Bar Gallery,
Dublin

2005
Summer Show, Kerlin Gallery, Dublin

2003
A Century of Artists' Film in Britain, Tate Britain,
London
Art Now Lightbox, Tate Britain, London & Site
Gallery, Sheffield

2002
Summer Show, Frith St. Gallery, London
Joint show with John Armleder, Galleria Massimo
de Carlo, Milan

2001
Different/Diverse, Teatro del Fondamento,
Venice Biennale, Venice
50 Years of Irish Art, Irish Museum of Modern
Art, Dublin

2000
Intelligence, Tate Britain , London
Summer Show, Van Abbemuseum, Eindhoven

1999
Space, With de Witte, Rotterdam
Artists films and videos, curated by Maria Lind
for Museet d'Arte Moderna, Stockholm

1998
In the Meantime, Estrany de la Mota, Barcelona
White Noise, Bern Kunsthalle, Bern
Video, Projection, Film, Frith St. Gallery, London

1997
A Small Shifting Sphere of Serious Culture,
curated by Gregor Muir, ICA, London

1996
Wingate Young Artists Award, London
Pandemonium, ICA, London
Now Here, Louisiana Museum of Modern Art,
Humlebæk, Denmark
Glen Dimplex Award, Irish Museum of Modern
Art, Dublin
Making Waves, *Artisti Britannici a Roma*, curated
by the British Council, Rome
Body of Evidence, curated by Iwona Blazwick for
Toyama Now, Toyama Museum of
Modern Art, Japan

1994
The Curator's Egg, Anthony Reynolds Gallery,
London
The Nowness of Everything, Minories Gallery
Colchester, Colchester

1993
Sonsbeek International, Arnhem (Collaborative
  project with Blue Funk),
BT New Contemporaries, UK touring exhibition
Wonderful Life, Lisson Gallery, London
Riverside Studios Gallery, London

1992
Stranger Still, (collaborative project with Blue
  Funk) Space Plentitude, Brisbane,
  Australia
Eustace St., (site-specific collaborative project
  with Blue Funk), Dublin
A State of Great Terror (collaborative project with
  Blue Funk), Douglas Hyde Gallery,
  Dublin

1991
EKKER, City Arts Centre, Dublin and Perth
  Institute of Contemporary Art, Australia

1990
GPA Emerging Artists Exhibition, Dublin

Other Projects

2003
Artist-in-residence for one month (May) at the
  Henry Moore Sculpture Foundation,
  Leeds. New work commissioned as part of
  the residency

2000
Somewhere Near Vada, curated by Jaki Irvine
  for the re-opening of Project, Dublin
  Artists included Bas Jan Ader, Marcel
  Broodthaers, Adam Chodzko, James
  Coleman, Tacita Dean, Gary Hill, Zoe
  Walker, Fischli&Weiss

Selected Published Writings

2007
"The Shadow of Despair: on Cecily Brennan",
  Art Monthly, May
"Past and Future Films", *Feint Magazine*, curated
  by Vaari Claffey and Isabel Nolan
  . . . . p.34, 52–53
"Inner Worlds, Outer Space", a catalogue essay
  in *Adam Chodzko, Then* (Dublin, Breaking
  Ground)

2006
"Diego", in *Magnetic Promenade
  and Other Sculpture Parks* (ed. ChrisEvans),
  London: Studio Voltaire p.55

2005
Towards a Polar Sea, London: Frith St. Books
  (artist's book)

2001
Mike Nelson: Extinction Beckons,
  London: Matts Gallery,
Re: Dispersal, catalogue essay for work-
  Seth/Tallentire, The Orchard Gallery,
  Derry

2000
Somewhere Near Vada, Dublin: Project Press

1999
Instances: Anne Tallentire, catalogue essay published by the Cultural Affairs Committee
  of the Department of Foreign Affairs, to
  co-incide with the Venice Biennale, 1999.

Selected Bibliography

Milou Allerholm , "Jaki Irvine", *Palatten Magazine*, 1/96 no. 224, pp.46-49, 1996

Edwina Ashton, "The Spaces Between Things: Edwina Ashton talks to Jaki Irvine", *Untitled*, Autumn/Winter, no. 23

Kathrin Brehmin, *Yet on the Other Hand*, Baden-Baden: Staatliche Kunsthalle Museum (catalogue)

Kate Bush, "Between You and Me: Kate Bush on Jaki Irvine", *Frieze Magazine*, September/October 1995, pp.44-45

Virgina Button & Charles Esche, "Jaki Irvine", *Intelligence*, London: Tate Gallery, 2000, pp.70-72

Luke Clancy, "Video Games: Jaki Irvine at Project Arts Centre", *The Irish Times*, Sunday, June 15, 1996

Martin Coomer, "Jaki Irvine: Frith St.", *Time Out* April 2-9, 1997

Martin Coomer, "Jaki Irvine: Frith St.", *Flash Art*, Summer 1997, p.140

Martin Coomer, "Jaki Irvine: Frith St.", *Time Out*, Oct 25-Nov.1, 2000

Gabriel Coxhead, "Jaki Irvine, Frith St. Gallery, London", *Frieze*, pp.110-111

Aidan Dunne, "Jaki Irvine: The Hottest Sun, The Darkest Hour", *The Sunday Times*, July 25, 1999

Aidan Dunne, "Getting the most out of video", *The Irish Times*, June 30, 1999

Aidan Dunne, "Somewhere Near Vada", *The Irish Times*, June 21, 2000

Brian Fallon, "Venice Observed", *The Irish Times*, June 19, 1997

Catherine Grant, "Jaki Irvine: The Hottest Sun, The Darkest Hour-A Romance", *Make*, no. 90, pp.29-30

Sue Hubbard, "Jaki Irvine: Delfina Project Space", *The Independant on Sunday*, January 28, 2001

Ian Hunt, "Jaki Irvine: Frith St. Gallery", *Art Monthly*, no. 205, April 1997, pp.29-30

Ian Hunt, "Jaki Irvine: Delfina Project Space", *Art Monthly*, no. 244, March 2001, pp.38-39

Martin Herbert, "Jaki Irvine:Delfina Project Space", *Time Out*, no. 7-14, 2001, p.60

Daniel Jewesbury, "Jaki Irvine:Douglas Hyde Gallery", *Art Monthly*, no. 229, September 1999

Sarah Kent, "Video Games: Pandemonium", *Time Out*, March 20-27, 1996, p.51

Caoimhin Mac Giolla Leith, "Jaki Irvine:The Project Arts Centre", *Flash Art*, November-December 1996, p.109

Caoimhin MacGiolla Leith, "Jaki Irvine", *Circa Art Magazine*, June 1996, p.52

Caoimhin Mac Giolla Leith, "Jaki Irvine: Douglas Hyde Gallery", *Art Forum*, September 1999, pp.177-178

Caoimhin Mac Giolla Leith, *Plans for Forgotten Works*, catalogue essay. Henry Moore Foundation, Leeds

Michael Newman, "Beyond the Lost Object: From Sculpture to Film & Video", *Artpress*, no. 202, pp.45-50

Medb Ruane, "Eyelashes", *The Sunday Times*, June 16, 1996, p.53

Stella Santacatterina, "Jaki Irvine: Ivana's Answers", *Flash Art*, March/April 2001, p.116

Adrian Searle, " Jaki Irvine: Margaret Again", *Time Out*, May 31-June 7, 1995. p. 44

Anne Tallentire, *The Trouble with Speaking*, catalogue for the Irish Section of the Venice Biennale, 1997

Maria Walsh, review, Circa '96, Summer 2001, p.64

Maria Walsh, rReview of "Towards a Polar Sea", *Art Monthly*, November 2005

Marina Warner,"Only Clouds…", *Parkett* 61, 2001, pp.188-198

Marcus Verhagen, "Jaki Irvine", review of "In a World Like This" at Chisenhale Gallery, London, *Art Monthly*, no. 312, December-January 2007-2008, pp. 33-34

(continued from page 10)

I would like to take this opportunity to thank
everyone involved in producing this publication.
To the Kerlin Gallery, Dublin, Frith Street
Gallery, London and Double agents, Central St.
Martins, London, for their support. To the Arts
Council for their generous support under the
Title-by-Title scheme. To Michael Newman for
his extraordinarily insightful essay which goes
to the core of Jaki's practice, tracing threads
which provide a framework through which this
important body of work can be approached.
Emer McGarry, Assistant Curator at the Model
who has as ever worked with incredible dedication
to realize both the exhibition and book, and to
Will Holder for his incredible commitment to the
project. This book, while providing an opportunity to survey Jaki's career to date should also be
seen as part of an ever evolving and enquiring
practice. Finally I would like to thank Jaki
for the extraordinary generosity and flexibility
in her practice.

Sarah Glennie,

Director
The Model Arts and Niland Gallery, Sligo

Conceived and compiled
by Will Holder and Jaki Irvine

Designed by Will Holder

Edited by Emer McGarry

Produced by
model :: niland
The Model Arts and Niland Gallery,
The Mall, Sligo. Ireland
www.modelart.ie

in response to the exhibition
In A World Like This,
at The Model Arts and Niland Gallery, Sligo
and Chisenhale Gallery, London

The publication has been realised
with additional support from:
Frith Street Gallery
GOLDEN SQUARE

www.frithstreetgallery.com

Kerlin Gallery
www.kerlin.ie

: Double agents
(Central Saint Martins
College of Art and Design)
www.doubleagents.org.uk

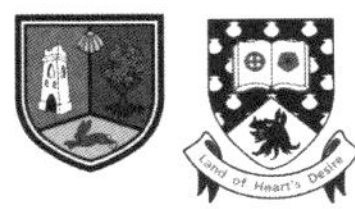

Sligo County Council
and Sligo Borough Council

This publication
has been generously
supported by the
Arts Council under
the "Title-by-Title" scheme.

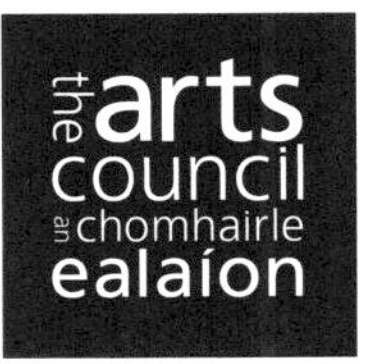

Design Coordination
Daniela Meda, Gabriele Nason

Editorial Coordination
Filomena Moscatelli

Copyediting
Margie Mounier

Copywriting and Press Office
Silvia Palombi Arte&Mostre, Milano

US Editorial Director
Francesca Sorace

Promotion and Web
Monica D'Emidio

Distribution
Antonia De Besi

Administration
Grazia De Giosa

Warehouse and Outlet
Roberto Curiale

No part of this publication may be reproduced, stored in a retrieval system or transmitted in any form or by any means without the prior permission in writing of copyright holders and of the publisher.

ISBN 978-88-8158-702-5

Printed in Italy

Edizioni Charta srl
Milano
via della Moscova, 27 - 20121
Tel. +39-026598098/026598200
Fax +39-026598577
e-mail: edcharta@tin.it

Charta Books Ltd.
New York City
Tribeca Office
Tel. +1-313-406-8468
e-mail: international@chartaartbooks.it

www.chartaartbooks.it

To find out more about Charta,
and to learn about our most recent publications, visit

www.chartaartbooks.it

Printed in September 2008
by Tipografia Rumor, Vicenza
for Edizioni Charta